M000300771

HOW TO CONVERT TO AN ELECTRIC CAR

Ted Lucas and Fred Riess

A HERBERT MICHELMAN BOOK

CROWN PUBLISHERS, INC., NEW YORK

Books by Ted Lucas

How to Build a Solar Heater

How to Use Solar Energy in Your Home and Business

Waterbed Verse

The Zoo Book

Inquiries should be addressed to Crown Publishers, Inc., One Park Avenue, New York, New York 10016

Printed in the United States of America

Published simultaneously in Canada by General Publishing Company Limited

Library of Congress Cataloging in Publication Data
Lucas, Ted.
How to convert to an electric car.
"A Herbert Michelman book."
Bibliography: p.
Includes index.
1. Automobiles, Electric. 2. Automobiles, Home-built. I. Riess, Fred, joint author. II. Title.
TL220.L82 629.22'93 79-24243
ISBN: 0-517-54055X (cloth)
0-517-53990X (paper)

Designed by Leonard Henderson

10 9 8 7 6 5 4 3 2 1

First edition

Contents

1 Enjoy Building Your Electric Car

Electrical vehicles are becoming increasingly popular in most of the industrialized nations of the world. In Britain, West Germany, France, Italy, and Japan, the high cost of gasoline and the threat of future shortages contribute to a growing use of electric cars, taxis, delivery vans, and buses.

Electric Cars Are Economical

Even though the price of gasoline in the United States isn't as high now as in Western Europe, Japan, and most of the "underdeveloped" nations, there is no doubt that the price of fuel for our automobiles will continue to climb. Today you can operate your own small electric car for about 2¢ a mile as against about 6¢ a mile for fuel in an average internal combustion engine (ICE) car.

An electric car is really a simple vehicle. It is not nearly as complex as that ICE car you're driving. Because the electric vehicle is an assembly with fewer parts than the conventional automobile, its reliability is excellent. The maintenance cost over a five-year period is lower. This was proved during the past few years by the Postal Service in operating several different kinds of electric vehicles. The British have been using electric vans for delivering milk in London for the past fourteen years. Comparisons show that these electric vans require far less maintenance and are more economical to operate than any competitive vans using either diesel fuel or gasoline.

In this book we're going to show you how, for a total materials cost of about $1,500, you can build an electrical vehicle (EV) with good performance. That is, a car that will operate at speeds up to 55 to 60 miles per hour and will have a range of at least 50 miles. This is the range you will get between battery charges.

Depending upon how many miles a year you drive to work, on shopping trips, to the movies, golf course, tennis courts or the beach, your electric car will pay for itself in a couple of years. Then you'll have money in the bank for each additional month you drive your home-built EV.

So it turns out that the longer you keep your electric car, the more money you will save by operating this fine small vehicle. We refer to your electric car in these terms because we're going to tell you how you can transform any one of a wide variety of conventional compact cars into an electric car which will not only give better performance, but will also, because it is less complex and has fewer parts, deliver more miles of trouble-free driving.

Satisfaction Guaranteed

A second important reason for building your own electric car is the personal satisfaction you'll get from doing this relatively simple job. Chances are that you will be the first person in your immediate area to have successfully converted a small "clunker"—an old car which barely runs—into a quiet, economical, nonpolluting electric car.

Your psychic income may be as great as your dollar savings. It will be a matter of genuine pride to show your friends and neighbors what you have accomplished in a couple of months of part-time work. Our experience shows that most people who have converted a compact "clunker" into a useful little car have been able to do the job in from 80 to 100 hours.

An interesting point is that most of these conversions have been made by individuals with only average mechanical ability. You don't have to be an engineer or a professional auto mechanic. If you follow the step-by-step procedures outlined in this book, just as we have, you'll find yourself driving away silently—the proud possessor of a vehicle that contributes practically no pollution, and saves you money.

If you don't want to build your own electric car, the information in this book will permit you to follow one of two other alternatives. You can buy electric cars, and we have described the characteristics of the typical EV's now available commercially. The other alternative is to buy the components for an electric car, after you have decided what kind of performance and range you want, and then have the electric vehicle of your choice built by one or more mechanics in your neighborhood.

Electric Cars Save Energy

The third important reason for building your own electric car is that you will help in the truly important job of conserving energy. There's been a lot of confusion about whether or not an electric car will really save energy. Some people have said that it actually takes as much fuel to create the electrical energy required to charge the batteries of your electric car as it does to drive a conventional gasoline-powered car (ICE).

Actually, this isn't true. It turns out that when you drive an electric car, as have the authors of this book, you usually charge your batteries in the period from 11 o'clock at night to about 6 o'clock in the morning. This charging is done automatically with a built-in battery charger and timer so that you don't have to worry about setting alarm clocks.

During this night period, the electric utilities in all parts of the world are operating at only about 45–55% of capacity. Thus, a very large number of EV's could be on the road without requiring any additional electric power-generating capacity. Another point is that electric power plants operate more efficiently when they're running at close to full capacity, so there will be substantial fuel savings when a large number of electric cars are on the world's highways.

There are some other very good reasons why each one of us should consider building or buying an electric car. We all hate the smog layers that hang over every major city. There is no practical way to get rid of that unhealthy, smelly, ugly blanket of smog until a large number of us are driving electric cars.

Just from a health standpoint, it's very important that we get as many electric cars, taxis, vans, trucks, and buses on the road as possible as replacements for ICE cars. Scientists have pointed out for years that smog induces lung cancer, emphysema, bronchitis, and asthma. It has also been proved that automobile exhausts are responsible for 50–60% of the smog that is such a killer.

Electric Cars Are Good for the National Economy

Americans are now driving automobiles nearly a trillion miles a year. This means that our ICE cars, gulping about 80 billion gallons every 12 months, spread more than 200,000 tons of pollutants, gases, chemicals, and solids into the atmosphere.

But aside from all this pollution, gas-guzzling automobiles are actually hurting our economy. The fact that in 1980 we have to import nearly 50% of our total petroleum requirements is the biggest factor in our huge negative balance of trade. This is a major reason why the dollar has been sinking in value. We are in an increasingly precarious condition as a nation, in terms both of our economy and of our military position, when half of the petroleum fuel we use has to come from overseas sources.

Of all the gasoline-powered cars owned by U.S. families, about 27 million are their second or third vehicles. If we could replace all these second and third cars with EV's, there would be an annual savings of nearly half a billion barrels of oil. This is a very sizable percentage of the total amount of petroleum which we import. Thus, the electric car represents a very important potential, both for you as an individual consumer and also for the national economy.

Encouragement from Uncle Sam

There is now an active program with federal sponsorship to develop improved electric cars and the components needed to make them very widely accepted. Congress has paid attention to the national surge of interest in electric cars. Our legislature in Washington drafted an act early in 1976, and then on September 17 of that year overrode a Presidential veto with Public Law 94–413, the Electric and Hybrid Vehicle Research, Development, and Demonstration Act of 1976.

After many years, when practically all the work on electric cars had been privately financed (most of it by individuals working in their spare time in backyard garages), $164 million in federal funds were made available for a five-year program. Objectives of this work, under the direction of the Department of Energy (DOE), were stated to be:

1. To promote electric- and hybrid-vehicle technology, including development of improved storage batteries, electronic controls, drive trains, and other components needed for more efficient EV's. A hybrid is a vehicle which is propelled by a combination of an electric motor and some kind of internal combustion engine, which may be a gasoline-driven engine or a diesel.
2. To demonstrate commercial feasibility of electric and hybrid vehicles. The first part of this program will involve sponsoring competitive designs of preliminary models. The second stage will result in putting 7,500 electric and hybrid vehicles in service on U.S. highways, under federal sponsorship.
3. To encourage inventors and small business, grants and loan guarantees will be provided for small as well as large vehicle manufacturers from the federal funds provided by Congress. Every attempt is being made to make sure that some of this money will go to small businesses. So if you come up with some good ideas while you're building your electric car, and feel the urge to become an entrepreneur, you may be able to get financial backing from Uncle Sam.

Some Basic Diagrams

So far we've presented some of the advantages of having your own electric car. In later chapters of this book you'll find information about electric motors, drive trains, control systems, and storage batteries that will be useful whether you build or buy an electric car or a hybrid vehicle.

You can grasp the basic principles of electric and hybrid vehicles from the diagrams in figure 1–1.

The first diagram, figure 1–1a, illustrates the flow of energy from the electric outlet in your garage to the wheels of the electric car. It's necessary to have a controller, usually with simple electronic circuitry, between the storage batteries and the electric motor so that the motor will operate efficiently. Then, as you might expect, the torque of your electric motor is applied through a suitable transmission to the front or rear axle of your car, depending upon whether you're modifying a front-wheel or rear-wheel-drive compact.

Figure 1–1b shows a series arrangement for a hybrid vehicle. The fueled engine, usually gasoline-powered, although it could be diesel- or propane-fueled, drives an alternator/rectifier or a DC generator. The power thus generated charges the batteries which operate the electric motor. When this kind of hybrid needs more power than is available from the heat engine, that added power is drawn from the batteries. At lower speeds or when idling, excess power is available from the small gasoline engine and the surplus is used to charge the battery.

Figure 1–1c is a diagram of the parallel hybrid system. The fueled engine drives the vehicle through a transmission that splits the power. When the demand for torque to drive the car's wheels is less than what the engine is producing, the transmission diverts power to a motor generator which charges the batteries. When you step down hard on the accelerator pedal, demanding more torque than the fueled engine can provide, the batteries deliver power to the electric motor. Now the transmission delivers power from both the fueled engine and the electric motor to drive this hybrid car at higher speeds or up a steep hill.

There are benefits from hybrid cars. The primary advantage of a hybrid design is a range extension beyond that of a pure battery electric while reducing fuel consumption and exhaust emission as compared to an ICE-only powered car. The hybrid heat engine is operated at a higher efficiency range. Many engineers who are familiar with electric and hybrid vehicles believe that hybrids will be the commercial interim step before most of us drive electric cars. Although this book is primarily devoted to telling you how to modify a small conventional car and convert it into a pure electric, you'll find that the material we have provided on components such as electric motors and storage batteries is equally useful whether you're interested in building a pure electric or a hybrid.

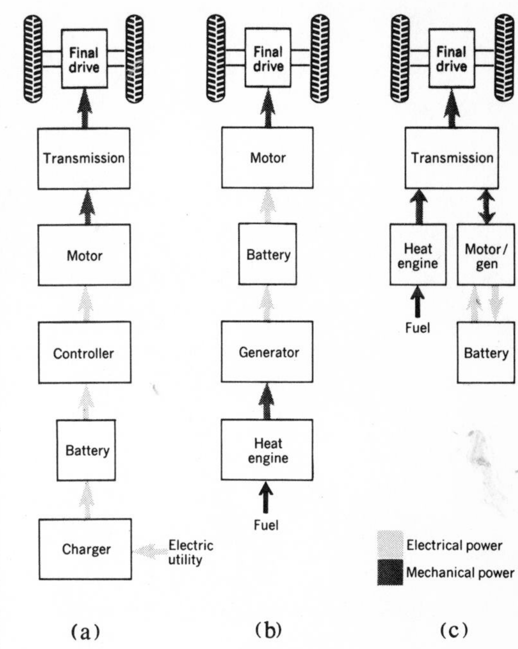

(a) DIAGRAM OF AN ELECTRIC CAR

(b) DIAGRAM OF A SERIES-TYPE HYBRID VEHICLE

(c) DIAGRAM OF A PARALLEL-TYPE HYBRID VEHICLE

Fig. 1–1. Typical electric vehicle arrangements

Why Modify a Clunker?

About now you might be wondering why we're suggesting that you modify a conventional small car—your own choice of a clunker—instead of starting from ground zero. The primary reason is economic: you will be able to build an electric car for not much over $1,000 if you start out with an old car, your clunker, and you use great care in getting components, some of which will be surplus. This car should have a reasonably good chassis. The condition of the engine is not important because you're not going to need it anyway. In general, it would be desirable if you can use the transmission and differential of your original clunker.

However, a variety of drive trains can be substituted for conventional transmissions, if you want to go a step further and make a more efficient EV. You will find it surprising, perhaps, to see how little it will cost you to buy a suitable clunker which you can modify to make an electric car. In the experience of these authors, used cars, which have essentially been junked, may be bought for as little as $25 to $50. In one large surplus operation, we have found small trucks which can readily be modified to make them suitable EV's. These trucks can be purchased for as little as $10 in some cases.

So if you want to get a truly economical start in building your own electric car, shop around in your neighborhood to find a clunker at a bargain price. Be sure that the vehicle has not been in a bad wreck and that the frame is not bent out of shape because this is a major repair job. You will not need a gasoline-driven engine—we'll be going on the assumption that you are building a simple electric vehicle.

It will be helpful, of course, if you can find a car that has good tires. In fact, it is desirable to use high-quality radial tires because they have less rolling friction. Therefore your EV will be able tc operate at higher speeds and draw less power from the battery pack, so you will get added range between battery charges.

Early in this century, nearly one-third of all the automobiles on the streets of major cities were electric cars. In fact, one of the early manufacturers of electric cars, Charles Baker, built a racer in 1902 with a design speed of 100 mph.

Electric cars were more reliable than gasoline-fueled automobiles but they were heavier and more expensive. Also, they were usually operated at a maximum speed of only about 25 mph and had a limited range of perhaps only about 30 miles. This was because the cars were relatively small, and the lead acid batteries of that period were considerably heavier and less efficient than the ones now available.

Another desirable feature of the early electrics was that they operated so slowly that the tires were good for many, many thousands of miles. Flat tires were rare because they used solid tires for many electric vehicles.

The reasons for going to electric cars now are far more important than they were early in this century. With the increase in population, air pollution caused largely by automobile exhausts has become a critical health problem for a high percentage of our population.

There is also the obvious fact that this planet is running out of petroleum. Because gasoline and oil are becoming increasingly scarce, the prices of these valuable commodities keep going up. Therefore, the operation of a gasoline-fueled car becomes more and more of a luxury.

In the meanwhile, when you can convert an old but usable chassis into an electric car for a relatively low cost in materials—something in the neighborhood of $1,500 or more, depending upon the performance you demand—you are creating a bargain when you build an electric car.

2 Basic Steps in Building Your Electric Car

By building your electric car from an old clunker you will have a valuable product that may become even more so in succeeding years. A recent survey made for the Electric Vehicle Council shows that, of about 132 million people over 18 years old in this country, at least 55 million would be interested in purchasing an electric car if it were available for around $4,000. The questionnaire was carefully phrased so that the people questioned, some 2,000 in a broad cross section of adults, were informed of the present limitations of electric cars. That is, it was deliberately stated that the electric car to be offered would have relatively short range, about 100 miles, and a maximum speed of about 50 mph.

Incidentally, surveys made in previous years showed only about 35% of the total motoring public interested in electric cars. That is, the total number of people interested in driving electric cars has risen dramatically since it is evident that the cost of gasoline is going to continue to rise in the foreseeable future. This is not a scare message at all; prices for gasoline in European countries and in most of Asia, Africa, and South America are higher than in the United States. In fact, in many advanced countries, including Japan, where the costs of gasoline and oil are substantially higher than in our nation, there are extensive government-sponsored programs to develop electric cars. Don't be surprised if the first mass-produced EV's offered by car dealers here carry a Japanese or European emblem.

We have been informed by a source close to the Japanese test drivers who have been driving experimental electric cars on U.S. tracks that some of the new electric models from Japan can travel more than 200 mph. Although this is not significant for the average driver in terms of the top speed you want to reach, it shows that the cars are becoming far more efficient and that their velocity is being extended past the normal top freeway speeds. Also, if an electric car can travel a few miles at 200 mph, it will very likely have a range of up to 100 miles at 55 mph.

Fig. 2–1. Renault Caravelle looks no different as an electric car

You Want Performance

The kind of electric car you can build from an ordinary clunker may be typified by the Renault sport coupe which Fred Riess made into a SEECOM electric car. SEECOM is an acronym for a Sensible, Economic, Electric COMmuter.

This modified Renault has four-wheel independent suspension and four-wheel disc brakes. The original curb weight, with its internal combustion engine at the rear and rear-wheel drive, was 1,750 pounds. See figure 2-1.

After conversion to an electric car, the total curb weight (that is, without passengers) is about 2,000 pounds. Although the weight was reduced because an electric motor and electronic controls were substituted for the internal combustion engine, that savings of some 50 pounds is overcome by the 300 pounds of storage batteries that were added.

Here is a brief summary of the performance specifications:

Acceleration: 0-40 mph in 15 seconds.
Top speed: About 60 mph.
Range: Approximately 50 miles at 25 mph under normal commuting conditions. This means frequent stops at traffic lights and typical urban driving. Range is about 20 miles at 50 mph.

Both the top speed and the range can be improved by adding more batteries, but at the expense of somewhat reduced acceleration because of added weight.

The electric motor used in the original modification was a surplus aircraft starter/generator motor weighing 75 pounds. It is a DC motor that is compound-wound. (This term will be explained with other motor characteristics in a subsequent chapter on motors.) The motor rotates counterclockwise and is not reversible as it was originally designed so that it was necessary to use a transmission for backing up. Power output is 10 HP continuously without any cooling. Fifteen HP is available continuously when it is fan-cooled. A photograph of this motor installed in the Renault appears in figure 2-2.

Fig. 2–2. Motor installation in Renault Caravelle

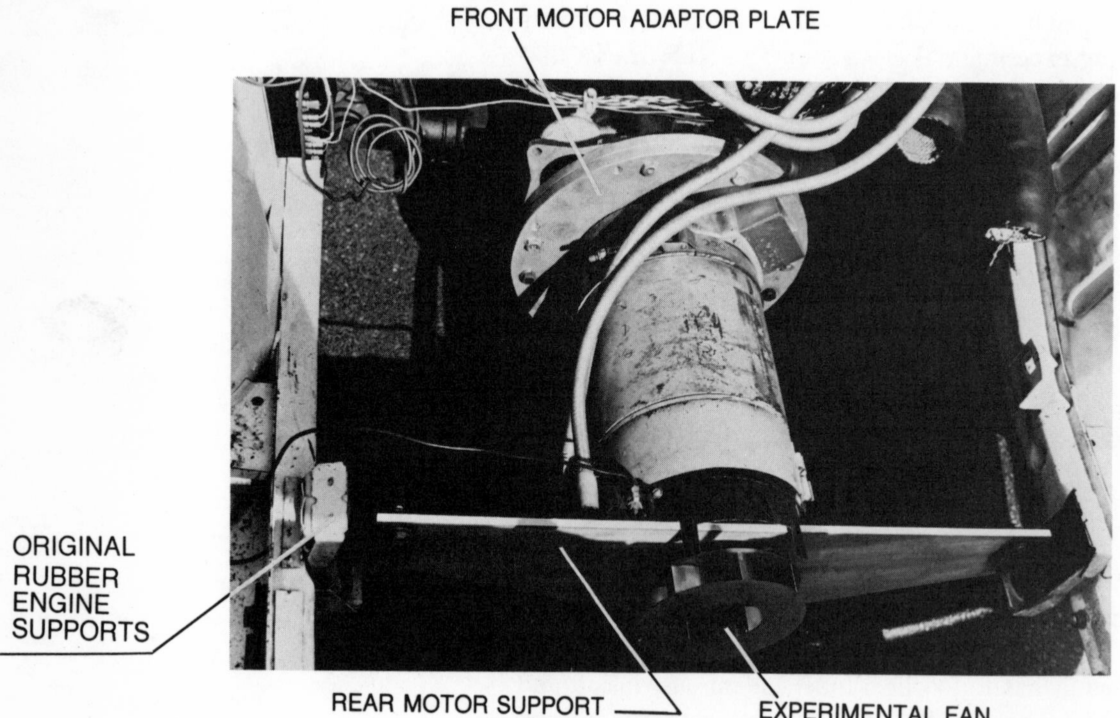

The transmission used with this car is the original manual four-speed forward and single-speed reverse. The electric car is normally used in second gear up to 40 mph, third gear to 50 mph, and fourth gear to 60 mph. First gear is used only for very steep grades. This Renault transmission is of the trans-axle type and will be described in the chapter on drive trains.

The battery pack for the Renault SEECOM electric car consists of eight 12-volt lead-acid batteries, each having a capacity of 85 ampere-hours at a 20-hour rate. They are connected in series-parallel to deliver 48 volts at 100 ampere-hours (two-hour rate), which corresponds to five kilowatt-hours of electric energy available.

The control system in the SEECOM is a silicon-controlled rectifier (SCR) chopper (see figure 2-3), which is described in detail in the chapter on electronic controls. It is a circuit which provides varying pulse widths at different frequencies, depending on the speed at which you want to drive the car. This is a convenient and efficient way in which to apply the DC from your storage batteries to the electric motor so that it will operate smoothly at various speeds and under varying load conditions. This kind of a control system has a range of 0–90% of the total power available from the storage batteries, and an efficiency of 98%. The control system also includes a shunt field control for regenerative charging. That is, the electric motor acts as a generator when you are slowing down so that some of the charge in your batteries is replaced every time you have to come to a halt, a feature that can extend the range of your electric car by a factor of as much as 15-20%.

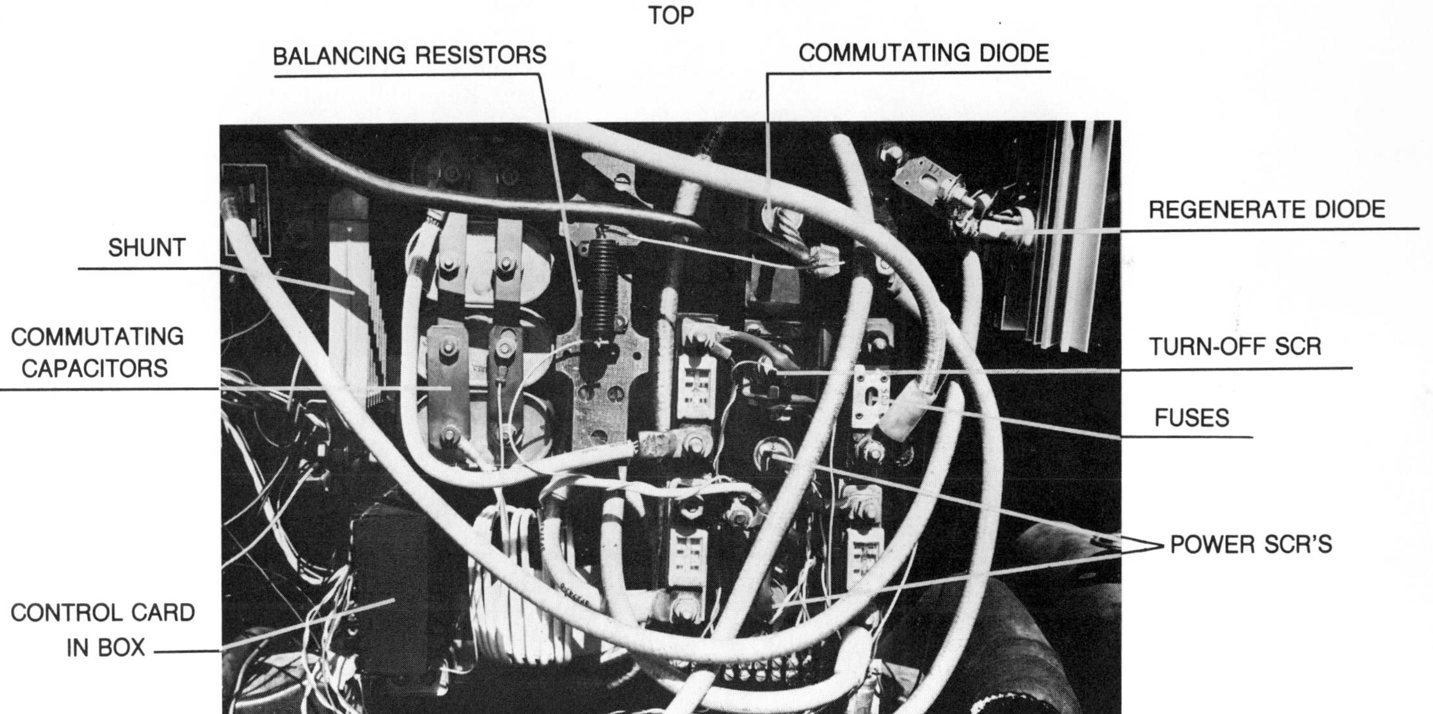

Fig. 2–3. Early version of SCR-chopper speed control. It used two 235A SCR's in parallel.

Instructions Applicable to Many Cars

Any kind of trans-axle vehicle may be converted efficiently into an electric car. By trans-axle, we mean a unit which has a transmission, differential, and drive shaft employing one or two universal joints. It is somewhat easier to convert a front-wheel-drive car with the electric motor and transmission in the front. However, as described in some detail in a later chapter, it is also quite possible for you to modify a compact car which has an engine and transmission mounted in the front followed by a drive shaft to the differential in the rear driving the rear wheels. Another variation is a rear-mounted engine connected to a trans-axle to drive the rear wheels.

STEP-BY-STEP PROCEDURE

The steps which you can follow in making your electric car will apply to a wide variety of compact cars. More details as to the modification of various cars are contained in chapter 8.

1. Obtain the detailed instruction manual for the car you want to convert. Study all the important drawings and pictures, as well as the written instructions, until you understand them completely.
2. When you are fully acquainted with the instruction manual, drain the engine and transmission oils. Also drain radiator water if you are modifying a car which has a radiator.
3. Disconnect the battery and all wires connected to the engine. Disconnect the accelerator cable or linkage and the fuel line. Remove the shrouds, splash-shields, fan and radiator, if the car is liquid-cooled.
4. Place loops of steel cable or chain at two different points around the engine. Then fasten the chain to a hoist above the engine or to two pieces of 2x4 wooden beams. You can place these wooden beams across the sides of the car if you protect the finish of the car with blankets or pads so that the engine, when it is hanging, will balance. An average 4-cylinder engine is heavy, weighing about 250 pounds.
5. Remove the rear engine support. Remove the bolts connecting the engine to the bell housing.
6. After reassuring yourself that the engine is supported securely, carefully separate the engine from its bell housing with the help of another person. Usually two sleeves or locating pins and the tip of the pilot shaft leading to the transmission must be cleared before you can remove the engine, so be extremely careful that you are free of this shaft before you move the engine up or down. Failure to do so might cause the shaft to break, and you would have a big job ahead replacing it. Follow these instructions carefully and you should have no problems. Remove the internal combustion engine and get rid of it. You have no further use for it!
7. Remove the gas tank and exhaust system. These are other items from your ICE clunker which you will need no longer.
8. *Making the front motor adaptor plate.* (See figure 2-4.)

   Note that making some of these parts will require machine tools. A band saw is needed for cutting 1" thick aluminum plate. A drill press is required for drilling holes easily and accurately. If you don't have access to a machine shop, you can lay out the parts you need made and get them from a local machine shop. Some operations are quite feasible with hand tools.

   a. Cut out 1" thick aluminum plate at least ¼" larger than bolt circle of bell housing (see drawing).
   b. Mark exact center and drill hole through center, the same size as pilot tip. The pilot tip is the end of the transmission shaft.
   c. The transmission in the car and the heavy aluminum plate should be prevented from slipping. Apply the correctly centered plate to the bell housing, using pilot tip of transmission shaft as guide, and clamp tightly.

CAUTION: Be sure the plate is centered and supported properly before clamping; otherwise the transmission shaft will be flexed and will not run concentrically.

   d. Mark drill centers through bell housing holes, using the same drill bit

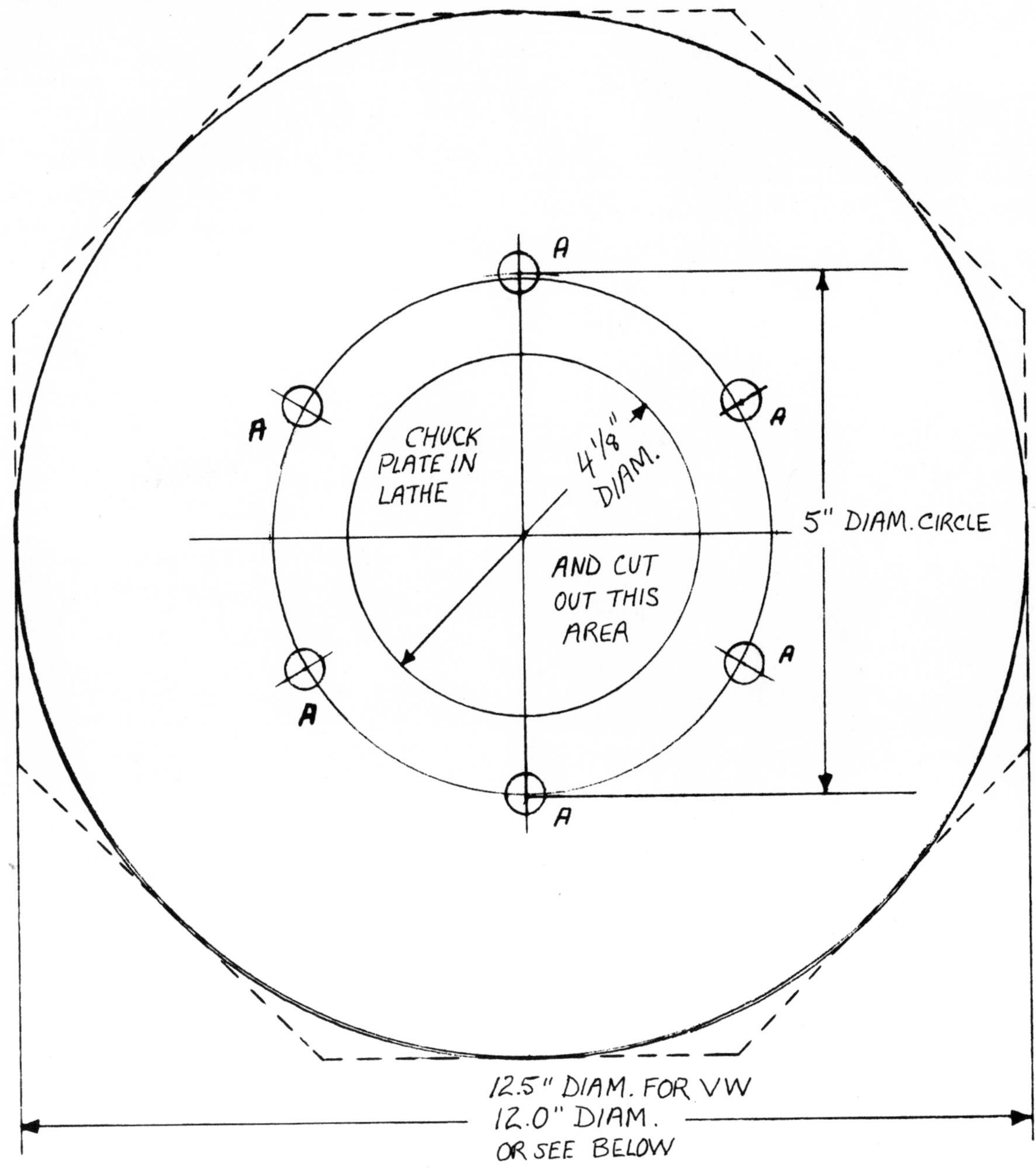

MATERIAL: 1" THICK ALUMINUM T-2024 (HARD) PREFERRED
DOES NOT HAVE TO BE CIRCLE - DOTTED OUTLINE CUT
WILL SUFFICE

HOLES: A - 7/16" DIAM.

Fig. 2–4. Front motor adaptor plate

THIS HAS TO BE MEASURED AND MACHINED VERY PRECISELY! TRANSMISSION MOUNTING HOLES NOT SHOWN. SEE INSTRUCTIONS. NOTE: BOLT CIRCLE WILL VARY DEPENDING ON THE MANUFACTURER OF YOUR AUTOMOBILE.

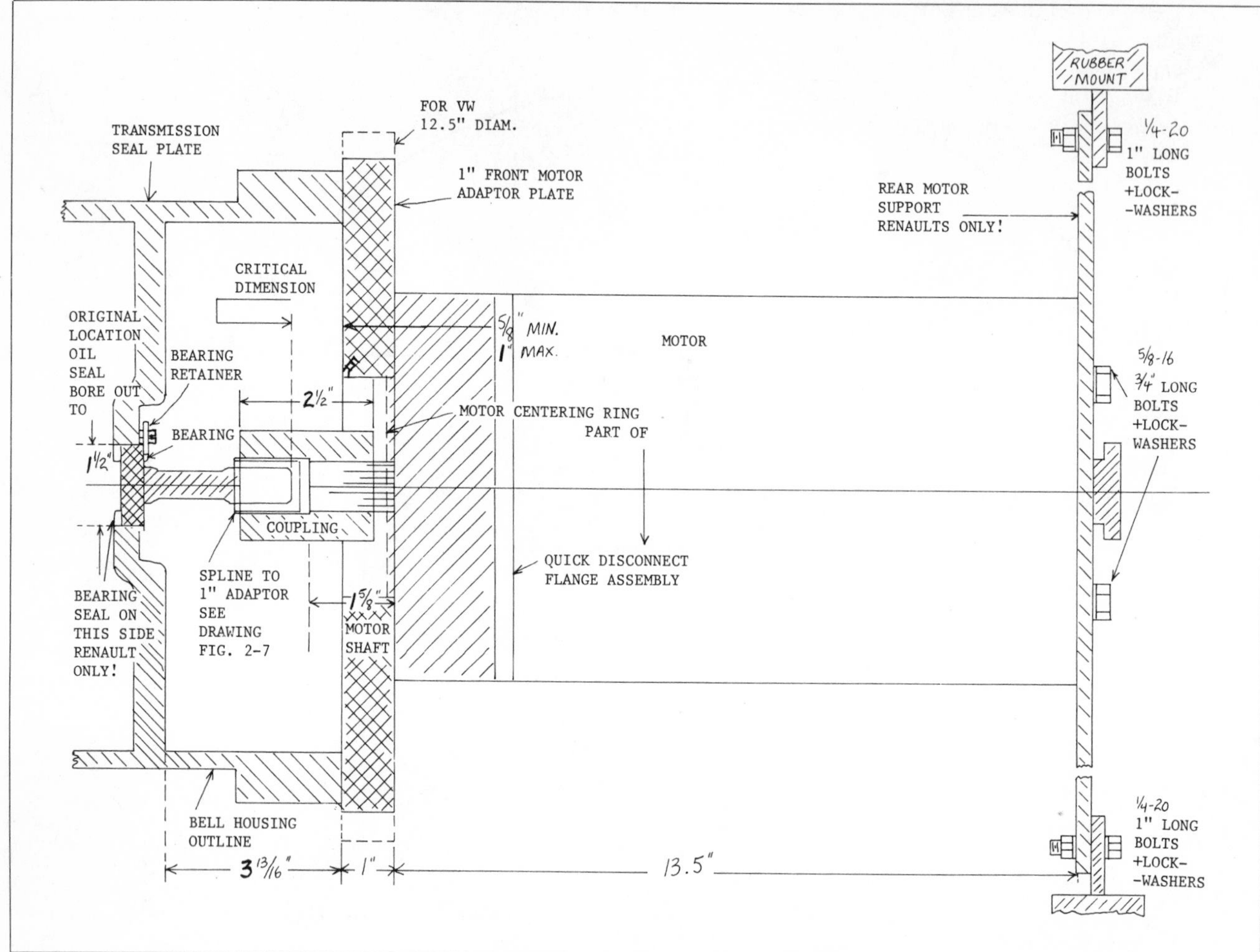

Fig. 2–5. Top view, cross section, motor assembly

size as hole size. By hand, apply some force while twisting drill bit back and forth. Remove plate.

e. Reinforce drill centers with center punch. Mark drill size for each hole (if different).
f. Drill out holes on drill press (use aluminum cutting liquid, available from hardware store); deburr holes.
g. Clamp disc in lathe and cut out 4 ⅛" diameter hole for motor centering ring (see figure 2–5).
h. Lay motor quick-disconnect ring on plate. The centering ring should be inserted now in hole made in Step g. The ring should be aligned with two holes exactly vertical (especially critical in rear-supported designs). See figure 2-5. Using ⅜" drill bit, proceed as per Steps 8d, 8e, and 8f in making holes.
i. The plate is now ready!

9. Make "CRITICAL DIMENSION" measurement as shown in assembly drawing, figure 2-5, and make minor variations to length of pilot tip cutoff in Step 12.

CAUTION: For next step use protective goggles. In VW's and other cars which do not have a readily removable transmission shaft, the pilot tip can be cut off, using a carborundum disc less than 2" in diameter mounted in a hand drill. The next five steps (10 through 14) apply to VW's, Renaults, or similarly constructed vehicles.

10. Remove bell housing; save screws and note exact locations for different size and length (metric). You will need them again when you reassemble the unit!
11. Remove transmission cover plate and follow directions as in Step 9.

12. Remove transmission shaft as described in Renault manual. Then cut off pilot tip as per Step 9 and the assembly drawing (figure 2-5), using a carborundum disc. Then reinstall shaft.
13. Remove oil seal in center of transmission cover plate, and bore out (if necessary, because it should be very close) to accept bearing. Also drill and tap for No. 6-32 screw as per drawing. See figure 2-6.
14. Now reassemble by reversing Steps 10 and 11. Apply some Form-a-Gasket No. 2 on inside of transmission cover plate for oil sealing.

Motor Assembly

1. Mount double-spline adaptor assembly on motor shaft and tighten set-screw. See figures 2-7 and 2-8.
2. Bolt together motor quick-disconnect plate and motor adaptor plate. (If motor you have does not have quick-disconnect feature, you have to bolt your motor to adaptor plate now!)
3. Bolt motor adaptor plate to bell housing.

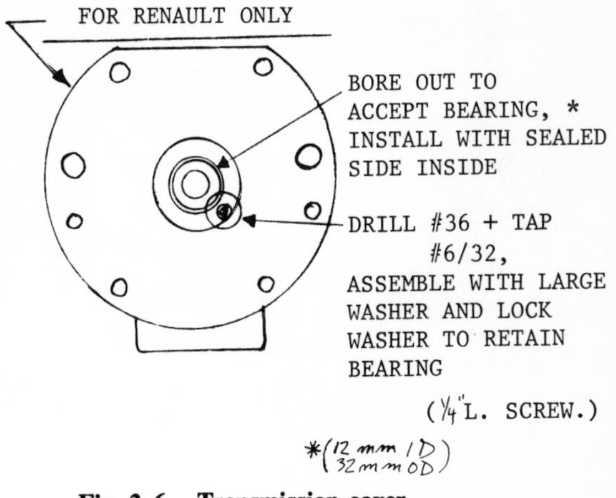
FOR RENAULT ONLY
BORE OUT TO ACCEPT BEARING, * INSTALL WITH SEALED SIDE INSIDE
DRILL #36 + TAP #6/32, ASSEMBLE WITH LARGE WASHER AND LOCK WASHER TO RETAIN BEARING
(1/4" L. SCREW.)
*(12 mm ID 32 mm OD)

Fig. 2–6. Transmission cover

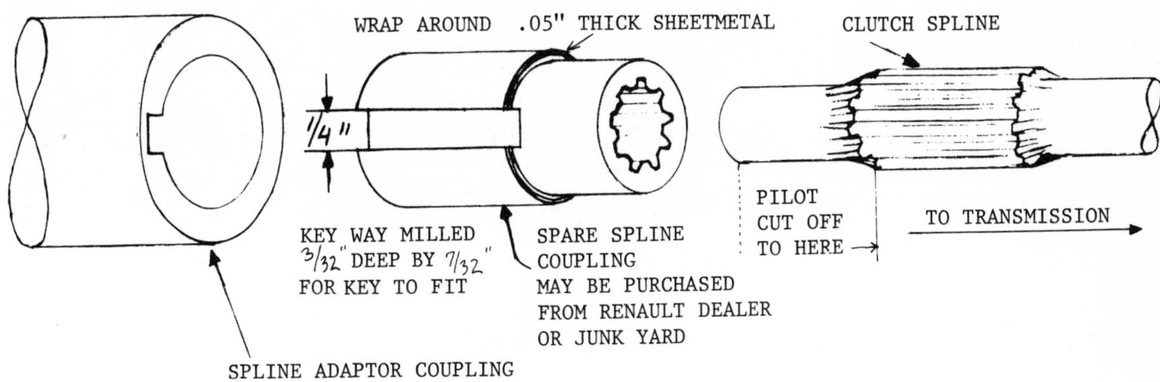
WRAP AROUND .05" THICK SHEETMETAL
CLUTCH SPLINE
1/4"
KEY WAY MILLED 3/32" DEEP BY 7/32" FOR KEY TO FIT
SPARE SPLINE COUPLING MAY BE PURCHASED FROM RENAULT DEALER OR JUNK YARD
PILOT CUT OFF TO HERE
TO TRANSMISSION
SPLINE ADAPTOR COUPLING

Fig. 2–7. Double spline adaptor coupling detail

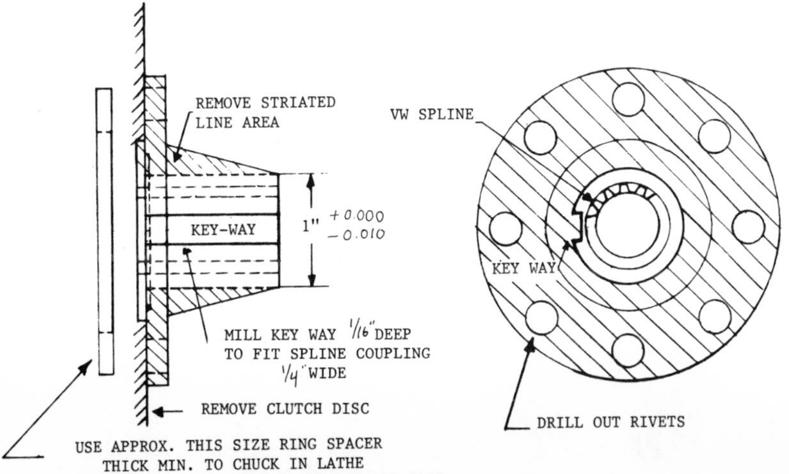
REMOVE STRIATED LINE AREA
VW SPLINE
KEY-WAY
1" +0.000 −0.010
KEY WAY
MILL KEY WAY 1/16" DEEP TO FIT SPLINE COUPLING 1/4" WIDE
REMOVE CLUTCH DISC
DRILL OUT RIVETS
USE APPROX. THIS SIZE RING SPACER
THICK MIN. TO CHUCK IN LATHE
TURN DOWN TO 1" - REMOVE EVERYTHING ELSE
THE RESULT IS A 1" DIAM. SLEEVE WITH A WIDE KEY WAY
WITH FEMALE SPLINE ON INSIDE TO MATCH TRANSMISSION SHAFT SPLINE

Fig. 2–8. VW spline adaptor sleeve shown; basically applies to most clutch-discs

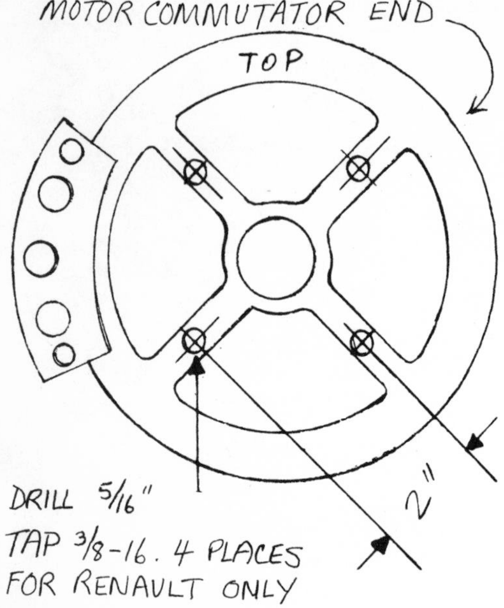

Fig. 2–9. Electric motor, rear view, showing holes to be drilled for rear motor support (if used)

Fig. 2–10. Rear motor support (use if required)

4. Using floor jack, carefully position motor about 30° counterclockwise (CCW) from mounting position (typical DC motor weighs about 75 pounds) and insert transmission shaft spline into spline adaptor. Push motor firmly toward transmission until it seats against quick-disconnect. Now twist motor clockwise (CW), while lifting locking pawl, until notch lines up with locking pawl. Now you can release locking pawl. Make sure the pawl is in the most CW notch. If you have difficulty seating motor, recheck Step 1, but push coupling in until it seats firmly and retighten set-screw. If you still have difficulty, recheck Steps 8 and 11 under the heading "Step-by-Step Procedure."
5. Position lock band in groove and tighten.
6. Bolt cables onto motor terminals.
7. Bolt rear motor support, where applicable, to motor. See figures 2-9 and 2-10.
8. Bolt motor support to original rubber motor mounts. Your motor is now installed!GV51,00181

Assembly of Electronic Controls

There are a variety of methods by which you can control the power to your electric motor from the array of batteries mounted in your car. In the chapter on electronic controls, you will find some typical circuits and instructions on building your own controls.

In the chapter on controls, there are various types of circuits, found to be effective with DC motors as well as some approaches to using AC motors. An inverter is required to convert the DC from your batteries to AC for typical induction or synchronous motors.

At this point it will be useful to look at figure 2-11, which is a block diagram showing how to connect your electronic controls to your batteries and electric motor. Further details are provided in subsequent chapters. For the moment, let us assume that you have made or purchased an electronic control system. We mention buying electronic controls because several manufacturers now supply off-the-shelf hardware which you can use efficiently for controlling the electric motor driving your car. For the do-it-yourselfer, figures 2-12 through 2-29 will be useful. Two choices of control methods are shown, with the parallel-series method recommended for the less electrically inclined person.

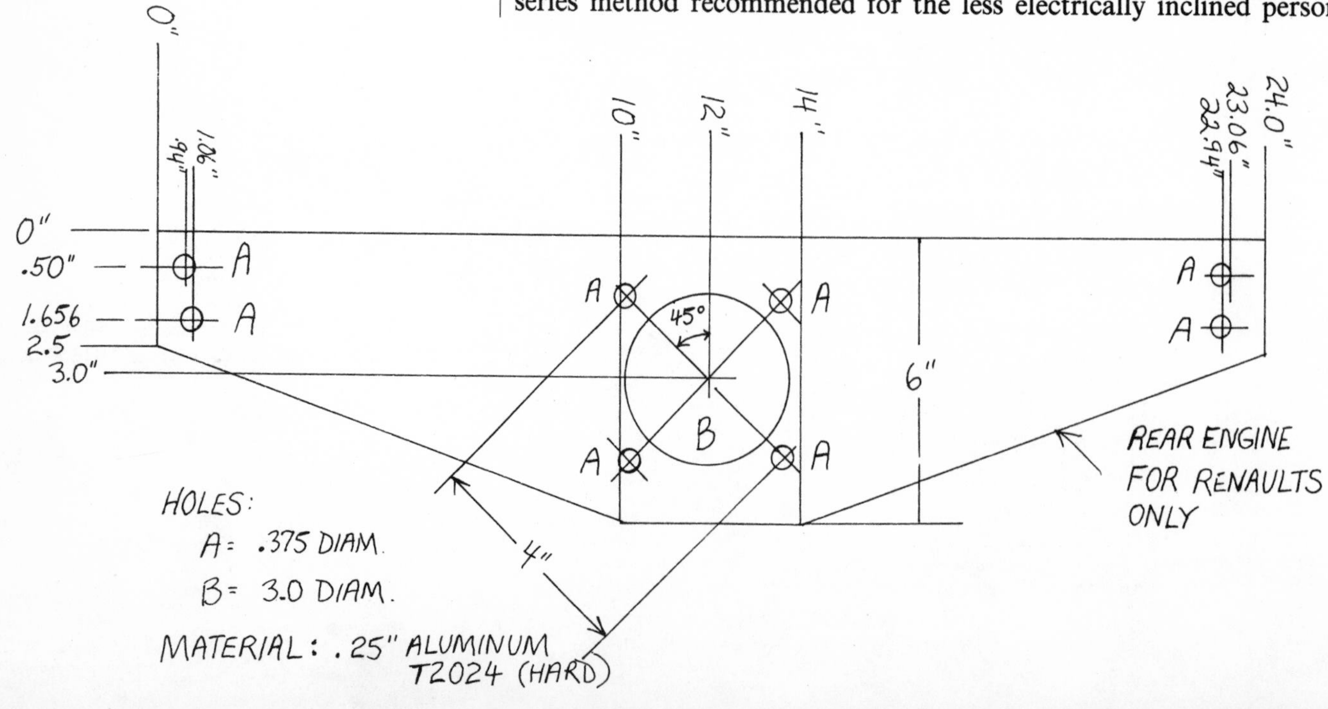

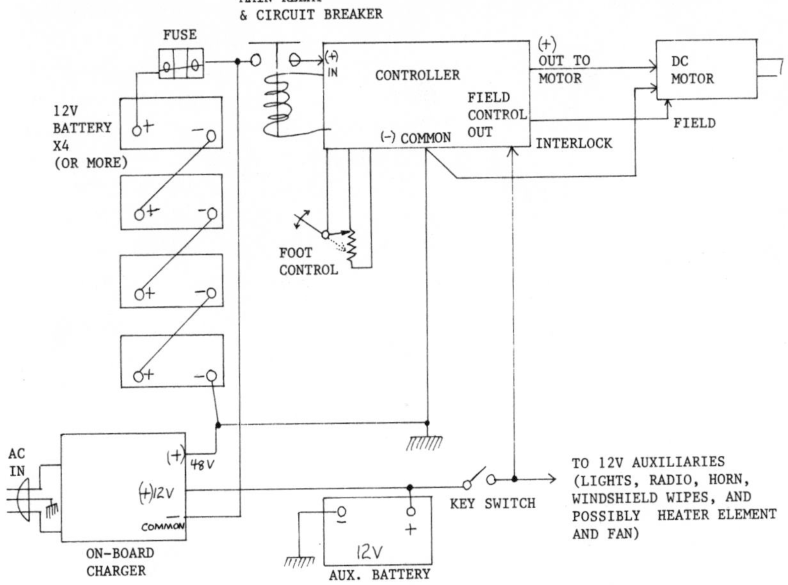

Fig. 2–11. Simplified block diagram of power circuit

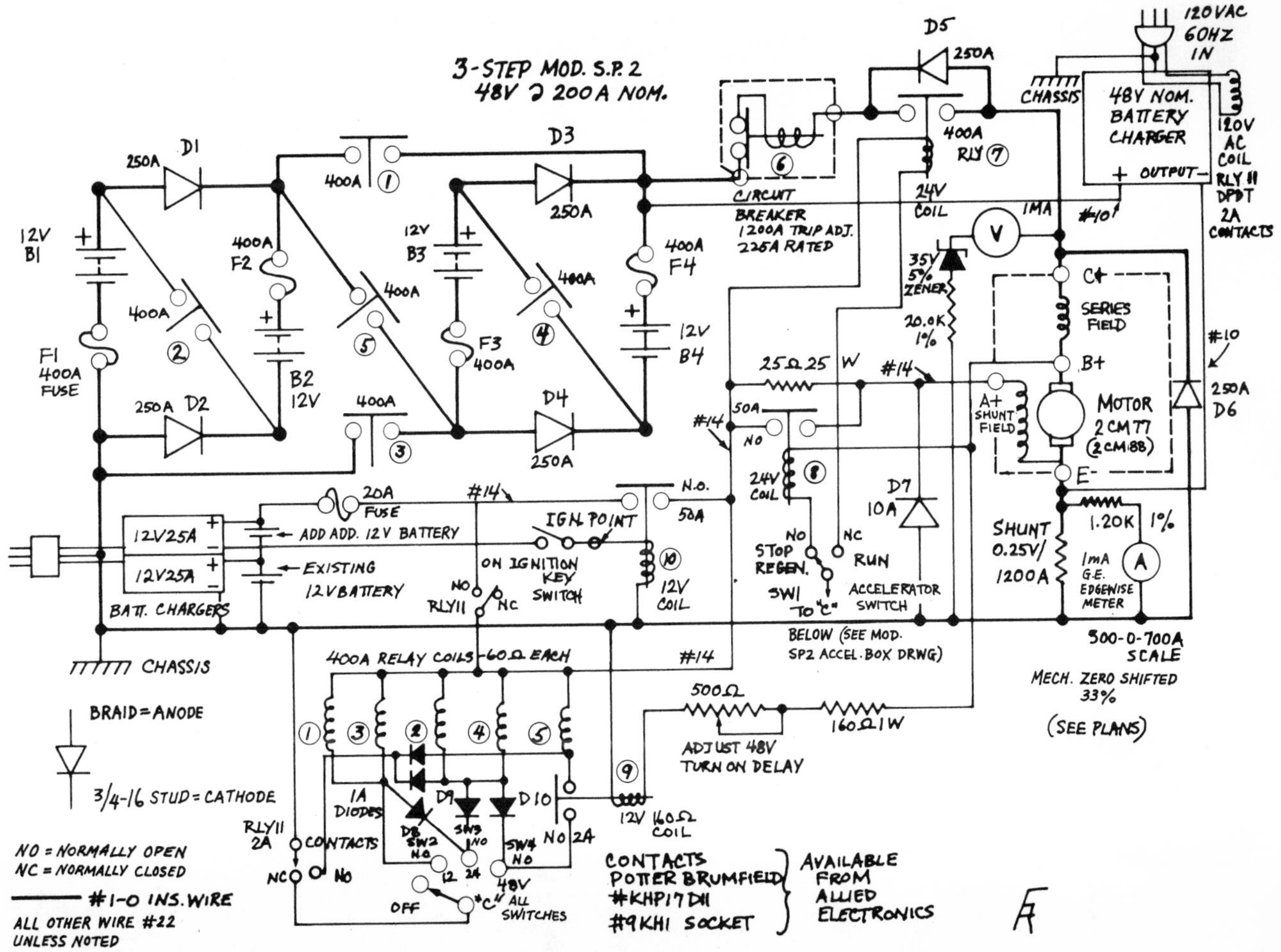

Fig. 2–12. SEECOM© electric car control schematic, 3-step mod. S.P.2, 48V @ 200A nom.

3-STEP MOD. S.P. 2
48V @ 200A NOM.

BRAID = ANODE
3/4-16 STUD = CATHODE

NO = NORMALLY OPEN
NC = NORMALLY CLOSED
#1-0 INS. WIRE
ALL OTHER WIRE #22 UNLESS NOTED

CONTACTS POTTER BRUMFIELD #KHP17D11 #9KH1 SOCKET } AVAILABLE FROM ALLIED ELECTRONICS

1MA G.E. EDGEWISE METER
500-0-700A SCALE
MECH. ZERO SHIFTED 33%
(SEE PLANS)

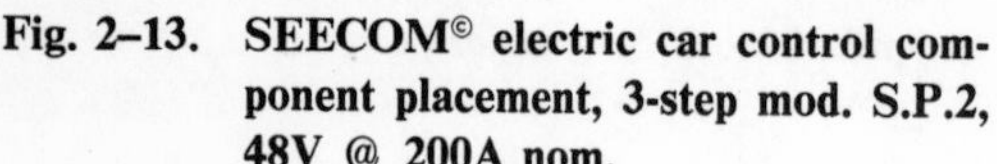

Fig. 2–13. SEECOM© electric car control component placement, 3-step mod. S.P.2, 48V @ 200A nom.

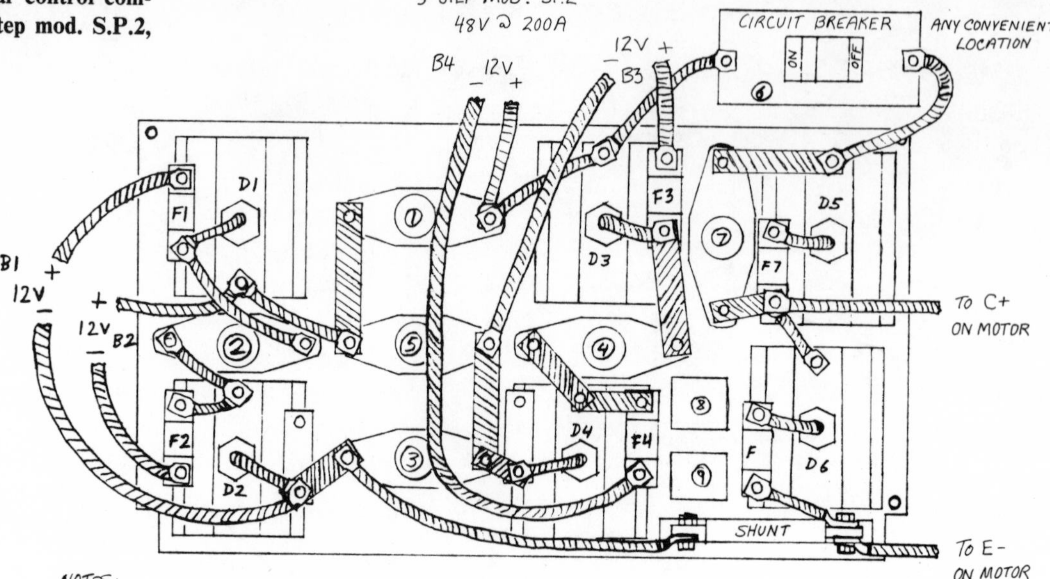

NOTES:

1. CONTROL WIRES NOT SHOWN.
2. D7 MOUNTED ON 1"x2" COPPER 1/8" THICK (NOT SHOWN).
3. ALL WIRES # 1-0 GLASS INSULATED, WITH 1-0 LUGS.
4. [hatched] STRAPS 1/16" THICK 1" WIDE COPPER OR EQUIVALENT.
5. PANEL CONSISTS OF 1/4" THICK PHENOLIC OR EQUIVALENT.
6. HEATSINKS MUST BE INSULATED!
7. SCRAPE OFF ANODIZED FILM FROM HEAT SINK CONTACT AREA.

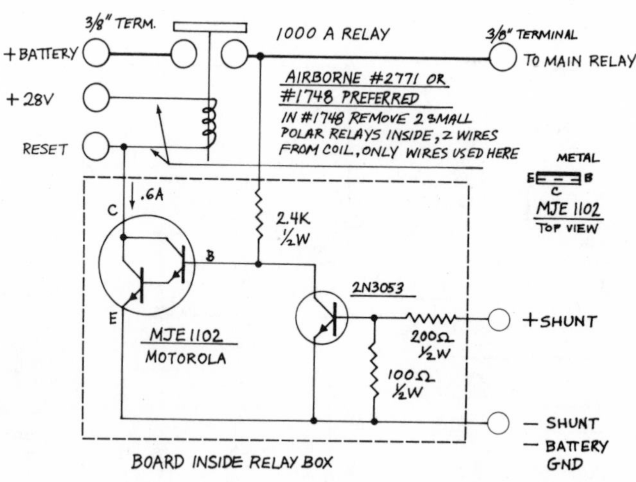

Fig. 2–14. Electronic circuit breaker—1200A trip (remote reset)

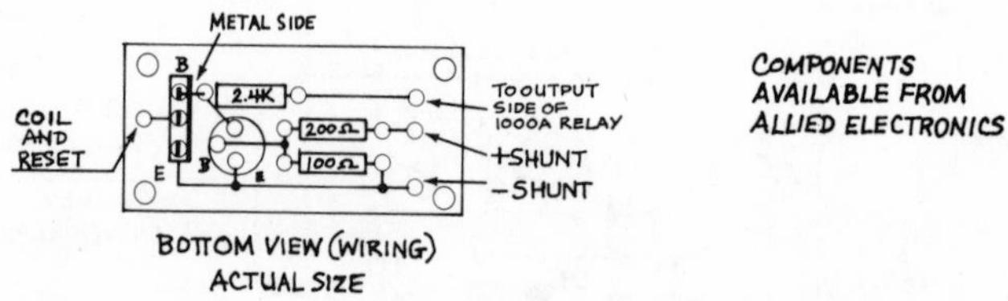

NOTE: THIS UNIT COULD BE REPLACED WITH A STANDARD INDUSTRIAL CIRCUIT BREAKER TYPE KA WHICH HAS ADJUSTABLE TRIP CURRENT. 2 POLE TYPE. BUT YOU WILL NOT HAVE REMOTE RESET.

AMPERE RATING	TRIP I. ADJUST RANGE LOW	HIGH
175A	875	1750
PREFERRED → 225A	1125	2250

SET FOR APPROX. 1200 AMPERES.

Test Procedure

CAUTION: Any time you work on the car, you should disconnect one 500-ampere fuse. During any live test, including the following, you should wear safety glasses or goggles.

After you have completely assembled and wired the control panel, recheck *all* your wiring to make sure there are no errors. Also make sure there are no heat sinks or pieces of metal touching. Be especially watchful of loose, unwanted pieces of wire. **SAFETY FIRST!**

To check out the unit, you will need a 48-volt battery pack (your batteries for driving the car) and a temporary load resistor. In addition to a voltohmmeter (VOM), an oscilloscope would be handy if you know how to use it. The load resistor consists of a 120-volt AC electric heater, which should have a rated current of at least 20 amperes (20A).

Follow the sequence of directions exactly and everything should go just fine!

1. Lay the control assembly on an insulated surface. Then, using two No. 16-gauge or heavier wires, connect one end of each wire to the proper motor output terminals of the controller and the other end to a female socket that is plugged into the heater plug. Be sure the wires on the socket do not short each other out!
2. Connect the battery after you make sure the control box rod is all the way out (it should be, since it is spring-loaded). The batteries should be fully charged, of course.
3. Connect the 24V terminal to the 24V point on the batteries—verify with VOM.
4. Connect a momentary pushbutton from the reset point on the circuit breaker box to ground.
5. Push the button. You should hear the contacts in the circuit breaker box close with a clack, and they should stay closed when you release the pushbutton.
6. Now remove the 24V wire from the battery—the circuit breaker contacts should drop out, as indicated by a dull, thudlike sound.
7. If satisfactory, repeat Steps 3, 4, and 5.
8. Very slowly pull out the rod from the control box; you should hear the main relay close with the typical clacking sound. At the same time you may hear a buzzing sound from the chopper section. Pull the rod out farther; the buzzing sound should increase in pitch. Now watch the heater coils (simulated load resistor) while you slowly keep pulling out the control rod; the coils should glow brighter and brighter.
9. Pull out the rod until it hits the stop; you should hear another clack, which comes from the bypass relay, giving you full power. In this condition, the chopper will stop making noise, and the heater coils will be at maximum power; they will draw from 48V DC, and there will be practically no power to speak of lost in the controller—ideal cruising condition.
10. Release the rod slowly, and the chopper will usually start buzzing again. If not, it's nothing to worry about; just release the rod completely, which will cause the main relay to drop out, and everything will stop. The next time you pull out the rod it will operate properly again.

This concludes preliminary testing. Disconnect the battery via the fuse. Disconnect 24V wire.

CAUTION: For the next test, jack up the driving wheels and/or place transmission in neutral.

11. Connect the motor instead of the heater, using No. 1–0-gauge wire or larger. If the motor is not in the car yet, support it with a couple of metal bands bolted to the bench. The reaction torque can be quite surprising if the motor should speed up suddenly.

12. Repeat Steps 3 through 10.

CAUTION: With no load on the motor, refrain from applying too much power to it for more than a fraction of a second, because it can overwind and possibly fly apart. Operating revolutions per minute (rpm) are usually less than 6,000 rpm under load.

13. If everything is all right, you are ready to install the control panel, wires, etc.
14. After you have installed everything, double-check every wire and make sure all power connections are tight (use wrench, about 5 ft-lb of force). Don't over-torque—the studs are plated copper, which is soft!
15. Put gear selector into neutral and push "GO" switch. Repeat Steps 3 through 10 except you now step on pedal. Then, if everything works properly, don't disconnect the battery or 24V tap, but take your foot off the accelerator pedal. The control switch is now in "STOP" position.
16. Put your left foot on the brake pedal and shift into second gear. Be sure there are no children or obstacles in the way. Switch to "GO."

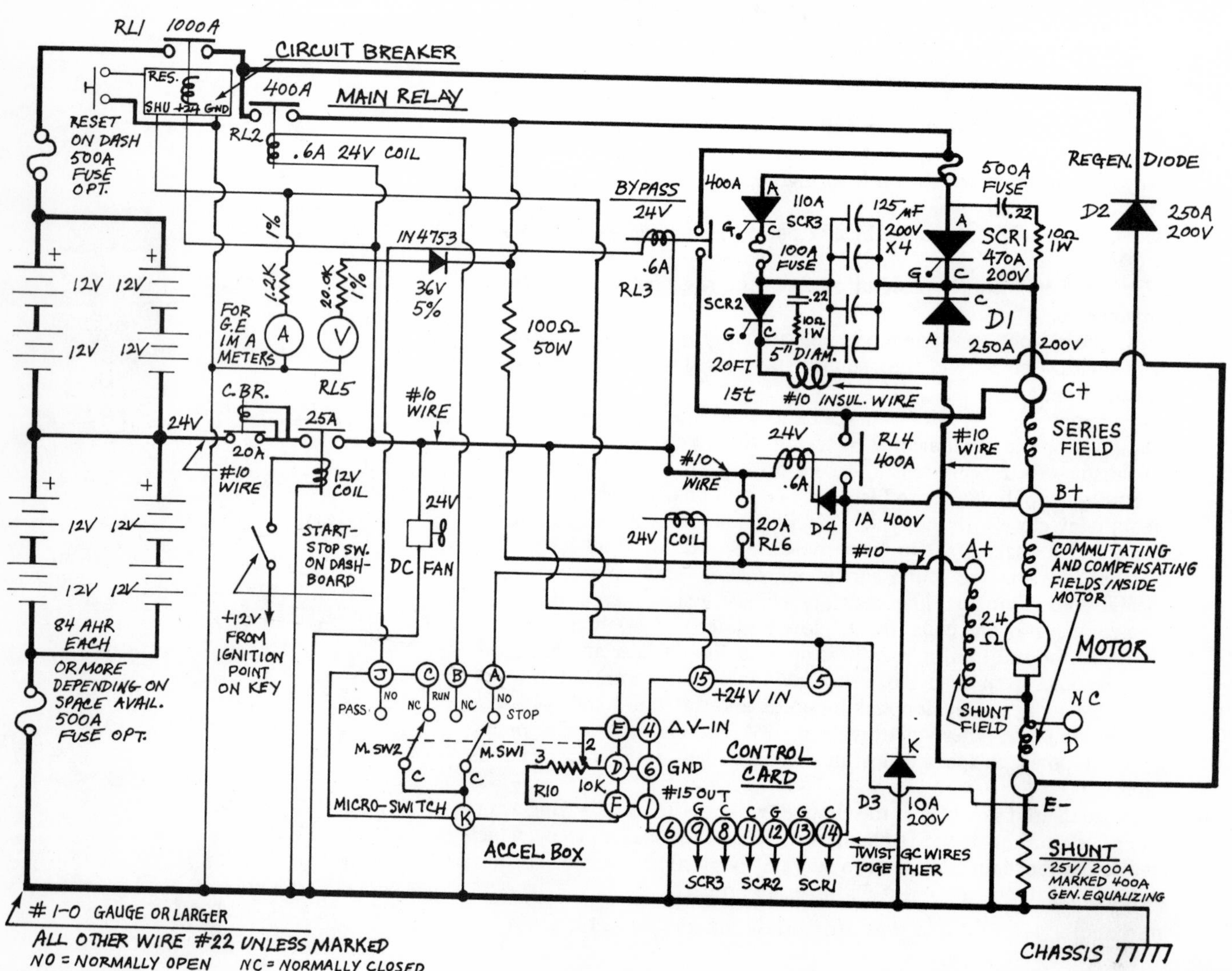

Fig. 2–15. Main power control circuit—SCR chopper

Gently push down on the accelerator pedal, while you ease off on the brake. You should start moving gently, accompanied by the buzzing sound of the chopper and the motor. You may shift gears by matching rpms.

To stop, you simply remove your foot from the accelerator pedal. Regeneration works automatically if you are going fast enough, or going downhill.

That is all there is to it!

One final word of advice: Save all your receipts. You may need them for registration, just like any other special vehicle registration. Also, in your joy in being able to outrun gas pumps, remember to plug in your battery charger as often as practical. This extends battery life and the car is always ready to give you maximum range.

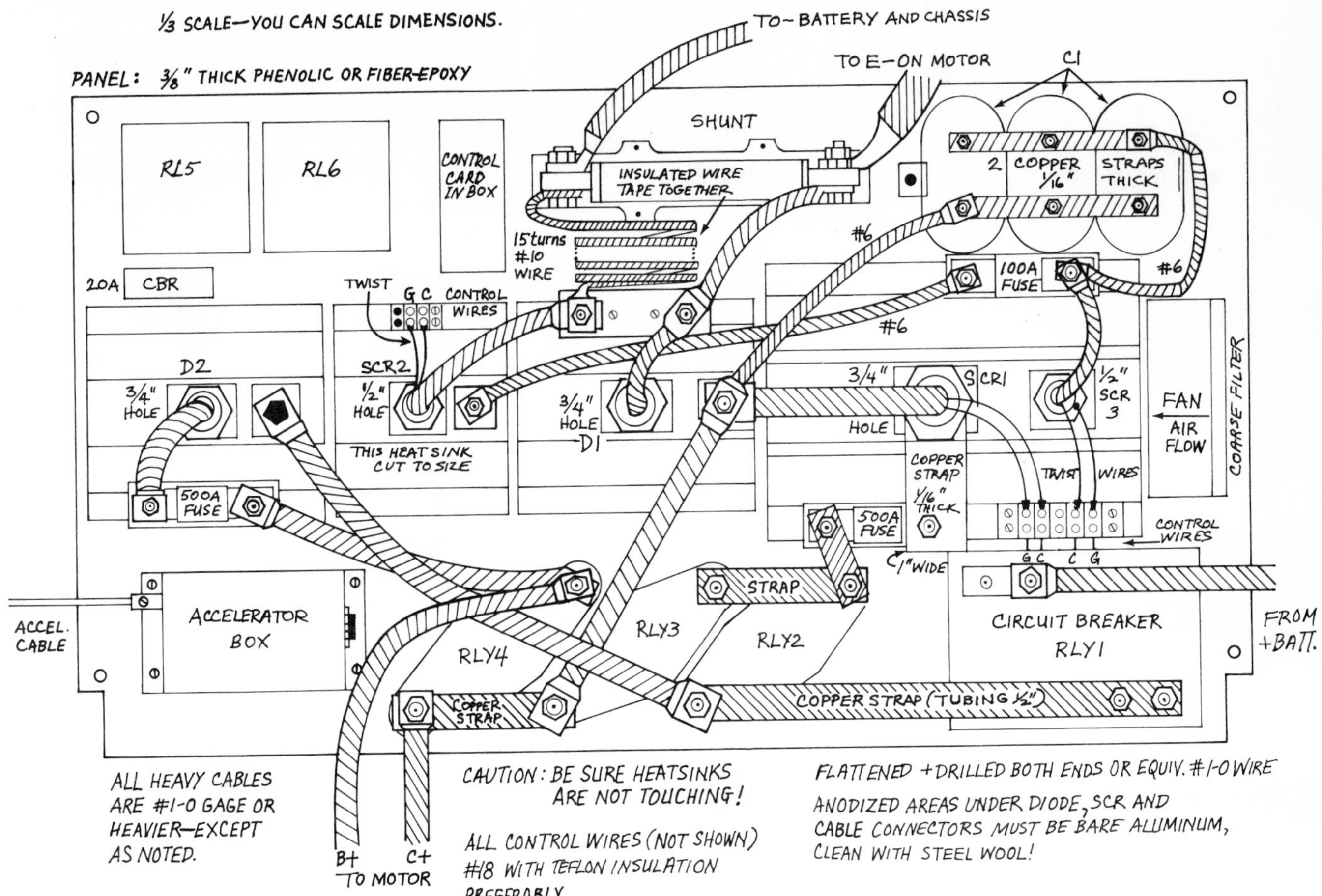

Fig. 2–16. Main power control panel of SCR chopper

QTY.	DESIG.	DESCRIPTION	MFG. NO.	SOURCE ORDER NO.		APPROX. PRICE EA.
1		MOTOR, SURPLUS GEN. *NO* QUICK DISCONNECT!	2 CM77 } SURPLUS			62.50
		OR MOTOR SURPLUS GEN. PREFERRED, QUICK DISCON.	2 CM77			84.00
		OR MORE POWERFUL, 2" LONGER, QUICK DISCON.	2 CM88			84.00
2	DI, D2	* DIODE, 250A 200V MIN. ANY MAKE	INT.RECT.1N2057	NEWARK	1N2057	18.90
1	SCR1	* SCR, 470A RMS,200V 15μ SEC t off MAX.! Contact SEECOM for latest and lowest price	WEST.T707023074	WEST.	T70702-3074	182.00
2	SCR2,3	* 110A RMS 200V SCR, ANY MAKE	WEST. 250D	WEST.	250D	26.00
3	C1	* AC CAPACITORS, 125μF 120V AC PAPER	GE 28F1104	GE	28F1104	37.29
6		* BRACKET FOR ABOVE NON-POLARIZED CAP.	302C920P115	GE		0.075
1		* HEATSINK—THERMALLOY FOR SCR1	6690B	ALLIED	957-3150	14.00
3		* HEATSINK—THERMALLOY FOR SCR2, D1, D2	6641B	ALLIED	957-3020	4.85
3	RL2,3,4	RELAY, 400A, 24V COIL SURPLUS	CUTLER-	SURPLUS	877	7.50
1	RL1	RELAY, 1000A, 24V COIL SURPLUS (ANY)	HAMMER	SURPLUS	1748	12.95
2	RL5,6	RELAY, 25A, 12V-24V COIL SURPLUS	OR EQUIVALENT	SURPLUS	1775	5.95
		or RELAY, 50A, 12V-24V SURPLUS	"	SURPLUS	1804	3.50
4		* FUSE-HOLDERS UP TO 500A FUSES	BURTON	SEECOM		1.50
3		* FUSES, 500A (ORDER SPARES)		SEECOM		2.50
1		* FUSES 100A (ORDER SPARES)		SEECOM		1.00
1		* SHUNT .25V/200A MARKED GEN EQU. RESIST. 400A (5 STRIPS)				
1		CIRCUIT BREAKER 20A		SEECOM		5.00
1		* FAN, 100CFM, 24V DC		SURPLUS		0.85
1	D3	DIODE 10A, 200V	INT.RECT. IN3210	NEWARK	1N3210	1.70
8		BATTERIES, 12V 84 AHR DIEHARD MAIL ORDER	SEARS	SEARS		38.00
1	D4	* DIODE, 1A, 400V, ANY MAKE				.50
1		* CIRCUIT BREAKER CARD SEE BELOW				
1		* CONTROL CARD SEE BELOW				
1		* ACCELERATOR BOX SEE BELOW				
1		SPLINE COUPLING		AIRBORNE	28	4.95
1		BALL BEARING	201KK	ALL BEARING		2.10

*** DESIGNATES SCR CONTROL COMPONENTS**

Fig. 2–17. Main power components using SCR controller

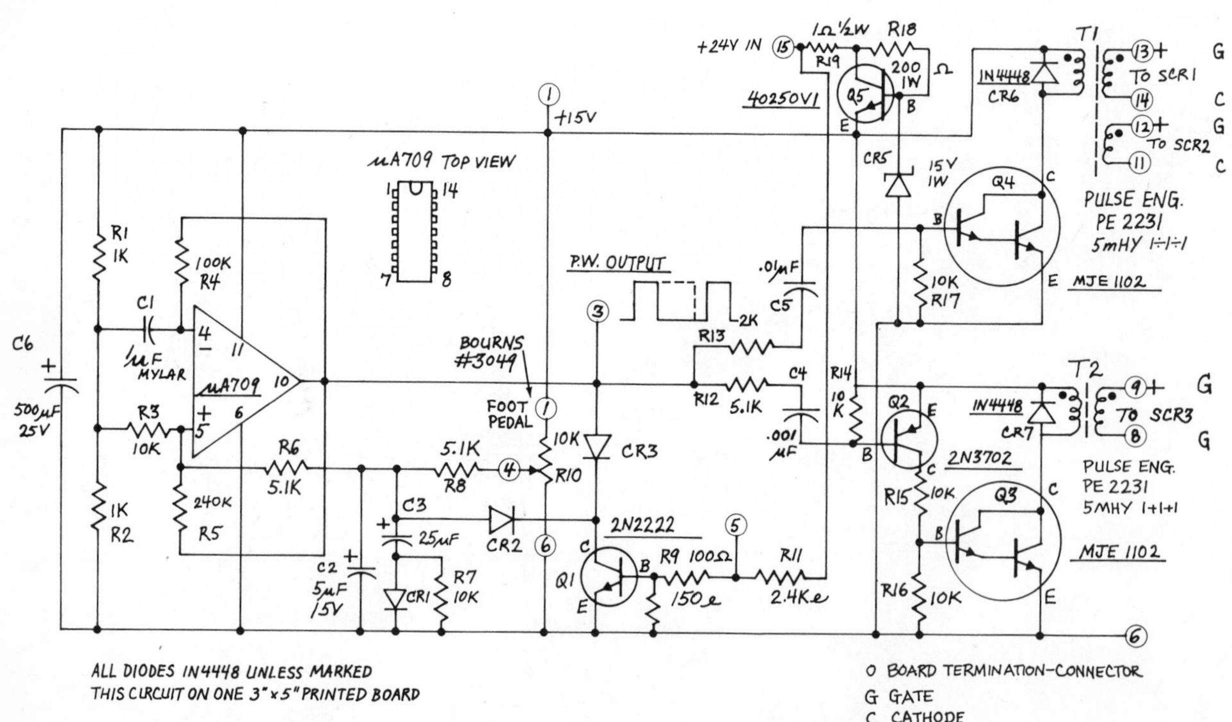

Fig. 2–18. Pulse width and frequency modulator card control card for SCR chopper

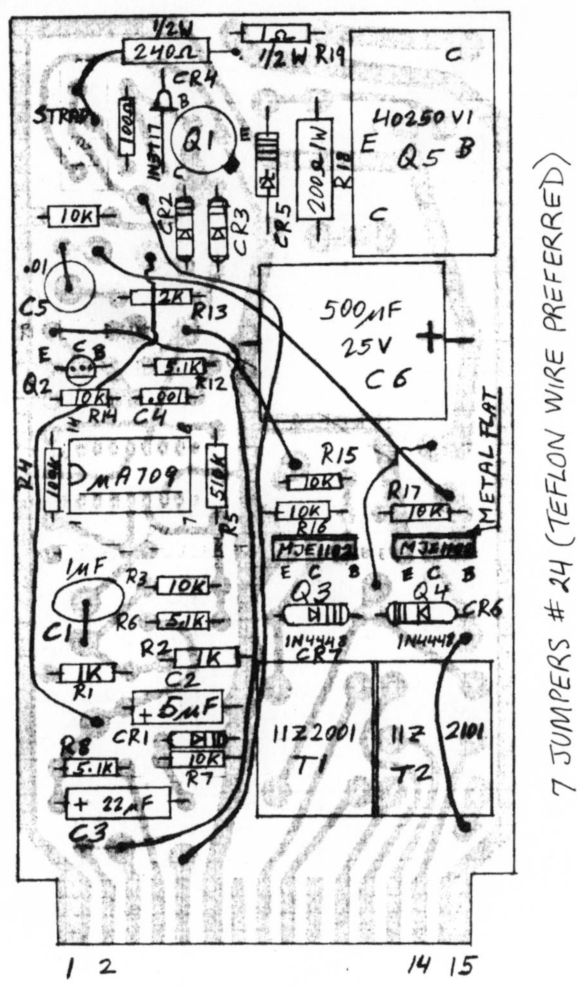

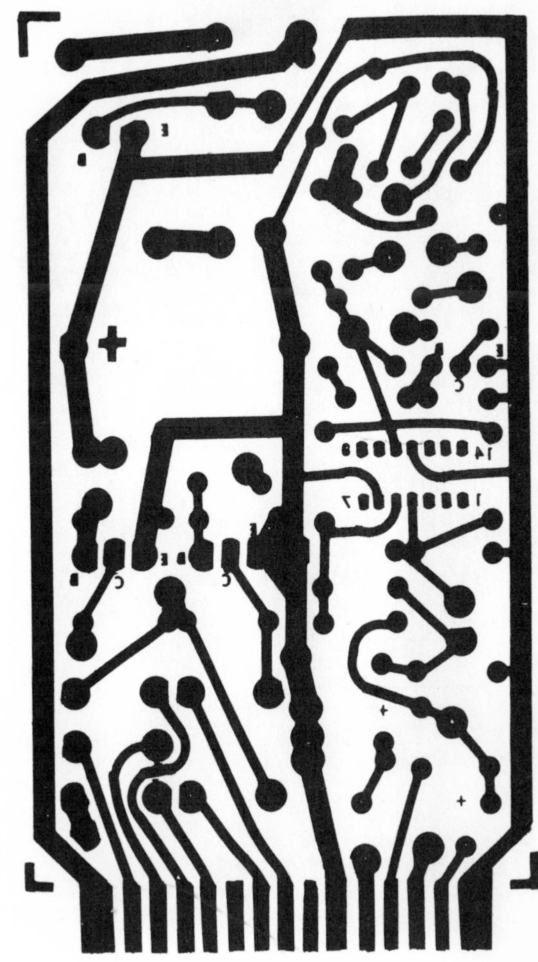

Fig. 2–19. Pulse width and frequency modulator card

QTY.	DESIG.	DESCRIPTION	MFG. NO.	SOURCE	ORDER NO.	PRICE EA.
		RESISTORS:				
2	R1, R2	1K Ω 1/4W 5% CARBON COMPOSITION	ANY	ALLIED	926C2100	.07
6	R3,7,14				926C2100	.07
	R15,16,17	10K Ω 1/4W 5% CARBON COMPOSITION		ALLIED	926C2100	.07
1	R4	100K Ω 1/4W 5% CARBON COMPOSITION		ALLIED	926C2100	.07
1	R5	240K Ω 1/4W 5% CARBON COMPOSITION		ALLIED	926C2100	.07
3	R6,8,12	5.1K Ω 1/4W 5% CARBON COMPOSITION		ALLIED	926C2100	.07
1	R9	100 Ω 1/4W 5% CARBON COMPOSITION		ALLIED	926C2100	.07
1	R11	2.4K Ω 1/2W 5% CARBON COMPOSITION		ALLIED	926C2200	.07
1	R13	2K Ω 1/4W 5% CARBON COMPOSITION		ALLIED	926C2100	.07
1	R18	200 Ω 1/2W 5% CARBON COMPOSITION		ALLIED	926C2200	.07
1	R19	1 Ω 1/2W 5% CARBON COMPOSITION		ALLIED	926C2200	.07
	R10	*LINEAR POTENTIOMETER—SEE ACC. BOX (10K)	BOURNS #3049	BOURNS	3049J-1-103	7.50
		CAPACITORS:				
1	C1	1 μF 10% MYLAR 100V	TRW TYPE X663F	ALLIED	960-3050	2.78
1	C4	.001 μF 10% MYLAR 100V	TRW TYPE 663UW	ALLIED	960-6010	.85
1	C5	.01 μF 10% MYLAR 100V	TRW TYPE 663UW	ALLIED	960-6070	.96
1	C2	5 μF 15V ELECTROLYTIC-ALUMINUM	SPRAGUE TE1152	ALLIED	926-1159	.71
1	C3	25 μF 15V ELECTROLYTIC-ALUMINUM	SPRAGUE TE1157.1	ALLIED	926-1170	.71
1	C6	500 μF 25V ELECTROLYTIC-ALUMINUM	SPRAGUE 507G0-25HE4	ALLIED	926-5620	2.29
		MISCELLANEOUS:				
1	μA709	OPERATIONAL AMPLIFIER μA709C D.I.P.	T1 SN52709N	ALLIED	SN52709N	1.80
1		* PRINTED CIRCUIT CARD				
5	CR1,2,3,6,7	DIODE IN4448, HIGH SPEED, 200MA 100V	SYLVANIA	ALLIED	IN4448	.96
1	Q1	TRANSISTOR, NPN, 2N2222	MOTOROLA	ALLIED	2N2222	1.13
1	Q2	TRANSISTOR, PNP 2N3702 SILICON	TI.	ALLIED	2N3702	.45
2	Q3, Q4	TRANSISTOR, DARLINGTON, POWER, MJE1102	MOTOROLA	ALLIED	MJE1102	2.21
1	Q5	TRANSISTOR, POWER, 40250V1 W/HEAT SINK	RCA	ALLIED	40250V1	1.49
2	T1, T2	PULSE TRANSFORMER, 11Z2101	SPRAGUE 11Z2101	ALLIED	925-9031	4.55
1	CR 5	ZENER DIODE, 15V, 1W	MOTOROLA		1N4744A	1.80

Fig. 2–20. Control card pulse width and frequency for SCR controller

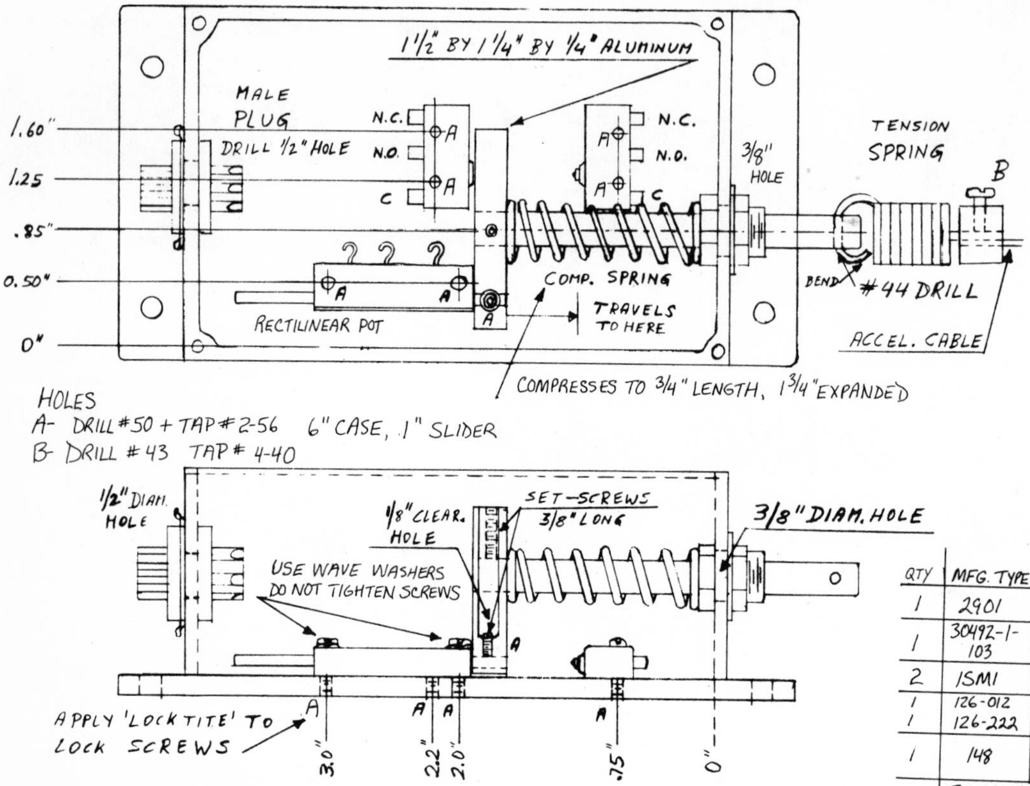

1 1/2" BY 1 1/4" BY 1/4" ALUMINUM

MALE PLUG
DRILL 1/2" HOLE

N.C.
N.O.
C

3/8" HOLE

TENSION SPRING

B

1.60"
1.25
.85"
0.50"
0"

RECTILINEAR POT

COMP. SPRING

TRAVELS TO HERE

BEND

#44 DRILL

ACCEL. CABLE

COMPRESSES TO 3/4" LENGTH, 1 3/4" EXPANDED

HOLES
A- DRILL #50 + TAP #2-56 6" CASE, .1" SLIDER
B- DRILL #43 TAP # 4-40

1/2" DIAM. HOLE

1/8" CLEAR. HOLE

SET-SCREWS 3/8" LONG

3/8" DIAM. HOLE

USE WAVE WASHERS
DO NOT TIGHTEN SCREWS

APPLY 'LOCKTITE' TO LOCK SCREWS

3.0" 2.2" 2.0" .75" 0"

Fig. 2–21. Accelerator box

PARTS LIST

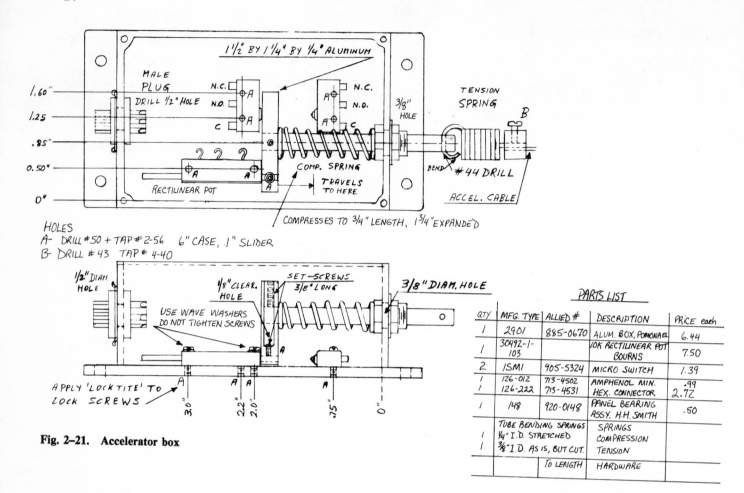

QTY	MFG. TYPE	ALLIED #	DESCRIPTION	PRICE each
1	2901	885-0670	ALUM. BOX, POMONA EL	6.44
1	30492-1-103		10K RECTILINEAR POT BOURNS	7.50
2	ISM1	905-5324	MICRO SWITCH	1.39
1 1	126-012 126-222	713-4502 713-4531	AMPHENOL MIN. HEX. CONNECTOR	.99 2.72
1	148	920-0148	PANEL BEARING ASSY. H.H. SMITH	.50
1 1	TUBE BENDING SPRINGS 1/4" I.D. STRETCHED 3/8" I.D. AS IS, BUT CUT TO LENGTH		SPRINGS COMPRESSION TENSION	
			HARDWARE	

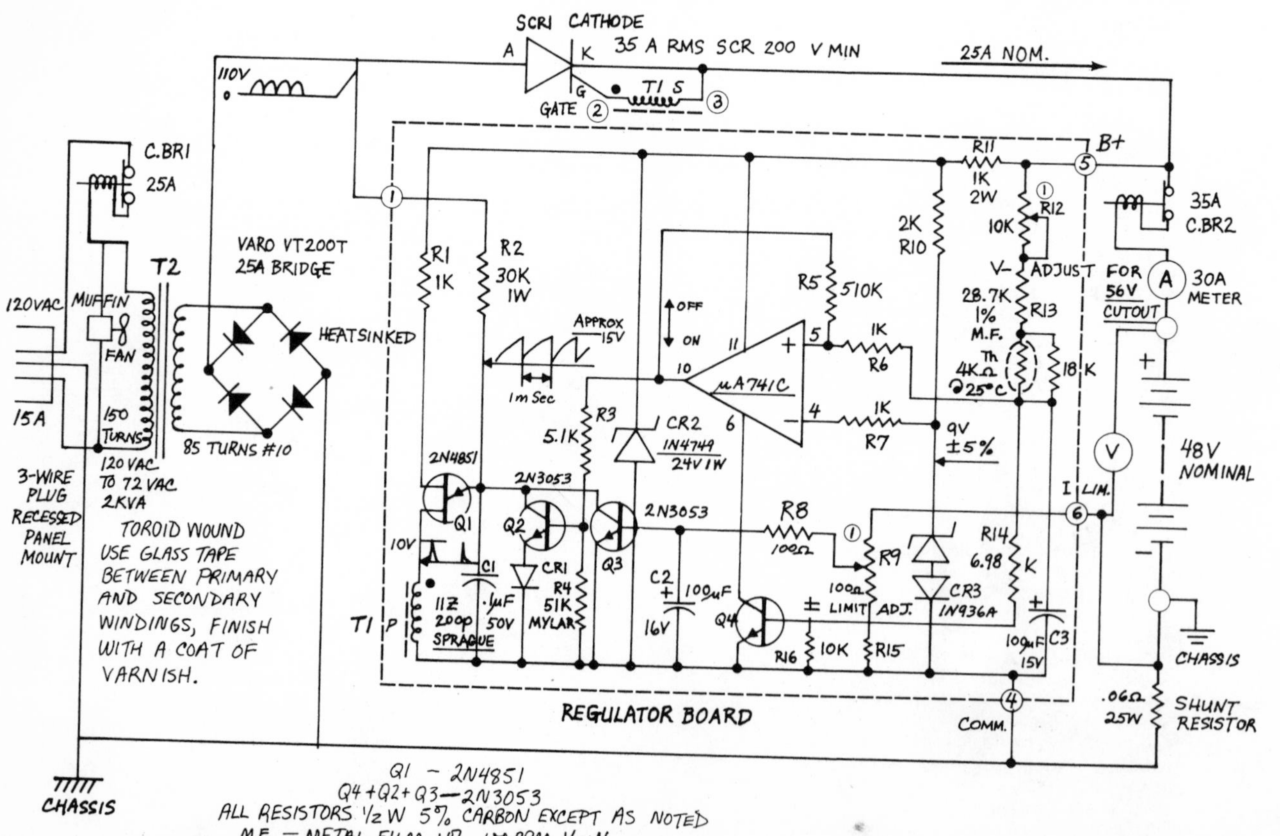

Fig. 2–22. 2 kW automatic charger

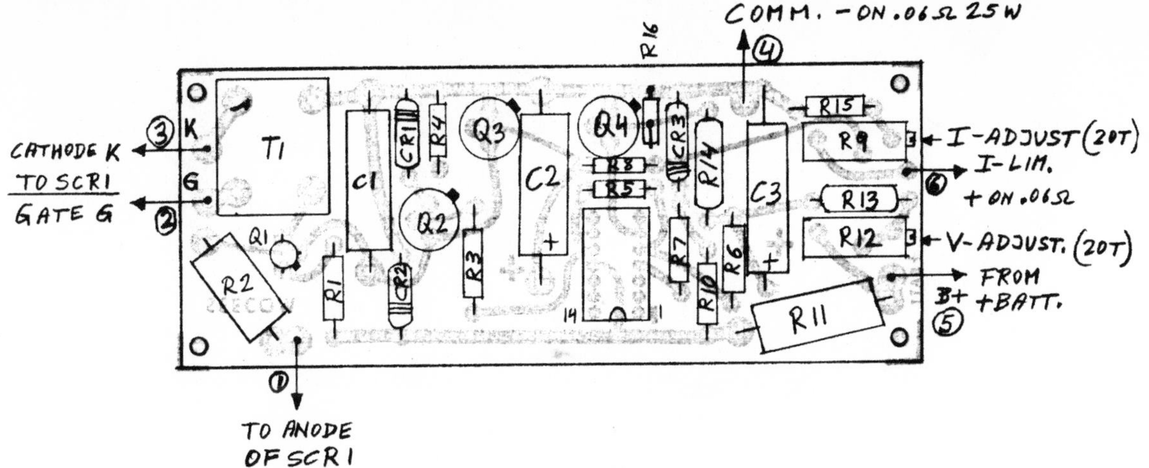

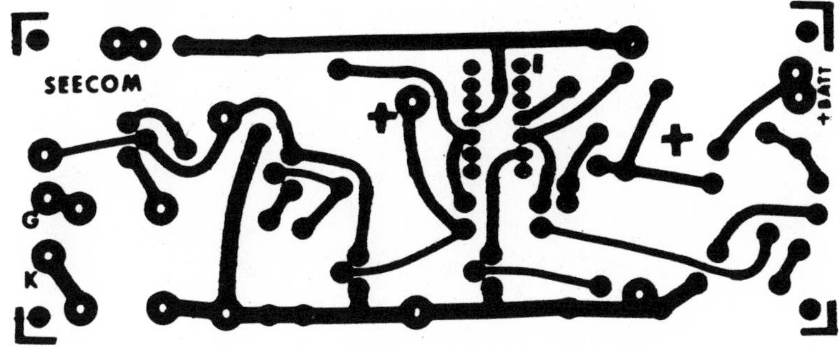

Fig. 2–23. Automatic charger regulator board wiring layout

QTY.	DESIG.	DESCRIPTION	MFR. #	SOURCE	ORDER #	APPROX. PRICE EA.
1		RECEPTACLE AMPHENOL "MS" #12 WIRE		ALLIED	712A 3102A-16-10P	1.94
1		CONNECTOR AMPHENOL		ALLIED	712A 3106A-16-10S	3.42
1	T2	2KVA VARIAC MODIFIED BY ADDING 85 TURNS #10 DOUBLE INSULATED VARNISH WIRE, OR EQUIV.	GE 9T92Y27	NEWARK	5F1009	45.00
1	CBR1,2	CIRCUIT BREAKER, DOUBLE POLE 30A 65V DC	HEINEMAN AM2-B3	ALLIED	812-0530	21.08
1	FAN	FAN, MUFFIN, 4 3/4" SQUARE, 1 1/2" DEEP, 80 TO 100 CU.FT./MIN	ROTRON MARK 4	ALLIED	907-6015	12.05
1	PLUG	PLUG, 3 WIRE, PANEL, RECESSED GROUNDING TYPE	HUBBEL 5240	SEARS		
1	BRIDGE	RECTIFIER BRIDGE, 25A, 200V	VARO VT200T	ALLIED	976-3162	8.00
	SCR1	SILICON CONTROLLED RECTIFIER, 35A RMS, 2N683 (any make)	RCA 2N 683	ALLIED	583-0683	4.48
1	METER	25A (30A) EDGEWISE				
1	METER	0-60V (OPTIONAL-ON DASH ALREADY)				
1	SHUNT	RESISTOR, .06Ω, 25W (0.12Ω 10W IN PARALLEL)		SEECOM	.06Ω	3.00
	WIRE	ABOUT 5 FEET #12 AND #22 TEFLON HOOK-UP WIRE				
	MISCELLANEOUS ALUM. PARTS, #10-32, 1/4" SCREWS, SEE MECH. DRAWING					
		REGULATOR BOARD				
		RESISTORS				
3	R1,6,7	1KΩ 1/4W 5% CARBON COMP.	ANY	ALLIED	926C2100	.07
1	R3	5.1KΩ 1/4W 5% CARBON COMP.	ANY	ALLIED	926C2100	.07
2	R4,16	10KΩ 1/4W 5% CARBON COMP.	ANY	ALLIED	926C2100	.07
1	R5	510KΩ 1/4W 5% CARBON COMP.	ANY	ALLIED	926C2100	.07
1	R8	100Ω 1/4W 5% CARBON COMP.	ANY	ALLIED	926C2100	.07
1	R10	2 KΩ 1/4W 5% CARBON COMP.	ANY	ALLIED	926C2100	.07
1	R2	30KΩ 1W 5% CARBON COMP.	ANY	ALLIED	926C2300	.09
1	R11	1KΩ 2W 5% CARBON COMP.	ANY	ALLIED	926C2400	.15
1	R13	33.2K 1/4W 1% METAL FILM		SEECOM	33.2K	1.00
1	R14	6.98K 1/4W 1% METAL FILM		SEECOM	6.98K	1.00
1	R9	100Ω TRIMPOT 20 TURN		SEECOM	100Ω TRIM	1.50
1	R12	10KΩ TRIMPOT 20 TURN		SEECOM	10KΩTRIM	1.50
		CAPACITORS				
1	C1	0.1μF 100V MYLAR	TRW	ALLIED	960-6135	1.07
2	C2	100μF16V ELECTROLYTIC	SPRAGUE TE1162	ALLIED	926-1179	1.05
		MISCELLANEOUS				
1	Q1	UNIJUNCTION TRANSISTOR	MOT'LA 2N4851	ALLIED	2N 4851	1.10
3	Q2,3,4	2N 3053 TRANSISTOR	RCA	SEECOM	2N 3053	.70
1	CR1	DIODE, SILICON, SIGNAL	2N3053	SEECOM	IN4448	.96
1	CR2	ZENER, 24V 1W	IN4448	SEECOM	1N4749	1.25
1	CR3	ZENER, 9V, 400mW REF.	MOT'LA IN4749	SEECOM	1N936	1.50
1	μA741C	OPERATIONAL AMPLIFIER, DIP	μA741C	SEECOM	μA741C	1.00
1		PRINTED CIRCUITBOARD		SEECOM		3.00
1	T1	PULSE TRANSFORMER	SPRAGUE 1122001	ALLIED	925-9021	3.85
1	Th1	Thermistor, 4 kΩ@ 25 C	Fenwal Gb34P2	ALLIED		2.00

Fig. 2–24. 2 kW automatic charger parts list

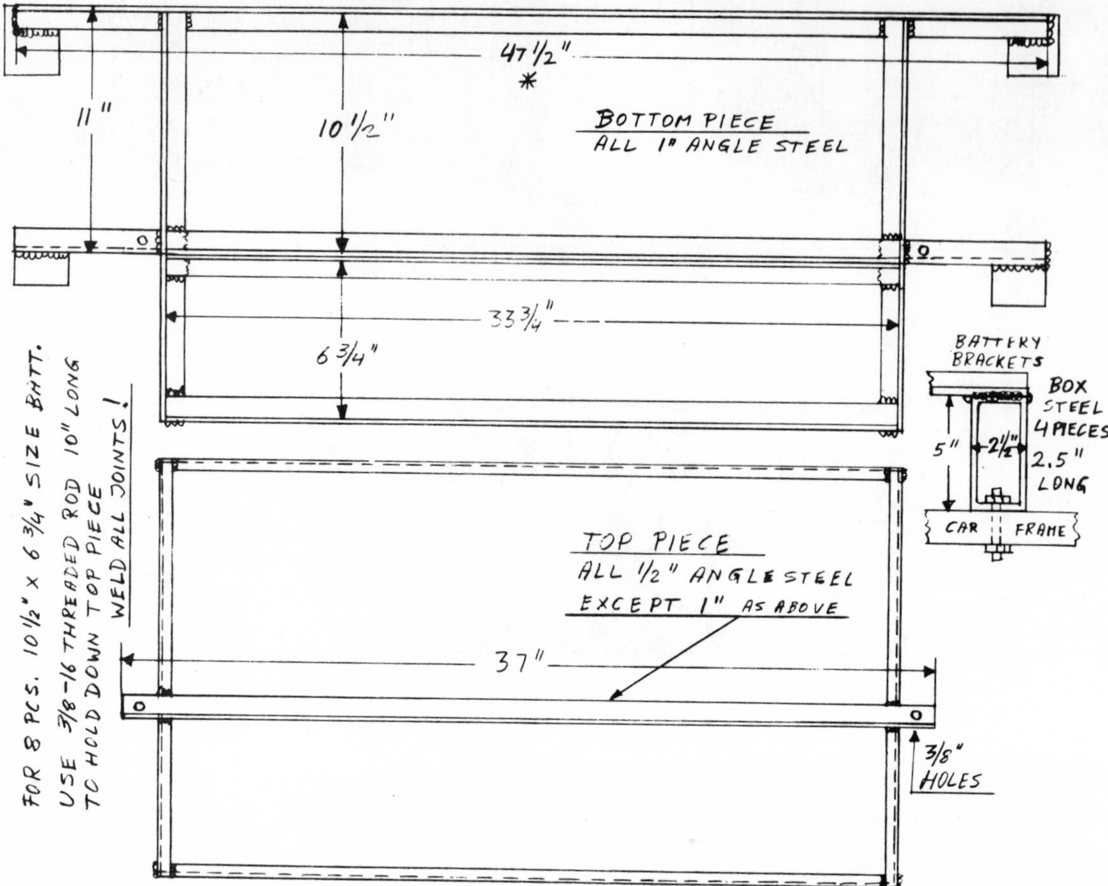

Fig. 2–25. Battery brackets

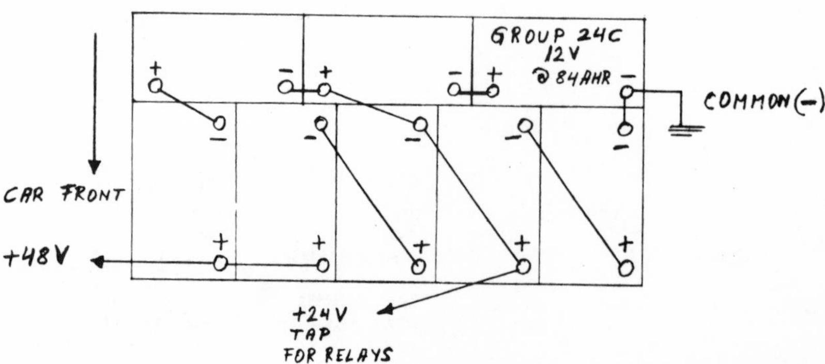

Fig. 2–26. Battery connections shown for 8 batteries

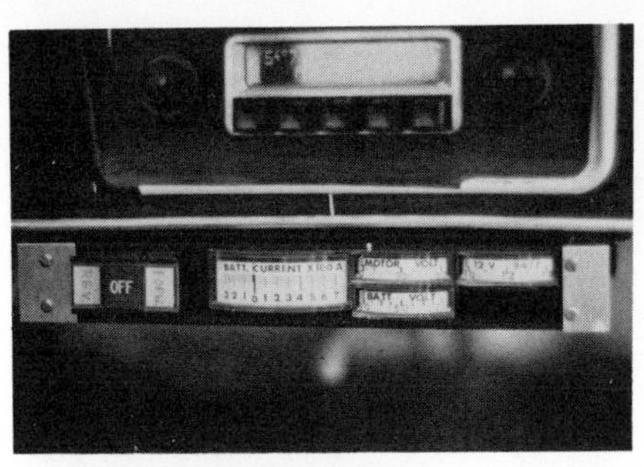

METER PANEL

ACCELERATOR BOX

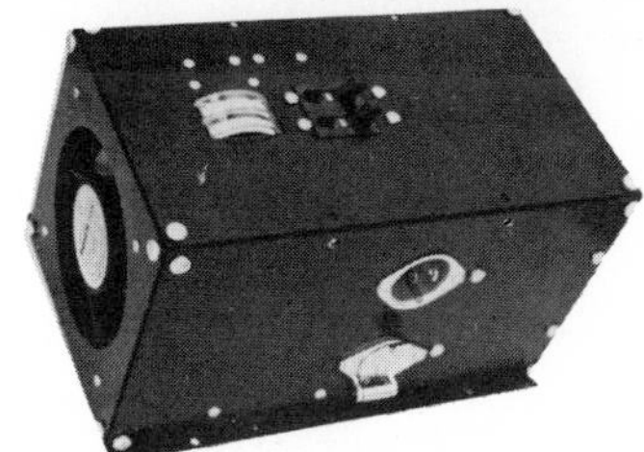

2 KW BATTERY CHARGER

CLOSE-UP VIEW OF CONTROL PANEL

INSIDE VIEW OF BATTERY CHARGER. USE FOAM RUBBER TO INSULATE TOROID TRANSFORMER ON FOUR SIDES. USE FOUR ½" SPACERS TO MOUNT PC (PRINTED CIRCUIT) BOARD.

SCR CHOPPER. EARLIER VERSION USING TWO 235A SCR'S IN PARALLEL.

Fig. 2–27. Actual components used in conversion of Renault to an electric car

---

Fig. 2–28. Typical battery and motor installations

FRONT TRUNK AREA SHOWING FOUR 6V BATTERIES AND 14V AUXILIARY LIGHTING BATTERY. CHARGER IS IN UPPER LEFT-HAND CORNER.

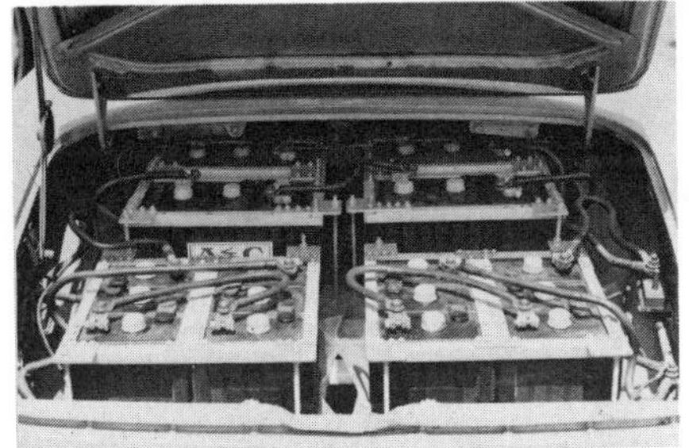

REAR ENGINE COMPARTMENT SHOWING EIGHT 6V BATTERIES ABOVE MOTOR ASSEMBLY SHOWN BELOW.

FOUR MORE 6V BATTERIES ARE LOCATED BEHIND SEATS TO MAKE UP 48V @ 280 AHR. BATTERIES WEIGH ABOUT 800 LB.

ANOTHER VERSION SHOWING NICKEL CADMIUM BATTERIES GIVING IMPROVED PERFORMANCE AND LIGHTER WEIGHT. TWO x 28V @ 100 AHR.

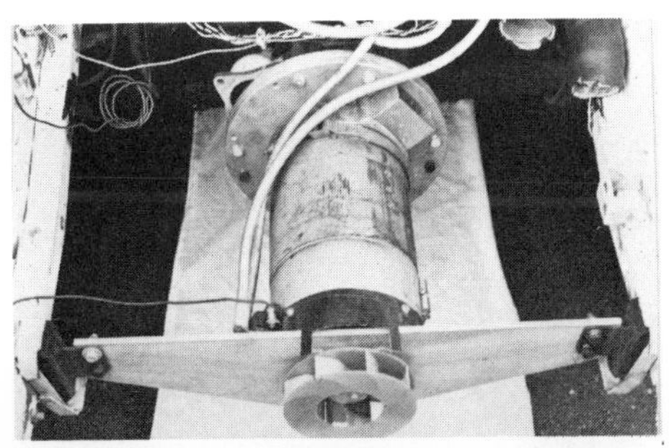

MOTOR INSTALLATION DETAIL, SHOWING FRONT MOTOR ADAPTOR PLATE, LOCK RING, REAR MOTOR SUPPORT, AND EXPERIMENTAL FAN WITHOUT SHROUD.

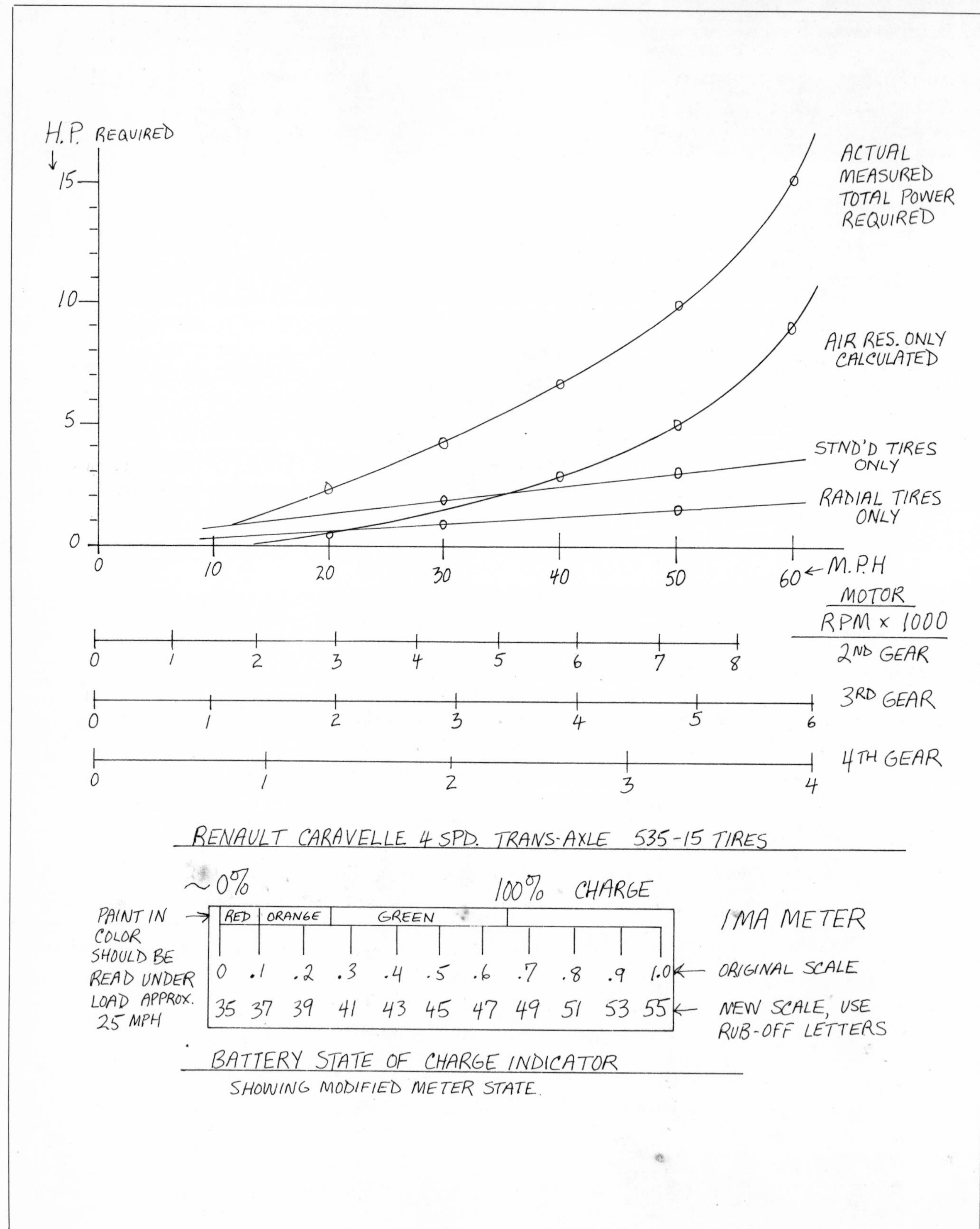

Fig. 2–29. Typical power requirement and motor RPM vs. speed

3 Electric Motors

DC Motors

An electric motor converts electricity into rotary energy. In an EV, the electric energy required to drive the motor is obtained from a battery in which it is stored as chemical energy.

The general types of electric motors which are used to drive EVs are classified as follows:

1. Series DC motor
2. Separately excited DC motor (shunt wound or compound wound)
3. Induction motor
4. Synchronous-type motor

As a general comment, most electric cars built to date have used DC motors because the combination of a battery supply, which provides DC power, and an electric motor which accepts direct current, is the simplest to build. However, there is considerable interest now in various types of AC motors because they can be more efficient, among other advantages, and improvements have been made in the electronic inverters which are required to convert the battery direct current to AC for use by either induction or synchronous motors.

In subsequent sections we shall describe briefly some of the characteristics of the four main types of motors listed previously, giving you their advantages and disadvantages. Also, you will find out more about various makes of electric motors that are now commercially available for use in the electric car you want to build.

A DC electric motor consists of two or more stationary magnetic fields, which may be wound coils or permanent magnets, and a rotor which has two or more wound coils and a device (commutator) to reverse polarity of electricity to the rotor coils one or more times every revolution. Torque is generated by the alternating interaction of the generated magnetic fields. See figures 3-1 and 3-2.

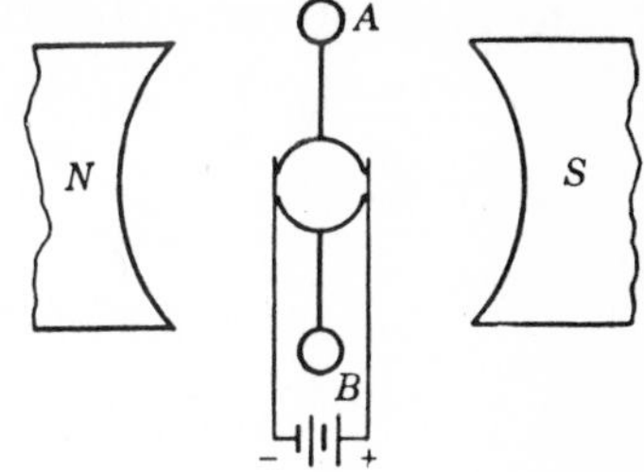

Fig. 3–1. Elementary dynamo with a two-segment commutator

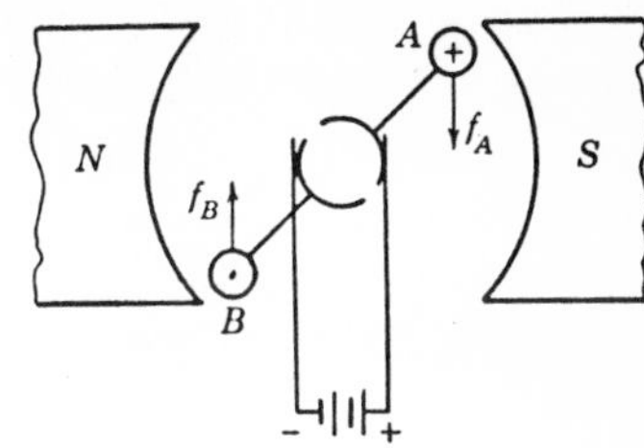

Fig. 3–2. Elementary dynamo with two-segment commutator with armature in position where torque is produced

The quantity of fields is generally referred to as the number of poles. That is, two fields are two poles, four fields are four poles, etc. Motors always have an even number of poles. A greater quantity of poles will deliver greater and more even torque since the angle and distance between rotor poles and field poles are less, with a resultant increase in magnetic force.

A DC motor generates a counter-electromotive force (CEMF) after start-up because of current buildup in the armature which tends to oppose the flow of current from the battery through the field windings and the armature. Therefore, as described in the subsequent chapter on control circuits, it is necessary to have a method for limiting the current flow through the armature until the CEMF is adequate to protect the motor from damage.

This basic structure has a number of variations and will be covered in more detail later on.

SPECIAL DESIGNS

Cylindrical Rotor. This type of motor is used when very rapid acceleration or sudden reversals are required, as in computer tape reel drives and servo systems in machine tool controls.

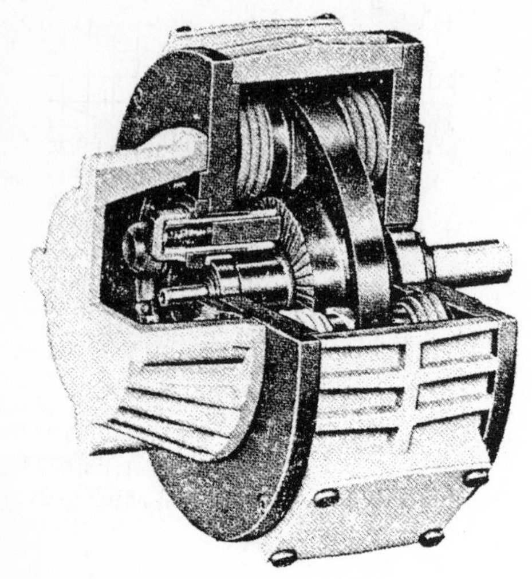

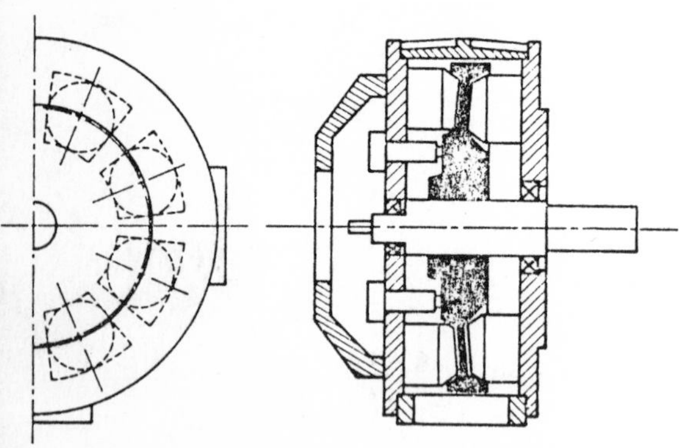

Fig. 3–3. Pancake permanent magnet (PM) motor (cutaway assembled and cross section) from Mavilor Motors

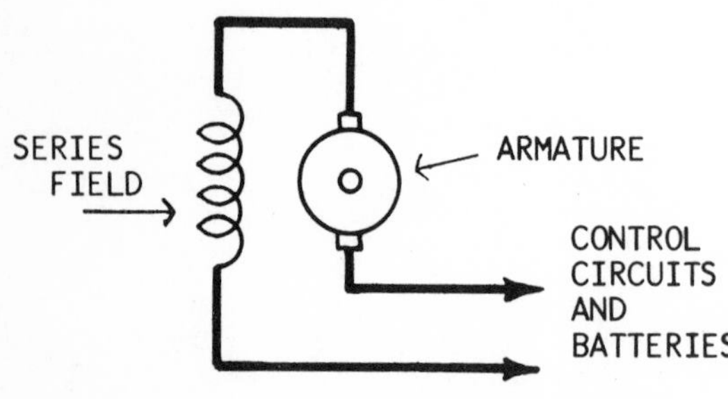

Fig. 3–4. Series DC motor diagram

As the name implies, the rotor consists of a stamped or wound cylinder usually molded or impregnated with a high-temperature epoxy to give the cylinder rigidity. To decrease mass, no iron laminations are used. This type is usually cooled by forced-air since there is little mass to absorb the heat generated. Operation under overload conditions is critical; a sophisticated controller with characteristics precisely matched to the motor to prevent damage to it is generally required.

Pancake Motor. This type of motor is very similar to the one previously described except that the winding is shaped as a disc instead of a cylinder. The field generally consists of permanent magnets arranged concentrically around a shaft on one or both sides. The field is axial (parallel to the shaft). The brushes normally ride on a portion of the stamped or printed winding, thereby eliminating a separate commutator assembly. This motor is also sometimes referred to as a printed motor. This motor has characteristics similar to the cylindrical motor. It can potentially be produced very inexpensively, although this has not yet been realized commercially. They are presently built in sizes to 5 HP. See figure 3-3.

At least one electric car has been built using two of these motors, one (5 HP each) per driven wheel.

Brushless Motors. In DC electric motors, the brushes are the most common source of trouble. In the last decade or so, semiconductors which can handle the high currents and voltages required for integral horsepower motors have become increasingly available as replacements for the brushes and commutators. This is generally accomplished by exchanging the rotor and stator; i.e., the rotor consists of two or more permanent-magnet poles and the outside stator field carries the main windings. Position sensors attached to the shaft route signals to semiconductor switches to control the currents in the windings in relation to the rotating magnet rotor. Properly designed, these semiconductor switches last indefinitely and the motor life is extended to the limit of the bearings used. This may be as much as 20,000 hours and could provide maintenance-free operation in an electric car for a million miles (50 mph times 20,000 hours). These semiconductor devices are known as transistors or SCR's (silicon-controlled rectifiers or thyristors).

SERIES-WOUND MOTOR

A series motor has its field coils connected in series with the armature as shown in figure 3-4, so that the current that flows through the armature also passes through the field windings. The field windings use a large wire size and few turns.

One useful feature of a series motor in an electric car is that there is a large increase in torque (that is, the rotational force of the motor shaft) for a given increase in current from the battery. This relationship between current and torque is shown in figure 3-5, and you can see that if you double the current, the torque is considerably more than doubled. That is, torque increases more rapidly than the applied current. It is a desirable feature of the series motor that it will provide a considerable amount of starting torque, since this enables you to get your electric car underway quickly with reasonable acceleration.

A series motor must be connected to a load or it may run away at an uncontrolled rate, reach much too high a speed and possibly destroy itself. However, under normal conditions a load is always applied to the electric motor when installed in your EV.

Since the speed of a series motor depends upon the amount of current applied to it, as well as the load, you will find that, as the load increases—the amount of torque output required—the motor draws more current, but its speed of rotation tends to decrease, as shown in figure 3-5. This characteristic makes the use of a series DC motor less desirable under variable-load conditions.

The chapter on controls also describes various ways for regulating the speed of a series motor by varying the amount of current that reaches the field and the armature. The series motor's direction of rotation may be reversed by a reversal of the field coil leads relative to the armature leads. Reversing battery connections of the motor will not reverse the direction of the shaft's rotation. A series-wound motor can operate on AC if properly designed to reduce heating in the field magnet structure. These are also known as universal motors.

In certain specific applications, a series motor can be designed to operate efficiently in both directions. However, it is not always as efficient in both directions, depending on where the brushes are mounted with respect to the field poles.

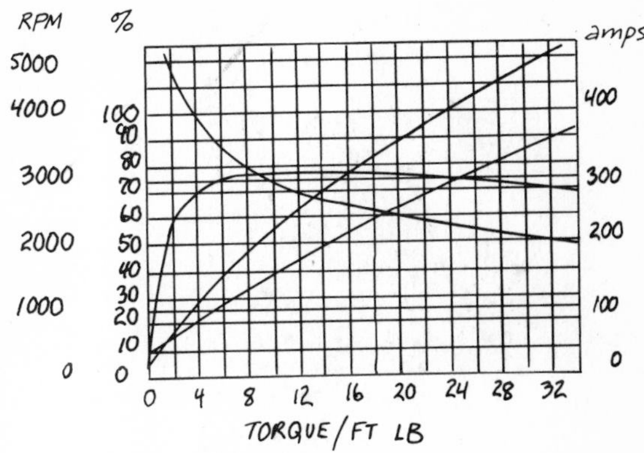

Fig. 3–5. Performance characteristics, HP, current consumption (amps), efficiency, rpm of a GE 3.5-HP series DC motor operated at 36V

SHUNT-WOUND MOTORS

In the shunt motor, the field windings are connected in parallel with or shunted across the armature windings, as shown in figure 3-6. Shunt windings draw current separately from your batteries.

The current through the shunt field winding of a shunt motor is usually rather small, typically about 5% of the current drawn by the armature. The resistance of these field coils is fairly high since conventional coils consist of many turns of small-sized wire. Since the current through this shunt winding comes from a fixed source of power (your batteries), the field strength will remain the same, no matter how the load varies.

The torque of this kind of motor is directly proportional to the armature current and the field strength. Therefore, with a fixed field strength, the shunt motor's torque varies in direct proportion to the armature current.

It turns out that, even with an increase or decrease in load, the speed of a shunt motor will remain quite constant. This is generally an advantage in EV operation. On the other hand, the starting current of the common shunt motor does not produce nearly as much starting torque as in the case of a series motor. An EV is therefore harder to start and has lower acceleration with a common standard shunt motor than with a series motor.

The no-load speed of the shunt motor is only about 10% greater than its speed under rated full load. This means that if you remove the load from a shunt motor, it will not destroy itself as a series motor tends to do.

The starting current in the shunt motor must also be limited, as is described in our chapter on controls. Since the armature current is so much greater under starting condition, it is essential to limit the armature current.

Another interesting feature of a shunt motor is that you can operate it at greater than the rated rpm. This is accomplished by reducing the

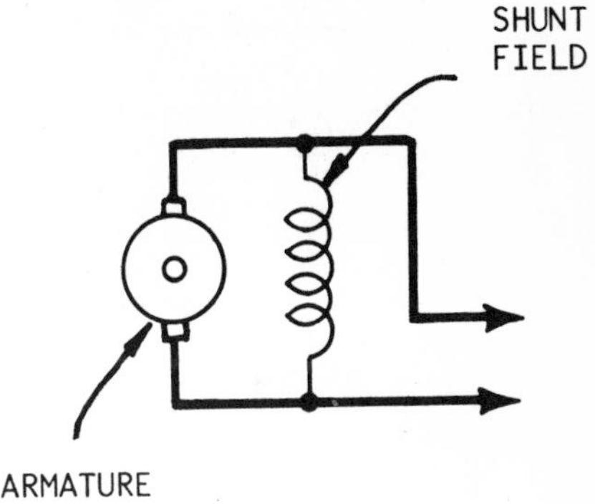

Fig. 3–6. Diagram of a shunt DC motor

field current, which in turn will increase the current drawn by the armature. However, there is a limit as to how low such reduction of the field current can be.

COMPOUND-WOUND MOTOR

This motor utilizes both series and parallel field coils, as shown in figure 3-7, and has many of the advantages of both. Two popular ways of arranging series and parallel windings are available in the two major types of compound-wound motors. In the cumulative unit, the current flow in each winding aids the other. The second type of compound-wound motor is called a differential unit, and in this case the current in the series windings opposes that in the parallel windings.

The cumulative type of compound motor is more widely used and has several advantages.

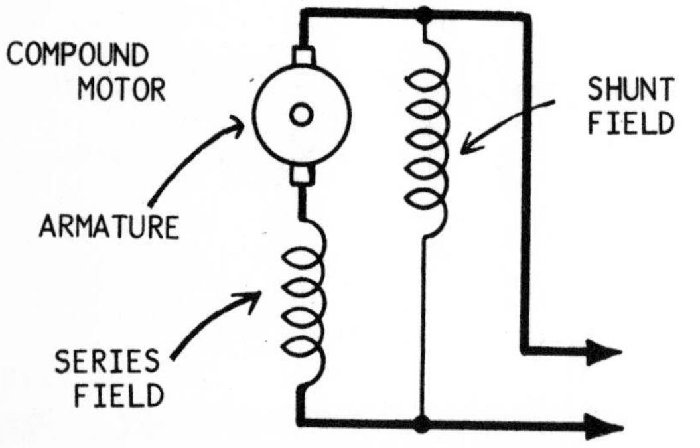

COMPOUND MOTOR
ARMATURE
SERIES FIELD
SHUNT FIELD

Fig. 3–7. Diagram of a compound-wound DC motor

When the two field windings are properly proportioned, you have most of the advantages of a series motor and a shunt motor without most of the disadvantages of either type.

The cumulative compound motor has a fairly precise no-load speed, as determined by the shunt winding, but its speed drops off more rapidly than in the case of the shunt motor when you increase the load.

Such a compound motor requires less current than a shunt motor for a given increase in torque, but it does not increase the torque as rapidly as does a series motor.

When the field coil windings of such a cumulative compound motor are external to the motor case, it is possible for you to install a bypass for the series coil. That way, when the motor has reached speed after providing you with the large starting torque of a series motor, you can short out the series coil and achieve the desirable operating characteristics of the shunt motor by itself. This kind of design can make use of a compound-wound motor very attractive.

Of interest to anyone who is planning to design an electric car or convert a clunker into a usable EV is the following material from an article written by R. H. Guess and W. R. Nial of General Electric, and M. A. Pocobello of Triad Services. This is a quotation from their paper entitled "Design of a Current Technology Electric Vehicle," which appeared in late 1977 at the Intersociety Energy Conversion Engineering Conference. The authors were describing work being done for the Department of Energy on electric cars.

Their description of the electric motor they selected is as follows:

> The DC separately excited motor (18 kW GE, 5 BT 2364 motor) that was selected for this Current Technology Vehicle has the most desirable control characteristic because the combination of armature voltage and field current control allows operation in the motor or generator mode over a wide voltage, current, and speed range without reconnection of windings. To obtain motoring speeds above the rated no-load speed at rated voltage, field weakening is employed. The desirable inherent characteristics of the series motor are achieved by utilizing the control flexibility of the separately excited motor. For example, two advantages of the series motor are the inherent field weakening at high speed and light load, and the inherent field compensation for armature reaction at high currents. These characteristics are added to the separately excited motor by a field controller capable of high field forcing which is connected in a feedback loop to maintain a set value of armature current.

Permanent Magnet (PM) Motor

This motor behaves like a compound DC motor but generally has a higher starting torque and it is often more efficient (see figure 3-8). Commercial PM motors are now becoming available and they have many advantages in terms of simpler construction and no losses in field coils.

This motor requires no field current because its magnetic field is provided by permanent magnets. The performance of a PM motor is very similar to that of a compound motor.

A good PM motor will have a starting torque that is greater than that of a typical compound motor and approaches that of a series motor.

A PM motor provides more electromotive drag when no power is applied than any of the other types of DC motors. This is because the fields of a PM motor are active, whether an armature current is applied or not. This feature turns out to be a desirable characteristic when you are using regenerative braking, and provides an accustomed braking effect for normal coasting of your EV.

The best PM motors will achieve greater efficiency than any of the other types of DC motors because no field current is required so none of this current is wasted in resistive losses.

If you want to operate a PM motor at a higher speed than its rated rpm, you will have to increase the voltage applied to the motor. The rpm increase with voltage increase is limited to the maximum rated or tested rpm.

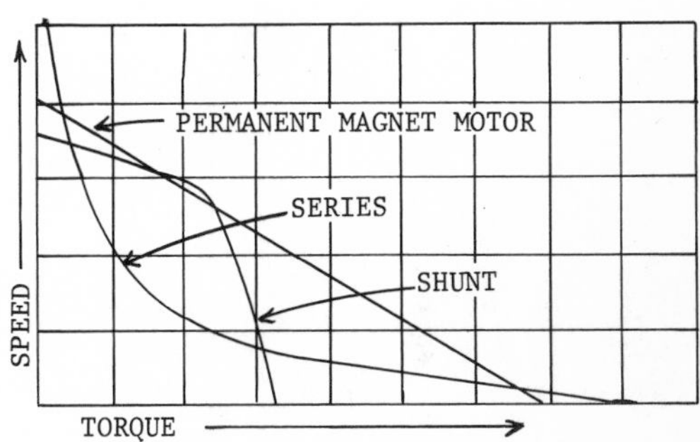

Fig. 3–8. A comparison of torque vs. speed of rotation of series, shunt, and PM DC motors

AC Motors

This type of motor uses alternating current (AC) like that generated and distributed by the power companies. Offhand, it appears that this type of motor would be unsuitable for electric car use since the available power in the car is from batteries which generate direct current (DC) and AC motors will *not* run on DC.

However, AC motors are produced in large numbers for industry and are therefore rather inexpensive. As the cost of semiconductor devices drops, a suitable low cost DC-to-variable-AC inverter could be devised. This inverter along with a conventional AC motor could provide many desirable characteristics to drive an electric car. Summed up, these characteristics are: low maintenance, low cost, low weight, high efficiency, good egeneration.

The configuration of these motors generally consists of stationary, laminated, wound-field windings of two or more poles, and a rotor in the center. Rotor design may vary depending on the characteristics desired. An alternating current is applied to the stator coils so that a revolving magnetic field is produced.

SYNCHRONOUS MOTORS

In a synchronous motor a permanent-magnet (PM) rotor will lock onto this rotating field and rotate with it. Since its rotational speed is locked to the AC frequency, this type is called a permanent-magnet synchronous motor. Thus, a two-pole motor, fed with 60 Hz, will produce 60 revolutions per second or 3,600 revolutions per minute (rpm) and a four-pole unit would give 1,800 rpm.

Other variations of synchronous AC motors are hysteresis and reluctance types. Instead of a smooth rotor, they have a salient (protruding) rotor which gets pulled along with the rotating magnetic field because the rotor tends to line up with the maximum magnetic field at any instance. These generally produce the least amount of torque and have very little starting torque when operated on fixed-frequency AC power. This is true also of the PM synchronous motor.

If the frequency were increased proportionally with the rotor rpm, a relatively high torque could be achieved throughout its entire speed range.

In this fashion, its characteristics approach the brushless motor previously discussed.

INDUCTION MOTORS

Originally invented by Nikola Tesla around the turn of the century, this is the world's most widely used and least expensive motor.

It consists of a stationary field winding, similar to the previously discussed synchronous motors, and a laminated iron rotor with a number of single-turn windings made of copper or aluminum, short-circuited at each end with a copper or aluminum ring. If aluminum is used for the conductors, the iron rotor is simply molded with that metal in its slots and rings around its ends, so that it appears to be in a cage. Therefore, it is also referred to as a squirrel cage rotor. In operation, the rotating magnetic field produced from the stationary field windings induces a voltage in these one-turn windings on the rotor. Since the windings are shorted, they produce a magnetic field of their own which interacts with the original rotating field to produce torque. There has to be a difference in speed between the rotating magnetic field and the rotor speed to induce a voltage in the rotor. This difference, called slip, consists generally of only a few percent of the rotor speed, depending on the resistance of the shorted windings on the rotor. Higher rotor resistance gives more slip and more torque, but a lower speed and efficiency. A typical 60 Hz, two-pole, 3% slip motor would have a loaded speed of 3,420 rpm and medium starting torque (about 250% of running). Efficiency would be highest with the least amount of design slip, but starting torque would be limited. Efficiency for a 10-HP, 60 Hz motor is typically about 85%, while its weight might be as low as 100 pounds.

A 10-HP motor would be suitable to drive a compact electric car to about 55 mph.

AC motors in sizes below about 2 HP are driven from single-phase AC power. Above 2 HP, three-phase power, resulting from a complex interaction of three single phases displaced 120 degrees from each other, is generally used. Three-phase motors produce greater starting torque than single-phase machines.

Solid-state semiconductors can be suitably interconnected and switched to produce simulated AC single or three-phase power from a DC supply. This AC power can be fed to a standard AC motor so that it can operate from the DC power of storage batteries. Motor speed is varied by changing the frequency of the controller. See figure 3–9.

Industrial motor speed controls with ratings up to thousands of horsepower have been available for about ten years.

These drives are made to be reliable in very heavy duty applications

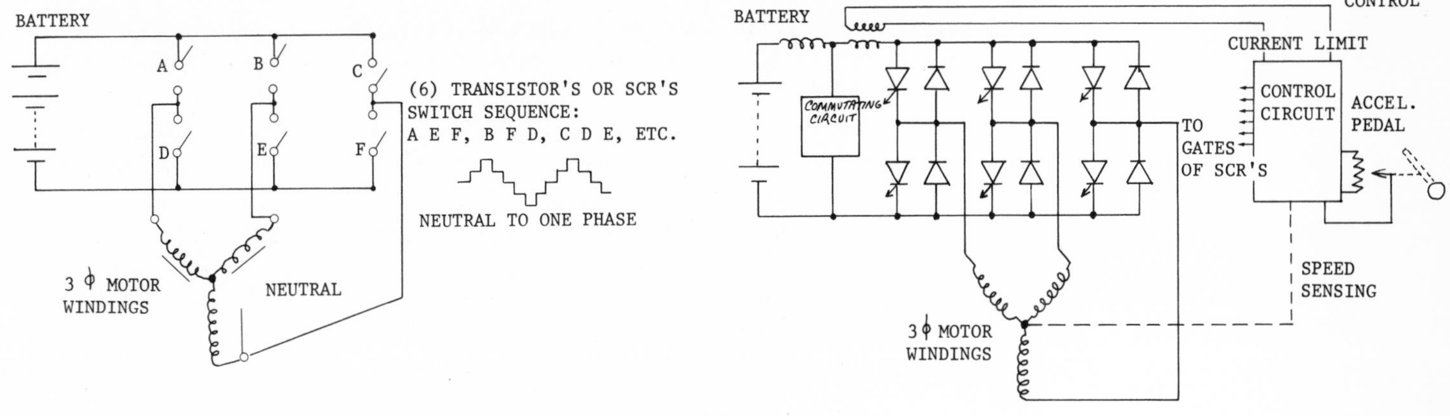

Fig. 3–9. Simplified schematic of three-phase AC inverter motor drive

and are therefore heavy and expensive. They also run off rectified 220 VAC or higher, which would be an unsafe high voltage for electric cars. A safe voltage for this use up to about 120 volts might be considered.

These motors could be rewound for lower voltages, but they would require heavier and more expensive semiconductors. Also, to achieve high starting torque without drawing too much current, a three-phase motor should be used. The penalty for this is a threefold increase in quantity of parts used, size, complexity, and cost. As a matter of fact, it takes a minimum of six power transistors or SCR's to generate three-phase power to drive an AC motor efficiently from batteries.

INVERTER-AC MOTOR

Potentially the simplest and least expensive system to use would be a single-phase inverter utilizing only two power transistors or SCR's and a specially wound but inexpensive variation of a single-phase motor. True, the starting torque would not be very great, so a torque-multiplying device would have to be used, i.e., a transmission. In reality, though, this is a blessing in disguise.

There is a fairly well known fact that while electric motors are able to produce very high starting torques, they also require high starting currents. Batteries perform very inefficiently under this condition, since they have a high internal voltage drop at high currents. The ampere-hour capacity also goes down drastically with high current draw; this applies especially to the lead-acid battery. This reduces range sharply.

For these reasons, many an electric car experimenter has found to his dismay that his car produced only about one-half of the anticipated range under actual operating conditions.

Comparing DC and AC Motors

For comparison purposes, at the time of this writing (1979) a 96 VDC 10-HP motor for electric car use costs about $800 in single quantities. A 10-HP three-phase 220 VAC induction motor costs about $250. One three-phase, variable-speed inverter drive for this AC motor might cost $1,000. It would be rated for 20-HP intermittent operation and 10-HP continuous duty at an input voltage of about 120 VDC to run a rewound, three-phase, low-voltage AC motor.

To keep things in proper perspective, the DC motor would also require an electric speed control to match the characteristics of the inverter-AC motor combination. The inverter-AC motor combination would also give superior regeneration, which would extend driving range by returning energy to the batteries while slowing down or going downhill.

Nevertheless, the cost in small quantities is high in either method used.

SELECTING AN ELECTRIC MOTOR

There are two prime criteria for selecting an electric motor for an electric car. First, there must be enough horsepower to achieve the desired top speed, since the horsepower requirement increases with increasing speed. Second, starting and low-speed torque must be sufficient to meet acceleration requirements. A motor solely to meet the second criterion would be too large and too expensive. A more effective method would be to add a mechanical torque multiplication transmission, as described in chapter 4.

Description of the Calculations Required for a DC Motor in Renault Conversion

In the example of the 1961 Renault which was converted by Fred Riess to an electric vehicle, the following points about its motive power are interesting. The Renault originally had a 40-HP, four-cylinder engine in the rear of the car, driving the rear wheels through a three-speed manual trans-axle. The peak torque rating of the engine was 36 foot-pounds at about 4,000 rpm, while the maximum of 40 HP is obtained at 6,000 rpm.

The electric motor was a surplus aircraft DC starter/generator originally designed to start aircraft turbines and supply electrical needs of military aircraft. Its rating as a generator is 30 volts and 400 amperes output, at speeds from 3,000 to 8,000 rpm. The motor utilized blast cooling at the rate of 100 cubic feet of air per minute, and a pressure drop of not less than 6 inches of water. Its rating as a starter is 24 volts at 1,000 amperes for up to 5 minutes, with a torque output capability of as much as 93 foot-pounds. Physical dimensions of this electric motor are 7 inches in diameter by 14 inches long, and it weighs 75 pounds. A similarly rated industrial motor might weigh about 250 pounds, and be about 10–12 inches in diameter by about 18 inches long (about a NEMA 254 frame).

This surplus unit (known as 2CM77, or 88, and made by General Electric) achieved its high power-to-weight ratio by utilizing the highest-temperature insulation materials available at the time of construction, in addition to the best technology known to achieve sparkless commutation. Also, high-grade steel material was used to achieve higher flux density and flux levels. The penalty paid for this increased performance was higher cost and lower efficiency. The motor also has a distinctive high-pitched whine at the higher applied voltages. Skewing of the armature poles at the time of construction would have reduced cogging and the resultant audible noise. Cogging is a term used to describe torque variation with shaft rotation, caused by straight armature poles being switched alternately as they pass the field poles.

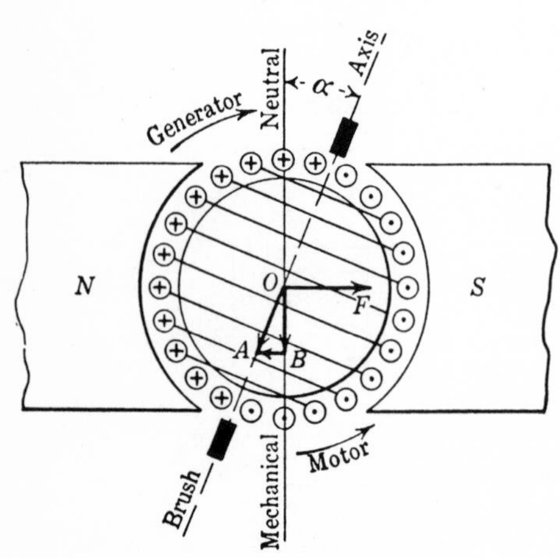

Fig. 3–10. Diagram illustrating the components of armature reaction

In the following discussion, the terms generator and motor are used interchangeably. When properly designed, there is very little difference in the machines and they can be used in either mode. In wound-field (series or shunt) machines, an effect called armature (rotor) reaction, resulting from the interaction of the two magnetic fields, causes the actual field to shift in one direction for a motor and in the other direction for a generator, with respect to the neutral location. See figures 3–10 and 3–11.

Theoretically, the brushes should be placed in the neutral position to cause sparkless commutation. Sparkless commutation is desirable since it minimizes erosion of the brushes and the commutator surface, in addition to reducing heating. In low-cost machines, the brushes are shifted from neutral to another location to achieve minimum sparking but this setting is only true for one particular current (torque) rating. Under high power levels and highly variable load conditions, this solution is not adequate.

To alleviate this condition, extra poles are added between the main poles. These commutating poles or interpoles carry a few turns of heavy wire which are connected in series with the machine's main terminals, and with proper polarity. The field thus produced neutralizes the armature reaction magnetic field under all loads and therefore allows sparkless commutation under all conditions—generating and motoring. See figure 3–12.

The GE motor selected for the Renault is compound-wound (types 77 or 88) and has an efficiency of greater than 75% at 400A output as a generator. Data curves from the manufacturer indicate the efficiency peaking at 80% with a 200A load. The terminal resistance is about 0.015 ohms. At a load current (generator) of 400A, the internal loss from the resistance is, according to Ohm's law:

$E = IR$

$I = 400A$
$R = 0.015$ ohms
$E = ?$ volts

$E = 400 \times 0.015$
$E = 6$ volts

This means that the generator is actually producing 30V (rated output) plus 6V, which equals 36V.

The *p*ower lost and showing up as heat which has to be *d*issipated is $P_D = IE$.

$P_D = 400 \times 6$
$P_D = 2{,}400$ watts

$I = 400$ amps
$E = 6$ volts

The *p*ower *o*utput produced is $P_o = (E_o)(I_o)$.

$P_o = 30 \times 400$
$P_o = 12{,}000$ watts, or 12 kW

$E_o = 30$ volts
$I_o = 400$ amps

The power lost from resistance in the winding in percent is:

$$\frac{P_{int} \times 100}{P_{out}} = \frac{2{,}400 \times 100}{12{,}000} = 20\%$$

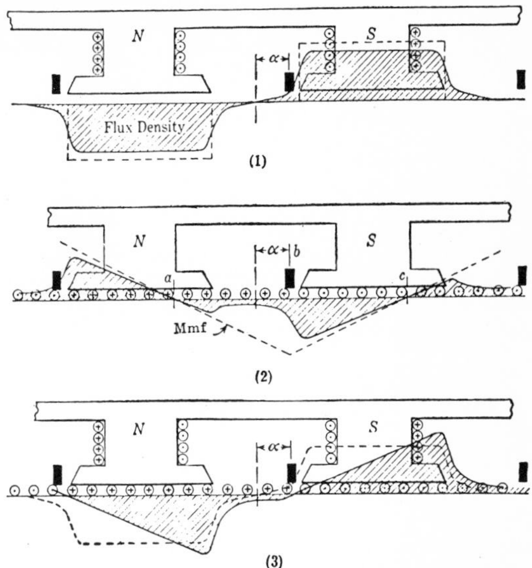

Fig. 3–11. Parts (1), (2), and (3) show respectively the distribution of the Mmf and flux for the field alone, and the combination of these when brushes are shifted.

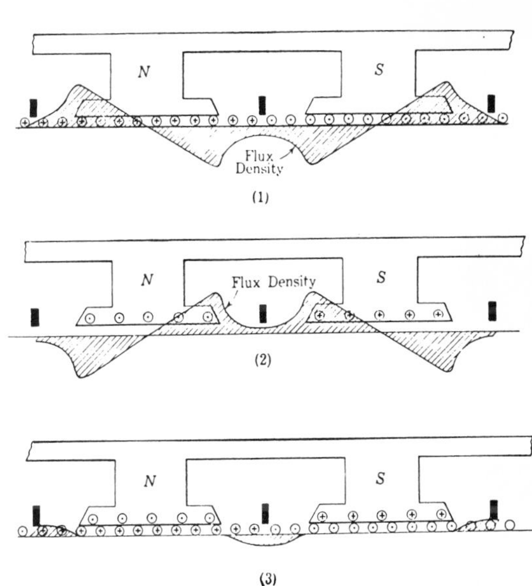

Fig. 3–12. Parts (1), (2), and (3) show respectively the flux caused by the armature current acting alone, the compensating winding alone, and the combination of the two.

This example shows the single biggest factor which prevents standard electric motors from achieving the theoretical 100% conversion efficiency. Some prototype motors have been built with zero-resistance windings utilizing the phenomenon known as superconductivity. Superconductivity is achieved in some special metallic alloys at near absolute zero temperature, which is –273°C. Maintaining this low temperature takes an elaborate setup and appears to be impractical for electric vehicle motor usage.

The balance of energy loss, in decreasing order, is contributed by brush friction, eddy current, hysteresis, windage, and bearing friction.

It follows, therefore, that to get high efficiency the winding resistance should be kept as low as possible. Practical limitations dictate the voltage drop (and the resulting power loss) to be about 10–20% of the rated voltage at the rated operating conditions. This will, in turn, dictate the full voltage starting current to be five to ten times the rated operating current. Since output torque is relatively proportional to current, the full voltage starting torque would also be five to ten times the rated operating torque.

Similarly, the short-circuit current of a generator would be five to ten times the rated current.

High starting torque is desirable in electric vehicles to get good acceleration with a given current, if this torque can be controlled. If full battery voltage is applied directly to the motor, assuming the battery can supply the necessary current, the vehicle would almost instantly achieve maximum acceleration and increase speed until the increasing horsepower requirement of the vehicle is matched by the decreasing horsepower output of the electric motor.

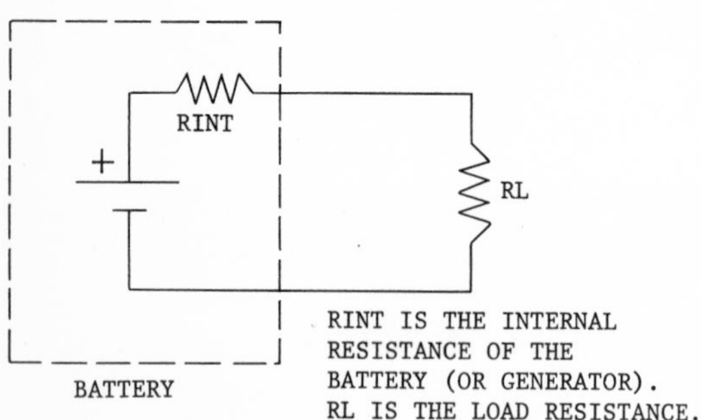

Fig. 3–13. Simplified schematic of battery and load

In the example given earlier, the Renault in second gear would attain about 40 mph, while in third gear it would reach about 50 mph. The current drawn would be about 250 amperes from 8 lead-acid batteries connected to deliver 48 volts. The peak power output of the Renault battery pack was about 24 kW, at 1,000 amps while the battery output had dropped to 24V output. The maximum power is transferred by any generator or battery when the output drops to one-half its open circuit value. See See figures 3–13 and 3–14. As the load resistance (R_L) is decreased, the current will increase to a maximum value when $R_L = 0$. In this shorted condition, all the battery (generator) voltage is dropped across its own internal resistance.

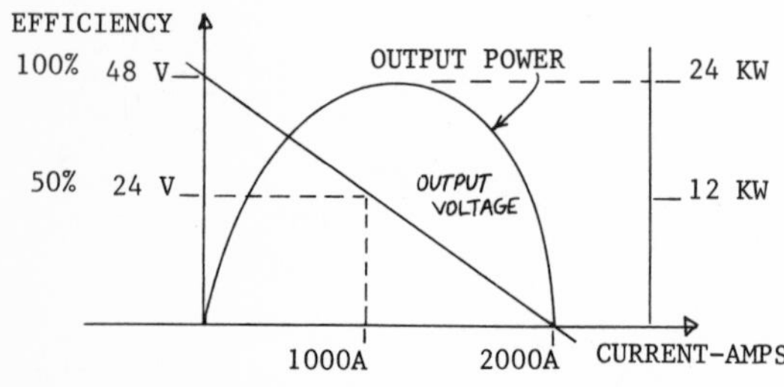

Fig. 3–14. Power transfer curve from battery to DC motor

Since power is equivalent to voltage times current (amperage), the net power transferred at the shorted condition is zero.

Example:

P_o = 2,000 X OV
P_o = 0 **I short = 2,000 amps**
V out = 0

Similarly:

P_o = 0 amps X 48V **NO LOAD**
P_o = 0 **V open = 48V**

Maximum output power:

P_o = 1,000 amps X 24V
P_o = 24,000 watts, or 24 kilowatts

From the drawing in figure 3–15 it is evident that power is transferred most efficiently from the battery to the load under light load conditions. Similarly, least efficient power transfer occurs under maximum current drain since, under this condition, all the battery voltage is dropped across its internal resistance—which all real batteries have. From figure 3–15 it also appears that maximum power available is synonymous with about 50% transfer efficiency. This power level is only recommended for very short periods since the high power dissipated inside the batteries would quickly destroy them. Generally, the batteries are discharged for any extended period of time well toward the left of maximum power condition, which also ensures a reasonable efficiency. For good, efficient battery utilization, the battery pack should have short-circuit current values many times greater than the stall current of the motor.

In figure 3–16, the efficiency of the battery drops to 75% under motor-stall condition. Under the rated motor operating condition, the battery would operate at maybe 95% efficiency, while the typical motor efficiency would be 80%. The overall system efficiency under rated condition would be 95% times 80%, which would be 76%. Under starting conditions the battery has a 75% efficiency, and the motor has 0% efficiency by definition, so the overall efficiency is 75% times 0%, which is 0%. Therefore, the overall efficiency varies from 0% while initially accelerating to 76% while cruising at rated condition.

Presently available commercial batteries have limited energy and power densities which changes the picture somewhat, as follows.

Assuming the motor efficiency to be about 75%, the overall efficiency is 0.75 times 0.75, which is about 56%. This is fairly typical for a high-performance electric car.

So far so good, if one wanted to accelerate from standing start at full acceleration, reach cruising speed in minimum time and spend most of the time at this speed. In most cases, though, this is undesirable. There are times when one does not want all-out acceleration, so the torque of the motor has to be limited by some means. Likewise, some means of allowing one to drive at only a fraction of cruising (top) speed has to be provided.

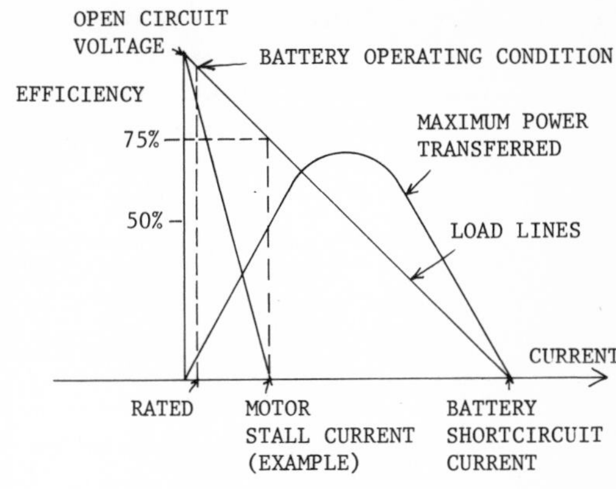

Fig. 3–15. Battery power rating vs. motor power consumption, under optimum conditions

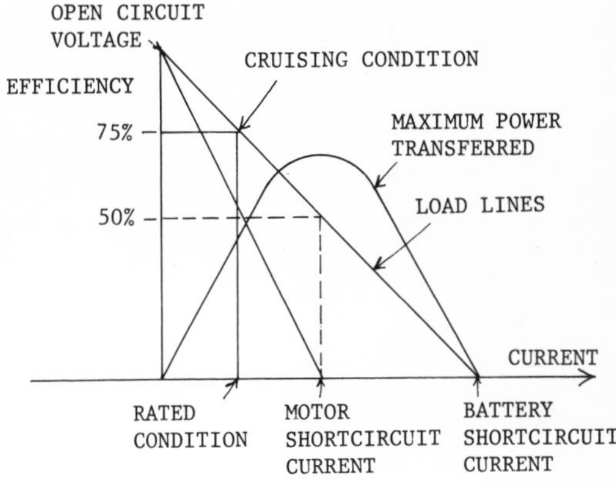

Fig. 3–16. Similar battery power rating vs. motor power consumption, under less favorable conditions

General Comments About DC Motors for Electric Cars

As shown in figure 3–17, DC series motors are the most widely used in electric cars because their speed torque characteristics are the best match for typical driving requirements. Under heavy loads, the torque-per-ampere ratio of a series DC motor is higher than that of any other standard type. As a result, a series motor drains your battery less during acceleration or while climbing up a hill than the other types of DC motors. As you can see from figure 3–17, series DC motors are the most popular among manufacturers of electric vehicles.

In the U.S. Department of Energy book *State of the Art Assessment of Electric and Hybrid Vehicles,* published in January 1978, it was pointed out that "when other motor types are chosen, the motor-controller-transmission combination attempts to emulate the series motor characteristics."

Where regenerative braking is desired, there are some advantages in using a separately excited DC motor. As described previously, the

Fig. 3–17. Electric vehicle motor classification from literature data tabulation. The motors used on the electric vehicles that were tested for this assessment are listed below. All are DC types, 15 of the 20 are series motors, 4 are shunt motors, and 1 is a compound motor. Also, 50 of the 83 motors reported in the literature survey of electric vehicles by DOE are series motors. There are 21 vehicles in which the motor types are not specified. The unavailability of suitable controllers has restricted the use of AC motors to experimental vehicles such as the General Motors Electrovair, the Exxon Industries experimental car, and the Linear Alpha Corp. van. The photo shows a 15-kilowatt (20-hp) DC series motor on a dynamometer test stand. Now that Exxon controls Reliance Electric, a major maker of AC motors, you can expect much additional work on AC motors for EV's.

	Domestic	Foreign
Motor type:		
Alternating current	5	0
Direct current		
Series	30	20
Separately excited	13	11
Compound	5	0
Other	2	2
Not specified	13	8
Motor size, kW:		
0–10	20	17
10–20	24	13
20–30	9	3
> 30	5	16
Not reported	10	1

TRACTION MOTORS USED IN TEST VEHICLES

Vehicle	Manufacturer	Type (DC)	Rating, kW
AM General DJ-5E Electruck	Gould, Inc.	Compound	14.9
Battronic Minivan	General Electric Co.	Series	31
CDA Town Car	Eaton Corp. (modified)	Shunt	----
Daihatsu	Tokyo Shibaura Electric Co., Ltd.	Shunt	14
EPC Hummingbird	Modified aircraft generator	Series	7.5
EVA Contactor	Not available	Shunt	7.5
EVA Metro sedan	Not available	Series	10
EVA Pacer	Baker Material Handling Co.	Series	14.9
Fiat 850 T van	Fiat	Shunt	14
Jet Industries Electra Van	Baldor Electric Co.	Series	7.5
Lucas limousine	Lucas Industries, Ltd.	Series	37
Marathon model C-300	Baldor Electric Co.	Series	6
Otis P-500 utility van	Otis Elevator Co.	Series	22.4
Power-Train van	Otis Elevator Co.	Series	22.4
Ripp-Electric	Otis Elevator Co.	Series	14.9
Sebring-Vanguard CitiCar	General Electric Co.	Series	4.5
Sebring-Vanguard CitiVan	General Electric Co.	Series	4.5
Volkswagen Transporter	Siemens AG	Shunt	17
Waterman DAF	Prestolite Electrical Division, Eltra Corp.	Series	6.7
Waterman Renault 5	Prestolite Electrical Division, Eltra Corp.	Series	6.7
Zagato Elcar	Scaglia	Series	2

major difference between series and shunt motors is the method of establishing the magnetic field along the axis of rotation. The field of the series-wound motor consists of a few turns of large-diameter conductors which are connected in series with the armature. By contrast, the shunt-wound motor field is made from many turns of small-diameter wire and these windings, composing the shunt field, are connected to a separate field controller.

To get regenerative braking using a series-wound motor, you must have a method of switching connections to the series field so that it is reversed during the braking operation. This requires heavy relay contacts. With a shunt motor and operating above its base speed, regenerative braking is possible merely by increasing the fairly small shunt field current. The chapter on control systems will show that it is highly desirable to design a controller which is matched for the specific motor you have chosen. According to the DOE report previously cited, every vehicle that uses a shunt or compound motor has a controller that was designed by or for the builder of that particular vehicle.

The efficiency of a series DC motor increases as voltage increases, figure 3–18. For instance, if a series motor is operating at partial voltage and speed, its efficiency may be considerably less than at the full voltage and speed. From figure 3–18, the peak efficiency of one of these motors at full voltage is 95%.

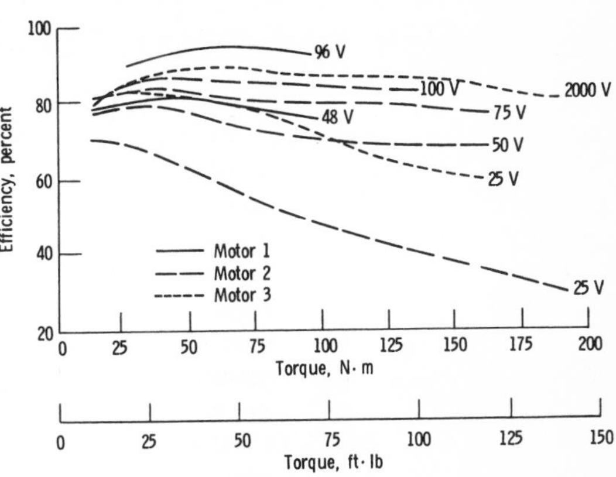

Fig. 3–18. Effect of voltage variations on series motor efficiency

Calculating the Speed of an Electric Motor

Dr. Ernest H. Wakefield, in his excellent book *The Consumer's Electric Car,* points out that the speed of an electric motor depends on several parameters. The armature of a DC motor rotates when electrical energy is applied to it and, while running, the back EMF is always less than the applied EMF. The difference is the voltage drop in the armature, which may be expressed as I_aR_a, where I_a is the armature current and R_a is the armature circuit resistance, including the series field. So the back EMF, E_b, is equal to E_a, the applied voltage at the armature, minus I_aR_a, or the equation is:

$$E_b = E_a - I_aR_a$$

The back EMF, E_b, is proportional to the flux per pole and also to the rpm or speed of the armature. An equation to express this is $E_b = k\phi$ (rpm), where k is a constant and ϕ is magnetic flux. So we now have an equation for rpm as follows:

$$\text{Speed in rpm} = E_a - \frac{I_aR_a}{K\phi}$$

This equation tells us that the speed of a DC motor depends on the armature voltage minus the voltage drop in the armature divided by the product of a constant k and the flux, ϕ, per pole. Dr. Wakefield points out that controlling the armature voltage E_a and the magnetic flux ϕ are the most common methods of varying the speed of a DC motor. This will be explained further in the chapter on control systems.

Some Sources for DC Electric Motors for EV's

Although we prefer not to make any recommendations as to specific types of DC motors, it may be helpful to provide some sources of the various kinds.

In ordering DC motors, the following information should be specified to the manufacturer:

1. The horsepower you desire and rpm, or torque and rpm at each point of your proposed duty cycle, or,
2. The horsepower you desire and rpm, or torque and rpm for level operation at no-load and at full-load conditions. Also provide the slope of the maximum grade in percentage. As an alternative,
3. If the motor designer is to calculate torque and rpm for you, then you should supply the following information:
   a. Your vehicle weight, empty.
   b. Your vehicle weight, loaded.
   c. Vehicle gear ratio (total).
   d. Gear efficiency.
   e. Vehicle rolling resistance. (Supply a description of the aerodynamics of your car's body for an estimate of frictional drag caused by air. Also use radial steel tires, inflated to the manufacturer's maximum recommended level in pounds, to minimize road friction.)
   f. Vehicle rolling radius.
   g. Vehicle mph for specific condition; that is, empty or loaded on level, on grade, and so forth. Mph values should be tied to the expected actual voltage at the motor.
   h. Battery and line resistance in ohms should be provided.

General Electric Company (3001 East Lake Road, Erie, PA 16531, phone (814) 455-5466) is the Direct Current Motor and Generator Department of GE. A cutaway view of a typical DC traction motor made by GE appears in figure 3–19.

General Electric provides some formulas in their brochure on electric vehicle motors which may be helpful in your design work:

1. Vehicle operation on the level:

   a. $$\text{Motor rpm} = \frac{\text{Vehicle mph} \times 88 \times \text{gear ratio}}{\text{Wheel dia in ft} \times \pi}$$

   b. $$\text{Motor torque} = \frac{\text{Vehicle wt in lb} \times \text{wheel dia in ft}}{100 \times \text{gear ratio} \times \text{gear efficiency}}$$

If you are concerned about climbing steep hills, then you must add an additional amount of motor torque for grades. A recommended amount to be added to the value of motor torque calculated from the previous equation is:

2. Additional grade torque =

$$\frac{\text{Vehicle wt in lb} \times \%\ \text{grade} \times \text{wheel dia in ft}}{2 \times \text{gear ratio} \times \text{gear efficiency}}$$

GE provides DC motors with series, shunt, or compound wound fields. There is no additional charge for the series or shunt designs, but there is an 8% increase for compound winding.

Comments by GE engineers are as follows:

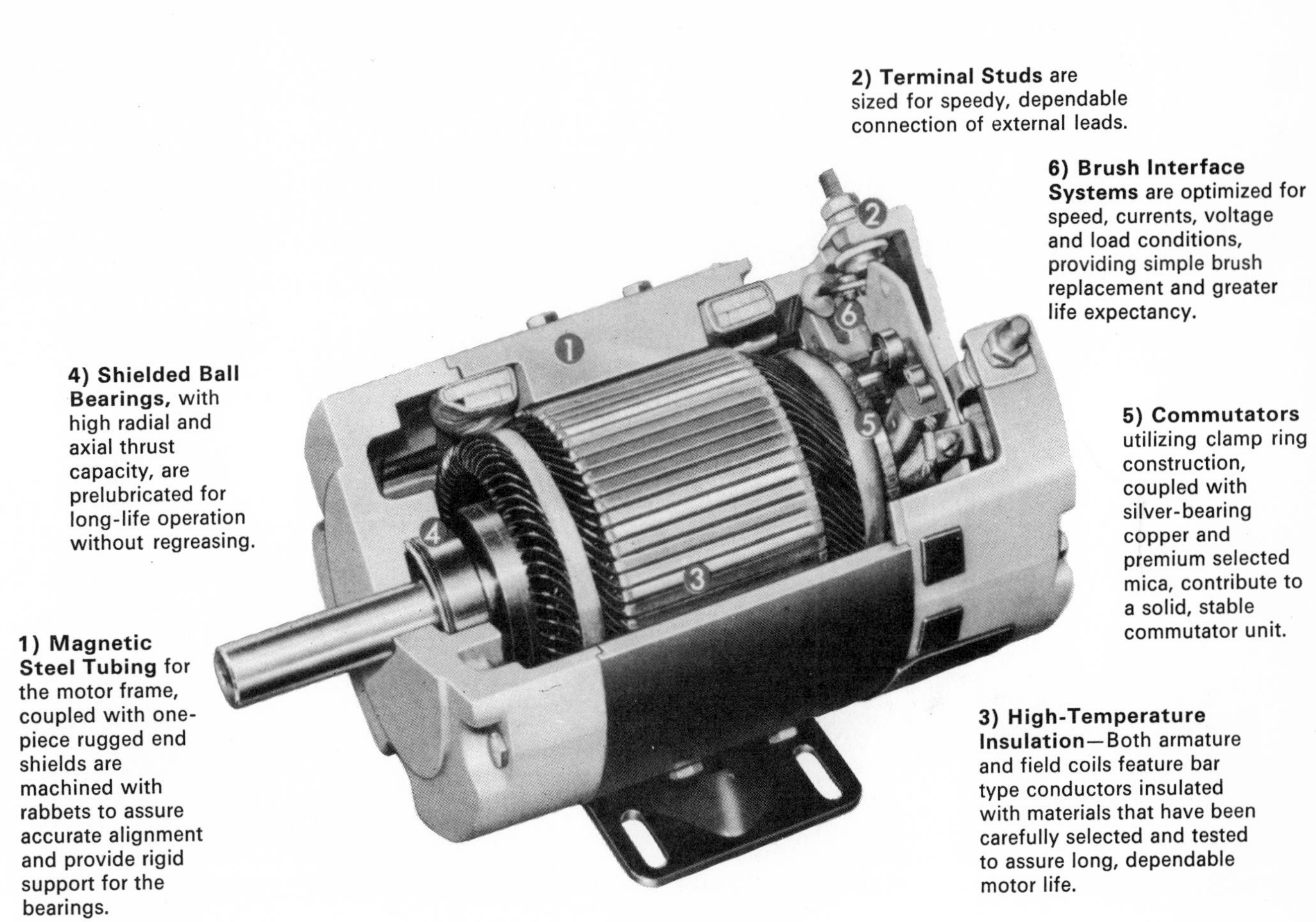

2) Terminal Studs are sized for speedy, dependable connection of external leads.
6) Brush Interface Systems are optimized for speed, currents, voltage and load conditions, providing simple brush replacement and greater life expectancy.
4) Shielded Ball Bearings, with high radial and axial thrust capacity, are prelubricated for long-life operation without regreasing.
5) Commutators utilizing clamp ring construction, coupled with silver-bearing copper and premium selected mica, contribute to a solid, stable commutator unit.
1) Magnetic Steel Tubing for the motor frame, coupled with one-piece rugged end shields are machined with rabbets to assure accurate alignment and provide rigid support for the bearings.
3) High-Temperature Insulation—Both armature and field coils feature bar type conductors insulated with materials that have been carefully selected and tested to assure long, dependable motor life.

Fig. 3–19. Cutaway view of GE DC motor for EV's

> Traction motors must be reversible, therefore field and armature connections are brought out separately. It is customary to use either SCR or resistance starting to obtain smooth acceleration. [See the chapter on control systems.] Various field designs are sometimes required, such as series-parallel or series-series. The overloads imposed by grade operations, if you are climbing up hills frequently, require motors capable of six times the rated output. Compound-wound motors are sometimes used to obtain lower speed regulation on small industrial trucks where the high light load speed of a series motor might be undesirable. In general, however, series-wound motors are used because of their high torque per ampere characteristic, and to cut down battery drain on grades because of the inherent slowing down as high torque is imposed.

The following table gives the horsepower rating, speed, and frame designations for GE electric traction motors ranging in horsepower from 2.0 to 36.

	HP	RPM	Frame Size
	2.0	1000	BT1322
	2.3	average	BT1324
	2.7		BT1326
	2.8		BT1341
Thermal rating TENV, one hour at 24, 36, 48, or 72 volts. Refer to Company for rating under any other conditions.	3.7	1000	BT1343
	4.5	Average	BT1344
	5.2		BT1346
	6.9		BT1362
	8.7		BT1364
	10.3		BT1366
	12.2		BT1368
	14.4		BT1372
	17.6		BT1374
	20.2		BT1376
	23.6		BT1378
	18	3100	BT2346
	18	2400	BT2348
Thermal rating separately ventilated, one hour at 120 volts. Motors may be rated at other horsepowers and speeds proportional to voltage in the range of 72 to 192 volts.	24	3000	BT2364
	24	2300	BT2366
	24	1800	BT2368
	36	2900	BT2374
	36	2100	BT2376
	36	1500	BT2378

Kaylor Energy Products (1918 Menalto Avenue, Menlo Park, CA 94025, phone (415) 325-6900) is a company founded by Roy Kaylor, a pioneer designer of electric cars, that supplies many EV components as well as conversion kits for VW's and other compact cars. The Kaylor part number KK-1 is a continuous-duty compound-wound shunt motor with a rating of 30 HP and a maximum output of 100 HP. This DC motor has a cooling fan, special lightweight flywheel, clutch disc pressure plates, splined pilot shaft, precision bearings, and machined cast aluminum adaptor plate to fit a VW transmission. This entire assembly is shipped F.O.B. P.O. Box 9400, Stanford, CA 94305.

A manufacturer of permanent magnet DC motors is *Indiana General Motor Products,* 1168 Barranca Drive, El Paso, TX 79935, phone (915) 593-1621. Although most of the PM motors made by this company, which is a division of Electronic Memories & Magnetics Corporation, are used for other purposes than electric vehicles, the company is interested in making larger sizes of PM motors for use in electric vehicles as the demand increases.

Gould, Inc., Electric Motor Division (1831 Chestnut Street, St. Louis, MO 63103, phone (314) 342-2500) is a division of Gould, a versatile manufacturer with many other automotive products, including batteries, plus both DC and AC motors for use in electric cars. DC motors range in rating from 1 HP to 20 HP, are totally enclosed, and are designed for long life. The single-phase AC motors range in power from 1 HP to 10 HP, while the three-phase motors range in value from 1 HP up to any size required up to 600 HP. In a typical application, a ¼-ton delivery van, for which the entire propulsion system was designed by Gould, the traction motor consists of an enclosed compound-wound DC motor, operating at 54 volts. This motor is 11.72 inches in diameter by 16.2 inches long and weighs 263 pounds. Note that it is an unusually heavy DC motor because of its requirement for heavy-duty service in a van. See figure 3–20.

Prestolite Electrical Division of Eltra Corporation (2 Pennsylvania Plaza, New York, NY 10001, phone (212) 695-1600) provides many DC and AC motors which can be used for electric vehicles. The company's Prestolite Battery Division is a leading supplier of lead-acid batteries for EV use, as described in a later chapter.

An electric motor used in some European applications is made by *Mawdsley's Ltd.* (Dursley, Gloucestershire GL11 5AE, England, phone Dursley 4131). A typical traction motor made by Mawdsley's develops 18 HP at 2,700 rpm for use on 72 volts DC. A performance curve on this motor, as well as a photograph, are shown in figures 3–21 and 3–22.

Soon to be in production on DC motors and generators for use in electric cars is *Fidelity Electric Company, Inc.* (332 N. Arch Street, Lancaster, PA 17603, phone (614) 397-8231). This company has been designing DC electric traction motors for use in cars, trucks, and buses. Sizes range from 1 HP to 20 HP, rated for continuous duty and self-ventilated at 1,800 rpm. Production on these DC motors is just getting under way.

Fig. 3–20. Typical DC traction motor made by Gould, Inc.

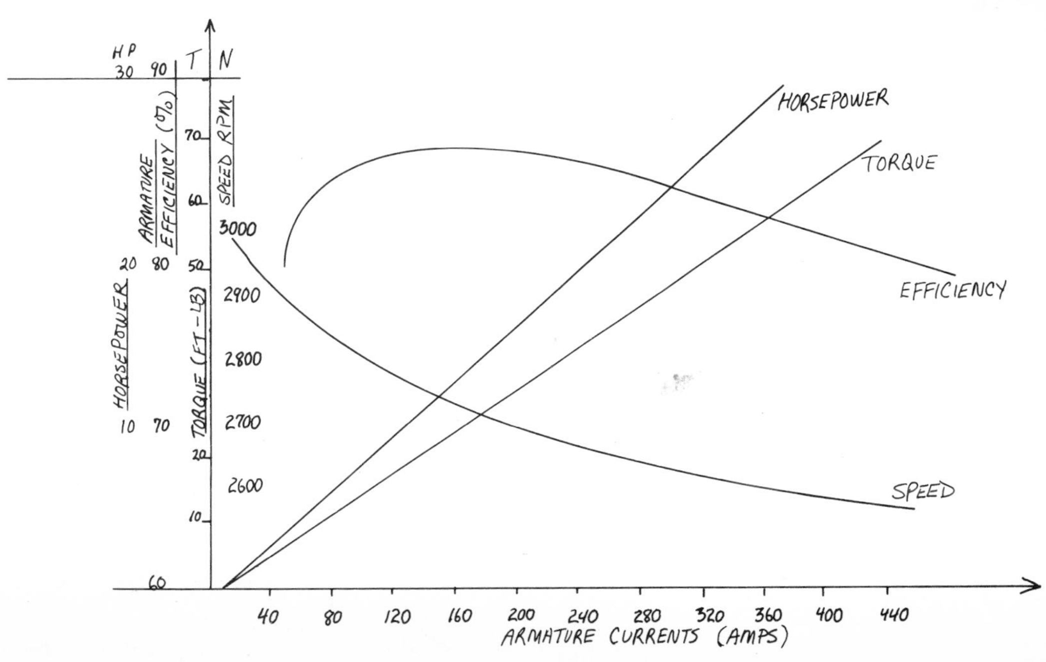

Fig. 3–21. Output characteristics for a compound-wound motor: 72 volts, 18 HP, 220 amps, 2700 rpm, 1HR-rated, open enclosure

Fig. 3–22. DC traction motor made by Mawdsley's Ltd.

An established producer of printed-circuit, permanent-magnet motors is *PMI Motors,* Division of Kollmorgen Corporation (5 Aerial Way, Syosset, NY 11791, phone (516) 938-8000). PMI makes printed-circuit, permanent-magnet DC motors rated up to 5 HP, operating at a speed of 2,500 rpm and at a voltage up to 125 volts DC, with a rated current of 28 amperes. These PMI DC motors have been used with the Flinders electric vehicle in Australia. The motor is light, weighing 70 pounds. In the Flinders application, one of these 5 HP motors is used to drive each of the front wheels of a Fiat 127 modified to be an electric car. The performance of the car is quite good, reaching a maximum speed of 75 kph (about 47 mph), with a range of about 80 kilometers (50 miles) in urban traffic.

Another manufacturer of somewhat smaller sizes of permanent-magnet DC motors is *American Bosch Electrical Products Division,* Ambac Industries, Inc. (P.O. Box 2228, Columbus, MS 39701, phone (601) 328-4150).

An additional source for permanent-magnet DC motors is *Mavilor Motors,* a division of Nuclear & Environmental Protection, Inc. (285 Murphy Road, Hartford, CT 06114, phone (203) 525-7743). These motors are totally enclosed and have the small, relatively flat shape shown in figure 3–23. According to the manufacturer, they have a very high torque-to-inertia ratio and can reach maximum speed in less than 20 milliseconds. They are available in eight standard types, from ¼ HP to 13 HP.

Among many suppliers of AC motors which can be used in EV applications is *Reliance Electric* (25001 Tungsten Road, Cleveland, OH 55117, phone (216) 266-7729).

Fig. 3–23. Mavilor Model MO 10000 PM pancake DC motor. Rated at 13 HP at 3500 rpm

Maintenance of Your DC Electric Motor

It is very important to inspect your motor regularly and to keep it clean. Be sure that your motor is free of dirt, grease, oil, and water. It is quite feasible to run a vacuum cleaner over your electric motor to remove any loose material. If there are sticky particles, wipe the motor off with a clean rag.

Inspect the brushes of your DC motor regularly to make sure that they are secure, but that they can move freely in their holders. Also make sure that there is even contact between the brushes and the commutator. Usually, brush life in a DC motor used in an electric car is several years. Shown in figure 3–24 is a commutator and brush housing.

You should make sure that the commutator on your motor is kept clean and polished looking. Wipe it occasionally with a dry cloth. Do not use oil on the commutator of your electric motor because the brushes, which are in contact with this commutator, are usually made of a graphite compound and are self-lubricating. If you find that the brushes on your motor are chattery, you can turn down the commutator simply by making a holder for sandpaper and sanding down the commutator to its original round shape. This should be done with the motor operated at low speed.

Inspect the bearings of your motor periodically. If there are ball bearings, there will usually be a fitting for a pressure grease gun. Wipe this fitting and the relief plug as well as the surrounding area clean. You can remove and clean the relief plug. While the motor is turning slowly, add grease until there is just a small amount coming out of the relief hole. Continue to run the motor for a short time since this will remove excess grease. Now replace the clean relief plug. Using a grease with about the consistency of petroleum jelly is desirable.

Check all nuts and bolts to make sure that fastenings are secure. Check fuses and contactors to make sure that they are in good condition, clean, and providing satisfactory electrical contact. With an ohmmeter, check to see that you have a complete electrical circuit between your batteries, motor, and the return cable to your storage batteries.

The next chapter contains a discussion of drive trains used with electric motors for more efficient operation of your EV.

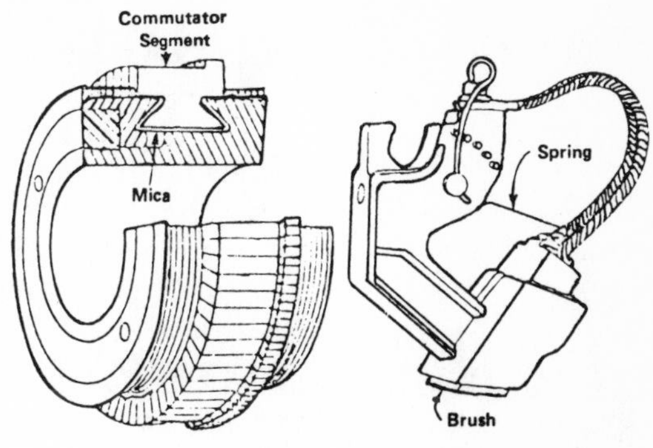

Fig. 3–24. View of commutator and brush arrangement

4 Drive Trains

Your electric car is going to need some form of speed reduction between the motor and the wheel drive axle because normally, motor speeds are considerably higher than those of the wheels. This is usually done through some sort of transmission which will allow you to match the motor output to the wheel requirements.

If the speed reduction can be accomplished by means of a differential alone, you can couple your electric motor directly to the differential. A drawing of a typical automotive differential appears in figure 4–1. This kind of differential is needed to keep both drive wheels loaded evenly when they rotate at different speeds, as, for example, when you are turning a corner. Differentials accomplish this by increasing the outside wheel speed while decreasing the inside wheel speed when the car is making a turn, to prevent wheel hop. Without a differential, because your outer wheels must go faster than the inner wheels in a turn, the outer wheels would tend to "hop" in an attempt to catch up.

Fig. 4–1. Typical EV differential from Spicer Clutch Division, Dana Corporation

It is quite possible to use the conventional differential in the small car which you plan to modify into an electric car. Or, if you are rebuilding a vehicle, you can buy a conventional differential from many sources. In the differential shown in figure 4–2, there is no relative motion or gear loss from gears 4, 5, and 6, except when the vehicle is turning a corner. The principal sources of energy loss are input gears 2 and 3, as well as the seals, bearing, and lubricants. A typical conventional automotive differential is about 95% efficient at 37 kW (50 HP), according to the DOE publication cited in chapter 3. In this case, it has losses of about 2 kilowatts or 2½ horsepower. In most electric vehicle designs, the differential and motor are either rigidly fastened to the drive axle or to the vehicle chassis. In the rigid installation, the differential housing is a structural member and must be capable of supporting its portion of the total vehicle weight, including the added weight of the batteries in your EV. The electric motor, differential, and axles constitute a considerable part of the total vehicle weight.

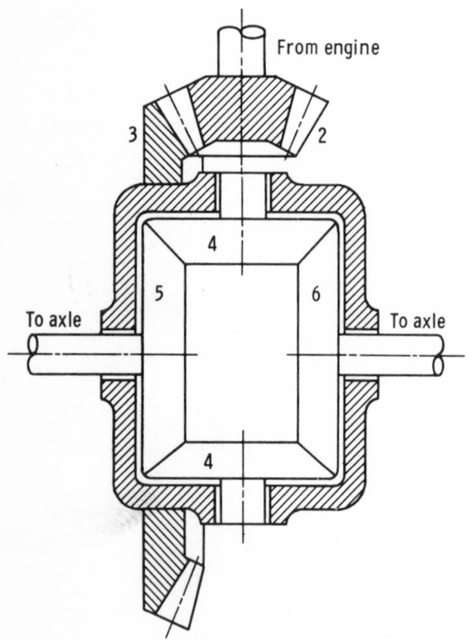

Fig. 4–2. Typical automotive differential, cutaway view

The alternate way of attaching the differential is to fasten it to the chassis. In this case, the output shafts are connected to the wheels through flexible couplings or universal joints. This approach requires more seals and bearings, which in turn cause more loss of energy.

Some axles contain differentials and gearboxes specifically manufactured for small, special-purpose vehicles, and these are particularly useful for electric vehicles.

Drive-Train Layouts

The most commonly used layout has the engine in front with an attached clutch or torque converter immediately followed by a transmission, which may be either a three- or four-speed manual shift or a three-speed automatic shift. The transmission is connected to the differential in the rear of the car via a drive shaft which has a universal coupling (U-joint) on each end. The differential distributes the power equally to the rear wheels, and is generally connected solidly to the wheels via two enclosed half shafts. See figure 4–3.

By contrast, in many compact cars the differential is in the front and included in the transmission to facilitate front-wheel drive. See figures 4–4 and 4–5.

The *advantages* of this layout are good utilization of space, low

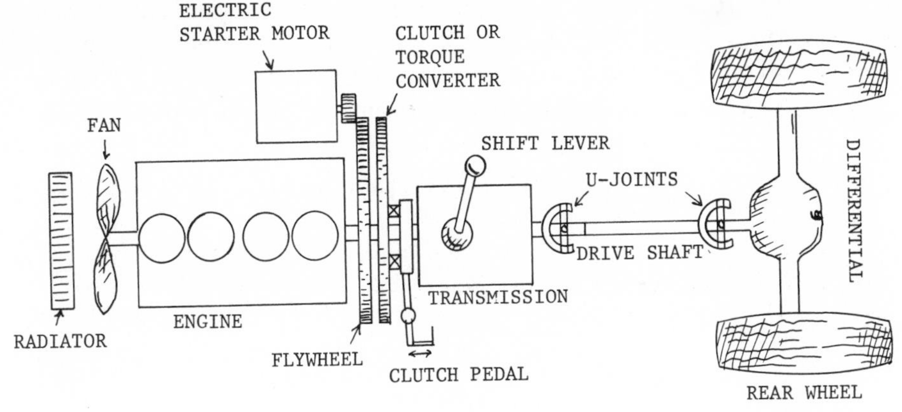

Fig. 4-3. **Conventional American car drive-train layout**

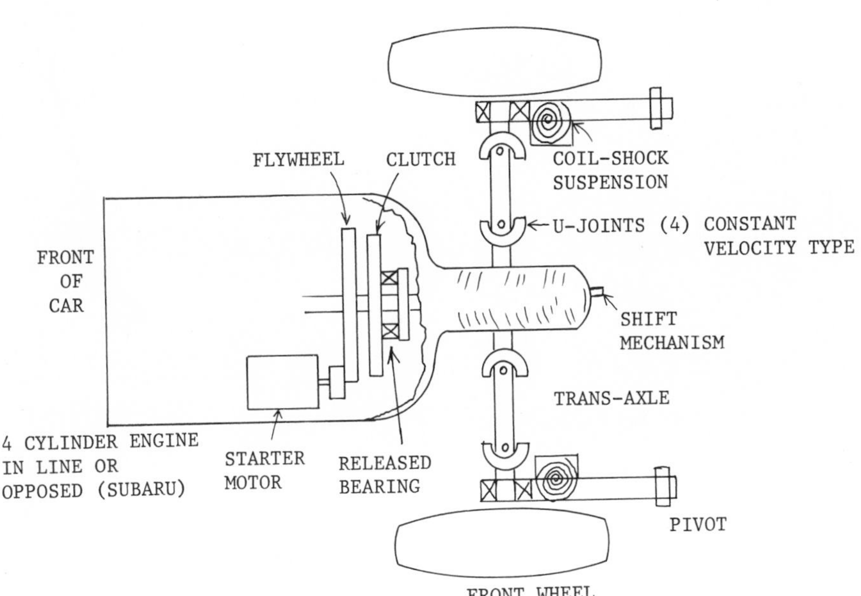

Fig. 4-4. **Front-wheel-drive power-train layout as used in Renault 12, 15, 17; Subaru (all); Saab**

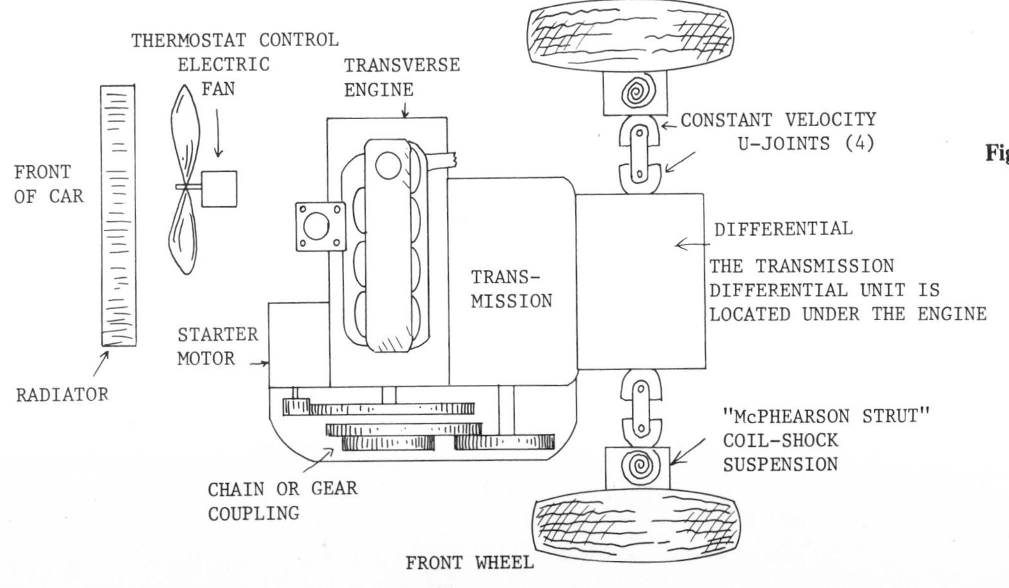

Fig. 4-5. **Front-wheel-drive layout gaining rapid popularity; presently used in Fiat 128; Honda 600 and Civic; VW Scirocco, Dasher, and Rabbit; Datsun F10; Plymouth Horizon and Dodge Omni; Austin America; Ford Fiesta**

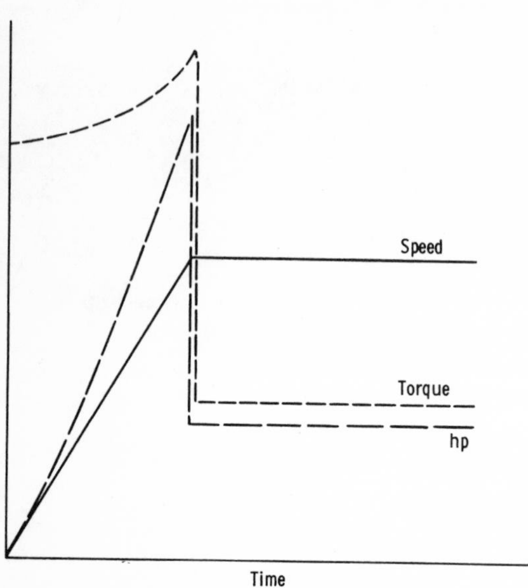

Fig. 4–6. General shape of speed, torque, and horsepower as function of time for typical driving cycle

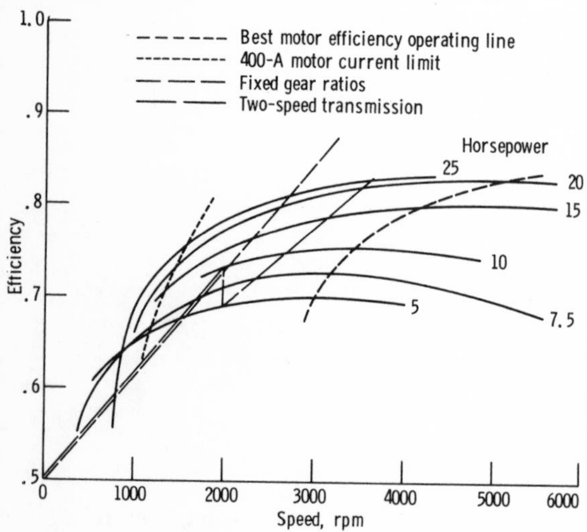

Fig. 4–7. Typical efficiency map for series-wound DC motor

reaction torque and vibration from the engine, direct engine cooling improvement, and simpler power train (as is the case of other engine-trans-axle integral packages) since with removal of a few bolts, the whole drive assembly can be detached through the bottom of the car.

Advantages of a Multi-Speed Transmission

It is particularly desirable to have a multi-speed transmission with an electric vehicle so that you can achieve greater motor efficiency in all modes of driving your car. In particular it will assure you of better acceleration and hill-climbing ability. If you were to use only electrical or electronic controls to vary the speed of your DC motor by varying the applied voltage, you couldn't get the most efficient operation from your DC motor. Nor could you get maximum power output under all driving conditions.

In figure 4–6 are shown the torque, speed, and power requirements at the input to the differential for an electric car accelerating at a constant rate from a standstill to a cruising speed of 45 mph. As shown in this figure, the motor's power requirements increase with vehicle speed until you reach your desired cruising speed.

Compare this with the efficiency versus speed and horsepower performance of a series-wound DC motor shown in figure 4–7. This figure shows that the efficiency of a DC motor improves at higher power levels and drops rapidly at low motor speeds, as we have previously discussed in chapter 3.

You will note also that figure 4–7 has operating lines for maximum motor efficiency. Whatever power you need, there is an optimum motor speed and torque for this horsepower to achieve maximum efficiency from your DC motor.

If your motor is directly coupled through a differential to the wheels, the motor speed is directly proportional to the vehicle speed and your motor efficiency will always be somewhat less than optimum. Therefore, it is desirable to provide some method of increasing the torque delivered to the wheels. This may be achieved in many different ways.

MANUAL TRANSMISSION

The simplest and most commonly used method is to use one or more discrete steps of gear reduction through a transmission. When the car is first accelerated, the highest gear ratio (and hence shaft speed reduction) is used. This gives the highest torque multiplication. While the car is accelerating, the ratio is progressively changed toward, typically, a 1:1 ratio. With a high-horsepower (high-torque) engine compared to total vehicle weight, fewer steps and/or a lower gear reduction ratio are required. When lower-horsepower engines are used, as in most imported cars, more gear ratio steps are required, typically four.

Disadvantages of a manual transmission are that manual changes of the gear ratio and operation of a clutch to disconnect the gear train from the engine while shifting are required. Generally, the three or four steps used for shifting in forward motion are adequate, but far from optimum. Eight, or even ten steps would be better, but a lot of time would be spent shifting, and the cost of the transmission would be much higher. These extra steps are not acceptable in cars, but in trucks, where optimum net hauling weight is important, 12 forward speeds are common.

AUTOMATIC TRANSMISSIONS

Automatic transmissions are rapidly replacing manual transmissions in most automotive applications, even though they have a number of disadvantages, primarily higher cost and lower efficiency.

While the manual transmission uses a single set of gears, two per speed ratio, the automatic transmission uses planetary gear sets which, with clutches and/or bands, allows one to shift gear ratios while under power. Additionally, the design has a torque converter or a fluid coupling and a system of hydraulic governors, pumps, valves, and piston actuators for the clutches and/or bands. The torque converter allows the engine to idle in gear while the car is stopped. It also gives a continuously variable torque multiplication from about 2.5:1 to about 1:1, although at the expense of lowered efficiency. Generally, only three speed ratios are used. The efficiency for a torque converter varies from zero at start to about 80% while cruising.

The shift points may be modulated through a mechanical linkage connecting the transmission with the accelerator pedal. More commonly, a vacuum line from the engine controls a diaphragm, which in turn controls a hydraulic valve. As the accelerator pedal is depressed, the manifold vacuum in the engine drops, which causes a delay in upshifting to utilize the increased torque with increased engine speed.

PLANETARY GEAR SETS

With the addition of a band-type clutch around the outside of the ring gear and a double set of clutches, the planetary gear set can produce freewheeling or idling (neutral), low gear reduction, reverse gear, and high gear of 1:1 (direct) in one compact package. All these operations may be achieved while under power with no fear of breaking gear teeth. In addition, a higher power rating is attained in the same size package as the simple two-gear parallel gearbox, since three points of contact are made by the planetary gears. The design distributes the forces on the gear housing in three directions, as opposed to only one in the simple gear arrangement. The forces are contained within the ring gear, so hardly any force is transmitted to the gear case. If the gears are hypoid gears, which are commonly used to reduce noise and extend life, instead of straight spur gears, a small axial force is developed.

Both manual and automatic transmissions are suitable for use in an electric car. The clutch in a manual transmission may be retained when doing a conversion, but it is not necessary unless a combined electrical and mechanical method for speed control is used. Such an approach was originally demonstrated by the late Warren Helle of La Jolla, California.

HELLE SYSTEM

Helle had used an old aircraft ground support generator rated at 120 VDC and 167A at 3,000 rpm. It weighed 100 pounds, had 6 poles, and an 80% efficiency at rated load, which was 20 kW. It required forced-air cooling at full power.

As a motor operated at about 144 VDC, it would be rated at about

25 HP continuously with air cooling. Installed in a Karmann Ghia (VW), which weighs about 2,000 pounds, with a clutch and shunt field control, it gave satisfactory performance. The motor would be initially started, with a very heavily saturated shunt winding, and would idle at about 1,500 rpm—similar to a gasoline-powered version. With low gear engaged, the field would be weakened and the car would accelerate. Then, as the torque fell off, the gears would be engaged in sequence via the manual clutch until the desired speed was reached.

Helle claimed a top speed of about 70 mph, but a governor limited that to around 55 mph in an effort to increase range. While downshifting, reverse action would take place and the motor would become a shunt-excited generator, returning some kinetic energy to the batteries. This phenomenon, known as *regeneration,* also provides a very effective braking action, thereby obviating the use of friction brakes except for the last few mph of slowing.

Helle did have problems with very hot motors and wasted current in the shunt winding. He was running with about 20 amperes in the shunt winding in an effort to bring the idling speed down to reduce glazing of the clutch at initial accelerating from standstill. This parasitic power loss was about 2.4 kW (120 VDC times 20 amperes), which could drive the car at 25 mph.

This system may be a viable power train in some applications with improvements.

To match engine horsepower to vehicle weight for satisfactory performance, all previous transmissions were connected to a differential which also gave one final gear reduction.

Continuously Variable Transmissions

Motor efficiency increases if you can provide a transmission with a continuously variable amount of torque. Therefore, as has been stated in numerous publications, including the DOE book *State of the Art Assessment of Electric and Hybrid Vehicles*, which came out in January 1978, a variable transmission (CVT) that can regulate motor speed continuously appears to be the ideal choice if its cost, weight, size, and reliability can be made comparable to those of conventional differentials and transmissions.

Basically three types of CVT's show promise for electric vehicle applications: variable-speed belt drives, hydromechanical CVT, and traction CVT. Variable-speed belt drives, as used in the Waterman DAF electric vehicle, are relatively simple and inexpensive. These belt drives have relatively good transmission efficiency, generally about 80% to 90% at full power, but are usually designed to handle less total horsepower than conventional differentials and transmissions. A typical rating for a variable-speed belt drive might be about 25 HP, corresponding to 18 kW.

DAF VARIABLE BELT TRANSMISSION

This system is one of the world's simplest, and potentially least expensive, drive trains in commercial production. Originally introduced in the 1950s, it is still used at the present time in the only Dutch car produced, coupled with a Renault engine in a compact car about the size of the smaller Renault models. See figure 4–8. These cars have competed successfully in some European road rallies, a testimonial to their ruggedness and reliability. The belts need to be replaced at intervals of six to twelve months, but since this replacement is quite easily made, such an interval appears to be quite acceptable to the average car owner.

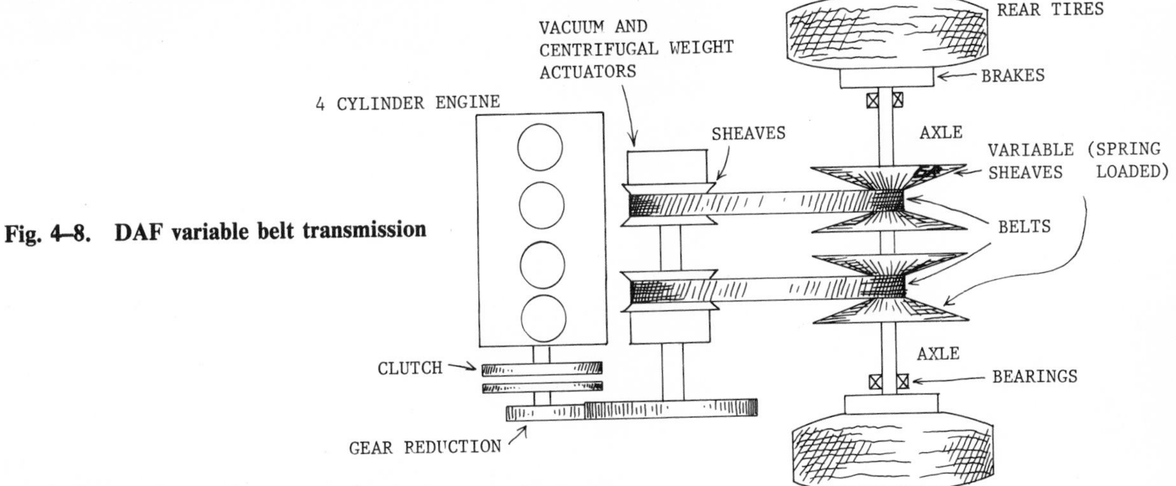

Fig. 4–8. DAF variable belt transmission

NOTE: Belt positions shown in figure 4–8 are in the starting position. This is one type of layout used. Other variations, which include differentials and single belts, have also been used or proposed.

Some of the advantages are:

1. Potentially inexpensive.
2. No high-technology materials or alloys necessary.
3. Fairly simple, flexible.
4. Speed may be adjusted automatically using torque or speed sensing, or both.
5. Infinitely adjustable speed ratio.
6. No fluids to leak.
7. Simple inspection of wearing parts, since the belts are the major parts which wear out.

This system is not perfect, and belt wear may be high, depending mostly on type of service and degree of overdesign. The efficiency may vary from approximately 90% to 50%, depending on design sophistication, but 80% seems to be typical. By comparison, a torque-converter three-speed automatic transmission may have an efficiency variation of 25% to 70% while accelerating to cruising speeds, and solid-state speed controls in an electric car may be typically 95% efficient when driving a DC motor. One other strong disadvantage is the larger physical size of such a variable belt drive, although its weight is about equal to that of a conventional automatic transmission.

However, the belt transmission and other infinitely adjustable transmissions, which will be covered later, share one very important advantage. Because of their large variation of torque multiplication, they allow the use of a much smaller engine for equivalent acceleration to cruising speeds, compared to a conventional automatic transmission. Conversely, using an electric motor of the same horsepower, the variable belt transmission provides superior acceleration and mileage.

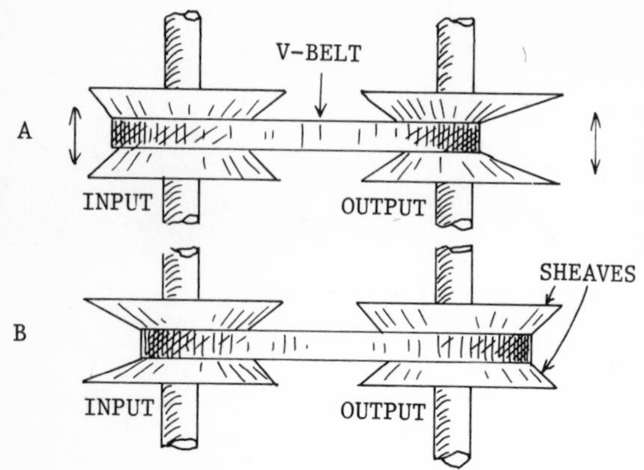

Fig. 4–9. Sketch showing operation of a variable belt transmission

Basic Operation. The simplest variable belt transmission or variable-speed device consists of a simple fixed sheave or pulley, a V-belt, and a special variable sheave that has two halves that slide on a splined or keyed shaft and some method to control this movement. See figure 4–9.

In the simplest design, the two halves are held together with a spring. To vary the output speed, the motor pulley is moved, causing a fixed-length V-belt to apply more or less pressure on the variable sheave and forcing it to open or close. The belt will therefore prescribe a different diameter on the variable sheave. The resultant speed is therefore the effective input pulley diameter divided by the effective diameter the belt prescribes, at any setting, on the variable sheave. See figure 4–10.

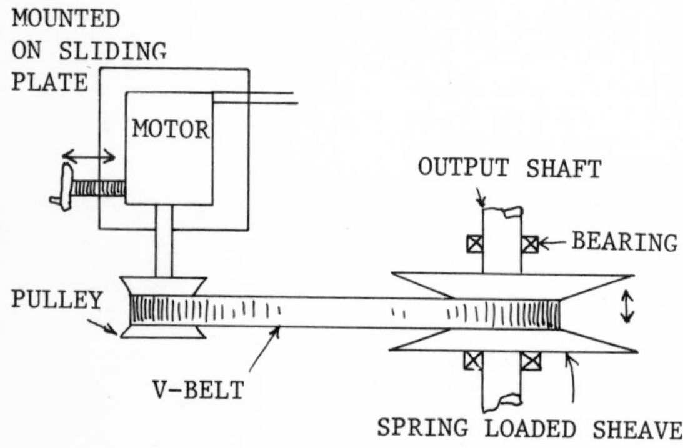

Fig. 4–10. Sketch of simple variable belt drive

SIMPLE VARIABLE SHEAVE

The characteristics of this simple adjustable drive are that the speed can be varied about 2.5:1, and torque varies inversely with speed. See figure 4–11. These characteristics apply if the spring force is strong enough to prevent the belt from slipping at the high-torque, low-speed setting by only a small amount—about 2% of speed. The motor has to be able to be moved back and forth as a function of the speed variation. This simple setup is used fairly extensively in industrial applications with low horsepower requirements, and where only limited speed adjustments are required. The most outstanding disadvantage is the fact that the spring, which is designed for the heaviest load expected, exerts the same force at all loads and therefore causes strong resistance to belt movement with resultant high losses under light load conditions. This problem can be alleviated with a mechanism that senses the torque required and applies just enough force on the belt to prevent it from slipping.

In more demanding applications, two variable sheaves are used. This design permits both input and output shafts to be fixed in relation to each other. Again, one sheave may be simply spring-loaded while the other is controlled through some mechanism that may be actuated in many ways: pneumatic, hydraulic, mechanical, manual, centrifugal or torque sensing, or electrical See figure 4–12. The tension of the belt tends to open the sheave, while the control force tends to close it. The balance between these two forces establishes the diameter on which the belt rides.

HYDROMECHANICAL CVT

A second type of CVT that looks promising is a hydromechanical unit utilizing a hydrostatic drive consisting of a hydraulic pump coupled to a hydraulic motor connected in parallel with a mechanical planetary gear unit. With this design, the power source for the transmission is

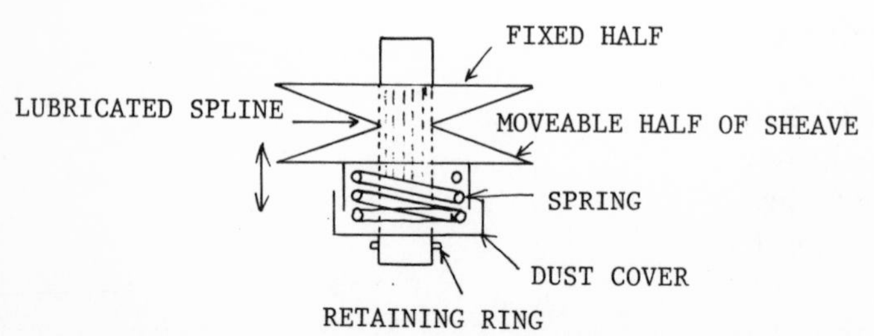

Fig. 4–11. Simple variable sheave

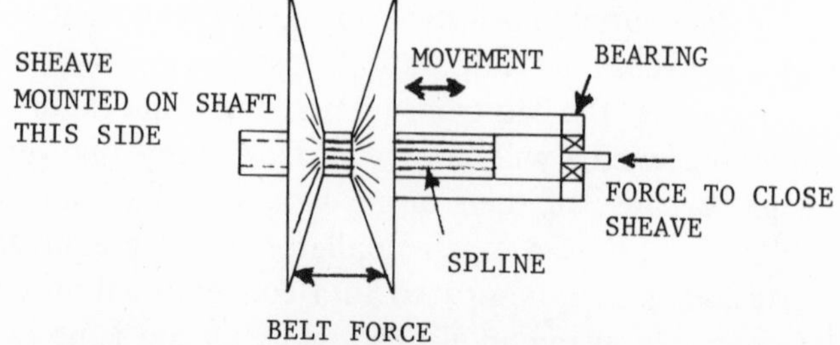

Fig. 4–12. Mechanically actuated sheave

split between the hydraulic and mechanical branches so that most of the torque is carried by the more efficient mechanical drive, so the overall efficiency of the transmission is improved. Orshansky Transmission Company has developed prototype hydromechanical transmissions which are now installed in both Hornet and Nova automobiles with internal combustion engines. However, there is no reason for this type of Orshansky transmission not to be used in electric cars. The mechanism is compact and has good high-power cruise capability.

TRACTION-DRIVE CVT's

A third type of CVT is called a traction drive. Such a transmission regulates the speed ratio by repositioning roller elements in such a way that the radii of the meshing rollers are varied. The primary limitation of such a traction transmission has been its low power capacity. Nevertheless, several adjustable-speed, industrial traction-drive units are available commercially. For example, such drives have been tested on a prototype basis with a toroidal configuration designed by Excellermatic, Inc., and General Motors Corporation in the United States. The DOE publication previously cited has commented that "traction-drive CVT's may hold the most promise for practical, efficient electric vehicle drive trains."

A very early application of this principle was made in a car in the 1920s. It used a leather material for the friction surface but had limited success because of rapid wear of the leather surfaces. See figure 4–13.

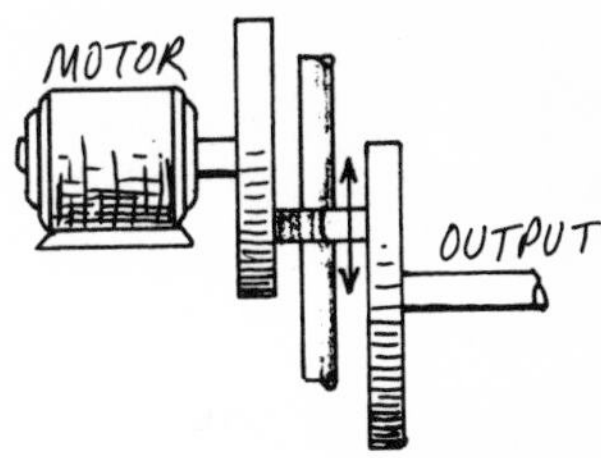

Fig. 4–13. Simple double-disc friction drive

This concept, with variations, has also been employed in industrial drives for decades, especially in Europe and Japan. Instead of using leather, metal-to-metal contact is made. In direct metal-to-metal contact, cold welding often results from the high pressures involved. Also, if the speed ratio is suddenly changed, or if there is insufficient contact pressure, something similar to skidding results. Skidding scores the steel surfaces quickly, causing a drastic increase in wear. A few years ago, several companies doing research on lubricating oils found that some lubricants could decrease wear drastically in metal-to-metal contact, even under very high loads. One of these fluids, called Santotrack by Monsanto Chemical Co., has some interesting properties. Under very high pressures, on the order of tens of thousands of pounds per square inch, such as is encountered in a traction drive, the metal contact surfaces deform and the fluid trapped between them temporarily solidifies and transfers the force. As soon as the fluid leaves the high-pressure area, it returns to a fluid state. There is therefore no direct metal-to-metal contact with its associated wear.

It is understandable, with the advantages of such systems, that a flurry of activity is going on to develop a transmission for automotive applications, but so far none is available commercially. One company in Texas, Tracor, has demonstrated this kind of transmission successfully in a Pinto. A substantial improvement in performance and mileage compared to the same car with a standard automatic transmission, estimated at as much as 100% under some driving conditions, was found.

Other EV Drive Trains

One of the most interesting drive systems has been designed by Lucas Industries of Birmingham, England, which has its U.S. headquarters at

5500 New King Street, Troy, MI 48098, phone (313) 879–1920. In a conversion of a van for electric operation, the drive is to the rear wheels through a rigid rear axle so that standard leaf springs from a 4,000-pound Bedford van can be used and higher-rated coil springs are fitted to the front suspension. The primary of the two-stage gear reduction, having a ratio of 2.38:1, is housed in a chain case attached directly to the motor. The complete unit is attached by means of anti-vibration mounting to the body behind the rear axle. The output from the primary reduction is transmitted to the secondary via a short transverse driving shaft with a rubber doughnut coupling at one end and a universal joint at the other. The secondary reduction of 2.81:1 is contained within the special rear-axle casing and drives the wheels through a conventional differential gear set and full-floating half shafts of unequal length. The main feature of this transmission system, described by the Manager of Special Projects for Lucas Industries, is that it is much more efficient than the hypoid unit previously used by Lucas Industries. It is more simple and efficient than the mechanical drive of the Lucas electric taxi, since the four constant-velocity joints on the front-wheel drive shafts of that vehicle are replaced by one doughnut coupling and one universal joint on the intermediate drive shaft. The use of 8-ply radial tires permits loading the rear axle to a weight of more than 5,000 pounds while using single rear wheels. This axle loading is feasible since prolonged high-speed motoring will not normally be encountered with this type of van.

A different type of variable belt drive has been designed by Robert S. McKee, McKee Engineering Corporation, 411 W. Colfax St., Palatine, IL 60067, phone (312) 358–6773. In the Mark XVI, a low-slung, lightweight sports car designed by McKee, the chassis consists of a box-beam backbone which houses the slide-in battery pack and supports the drive motor, independent suspension, and rack and pinion steering.

Two parallel, flexible belt drives, connecting the electric motor with the rear wheels, eliminate a conventional gearbox, clutch, and differential; universal joints are also eliminated. Each belt drive is infinitely adjustable from a low of 3.1:1 to a high of 0.77:1 (overdrive) and has a limited-slip differential action. The rear-wheel hubs have integral 4.88:1 gear reducers. As a result, the system has an overall drive ratio range of from 14.4:1 to 3.7:1, which is exceptionally good. The belt drive is controlled automatically as a function of rpm, and its low start-up ratio gives good acceleration with minimum power drain from the batteries.

In this case, McKee has used an 8-HP Tork-Link electric-drive motor powered by 12 standard 6-volt lead-acid batteries. See figure 4–14.

Some Other Variable-Speed Drives

Cone drives are available from Graham Transmissions, Inc., Menomonee Falls, WI. Another design is supplied by Simpo Kogyo Co., Ltd., Karahashi, Minami-ku, Kyoto, Japan.

Disc drives are available from Sentinel (Shrewsbury), Ltd., Shrewsbury, England, and also from Block and Vaupel, Wuppertal, Germany.

Ring drives are available from Master Electric Division of Reliance Electric, Dayton, OH, as well as from H. Stroeter, Dusseldorf, Germany, and Excellermatic, Inc., Rochester, NY.

Fig. 4–14. Series-wound, 8-HP DC motor gives McKee Engineering Corp. Mk–16 commuter car an acceleration capability of 0–30 mph in 9 sec; top speed of the vehicle is 60 mph; power reaches the rear wheels through an infinitely variable belt drive and 4.88:1 gear reducers in the wheelhubs.

Spherical drives are available from: New Departure Division of General Motors, Bristol, CT; Perbury Engineering Ltd., England; Cleveland Worm & Gear Division of Eaton Mfg. Co., Cleveland, OH; Excelecon Corp.; and Friedr. Cavalio, Berlin-Neukoelin, Germany.

Multiple-disc drives are available from Ligurtecnia, Genoa, Italy, and Reeves Pulley Division of Reliance Electric Co., Columbus, IN.

Impulse drives are available from Morse Chain Co., Ithaca, NY, and Zero Max Co., Minneapolis, MN.

Differential drives are available from Link-Belt Co.; Stratos Division of Fairchild Engine & Airplane Corp., Babylon, NY; and Lombard Governor Corp., Ashland, MA.

Lightweight EV Transmissions

A manufacturer of die-cast aluminum axles, including transmissions for use in electric cars, is the *Spicer Clutch Division,* Dana Corporation, P.O. Box 191, Auburn, IN 46706, phone (219) 925–3800. The new Model 18 Spicer unit has a conventional drive shaft and an axle-load capacity of 2,000 pounds. Gear ratios of 5.17:1, 7.83:1, and 12.25:1 are available. There is also a 6.83:1 for extended-pinion direct coupling to electric motors, while the ratios normally available are for companion-flange coupling. The Model IS18, which is available in the same gear ratios, is designed for independent-suspension drive.

These units weigh only 75 pounds and provide a load capacity of 2,000 pounds with a maximum torque output of 1,000 foot-pounds.

5 Control Systems

Review of Basic Motor Characteristics

A DC motor produces torque, rotational force, by the interaction of two magnetic fields. One, usually stationary, is normally referred to as the "field," the other, movable (rotating), is called the "armature."

If the field poles are energized electrically, they may be shunt-wound, meaning that they are wired in parallel with the armature and consist of many turns of fine wire since they have to sustain the fully applied voltage. Or, the field may be series-wound, meaning that it is connected in series with the armature and consists of a few turns of heavy wire since it must carry the full armature load current.

Assume, for the moment, that the field winding is producing a fixed magnetic field. This could be a shunt-type winding across a fixed voltage source, referred to as a separately excited shunt motor, while we apply a variable voltage to the armature. Horsepower is equivalent to torque times rpm, or to be precise:

$$HP = \frac{T \times rpm \times 2\pi}{33{,}000} \quad \text{where T is in foot-pounds}$$

As you can see, there has to be rotational speed in addition to torque to produce power.

The armature is a coil having a resistance (R_{arm}) with a voltage applied across its terminals. When this armature rotates, it cuts through the magnetic field produced by the poles, which tends to induce a voltage of the same polarity in the armature. This induced voltage, referred to as back EMF, opposes the applied external voltage. The resultant current into the armature is therefore a function of the motor rpm:

$$I_{arm} = \frac{E_b - V_{bemf}}{R_{arm}}$$

E_b = battery volts
V_{bemf} = back emf, volts
R_{arm} = armature resistance, ohms

The rating of a motor is expressed in terms of current and rpm, at a given voltage. Most motors are designed to have an armature resistance as low as possible, to minimize voltage loss across it. This voltage loss (I^2R, according to Ohm's law) reduces the effective voltage impressed across the armature coils and shows up in the form of heat, which contributes to inefficiency. This voltage drop is approximately 5 to 10% of the rated voltage. Referring to the formula for armature current, it is readily apparent that the armature current increases as the motor is stalled, since the term V_{bemf} approaches zero. Therefore, at stall condition the motor would draw 5 to 10 times the rated current. Since torque is also roughly proportional to armature current, the stall torque would also be 5 to 10 times the rated torque. This high torque would be rather unwelcome when parking or accelerating from start. It would increase the stress on the drive train and the electric components (including the motor), and would reduce range, since the batteries at high current flow are much less efficient.

Resistor Control

The most common and simplest method of limiting the current has been to introduce variable resistors in series with the armature. For example, at half the rated speed of the vehicle, half of the power is lost in the resistor in the form of heat, since half the voltage is dropped across the resistor, while the other half is across the motor. The main advantages of this system are low cost and smooth control. See figure 5–1.

The maximum current (starting) is the battery open-circuit voltage divided by the total circuit resistance. As shown in figure 5–2, as the variable resistance is decreased (and hence the total resistance goes down) the current increases and thus the vehicle speed increases.

Total circuit resistance effectively limits the maximum current and voltage to the motor and therefore controls the maximum torque output. Since the electric-motor speed, and therefore the vehicle speed, are related to the voltage applied to the motor, the vehicle does not reach top speed because some of the voltage is lost across the resistance. And here is the key word in this type of torque and speed control—*lost.* As mentioned previously, a limited amount of energy is available, so any energy wasted is undesirable. But this is exactly what happens in a resistance type of control, since any voltage lost is energy lost. If the vehicle is operated at half speed, half of the battery voltage and therefore half of the energy would be wasted by the resistance control. Any extended operation in this mode would therefore be highly undesirable. In the example of operating at half speed, half of the batteries' energy would be used to heat up the resistor. This heat would have to be dissipated without heating up the interior or any other part of the vehicle, except possibly on cold days.

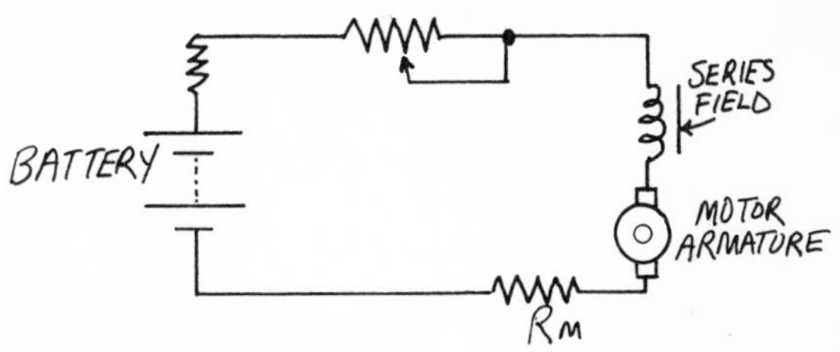

Fig. 5–1. Variable resistor control of a DC motor

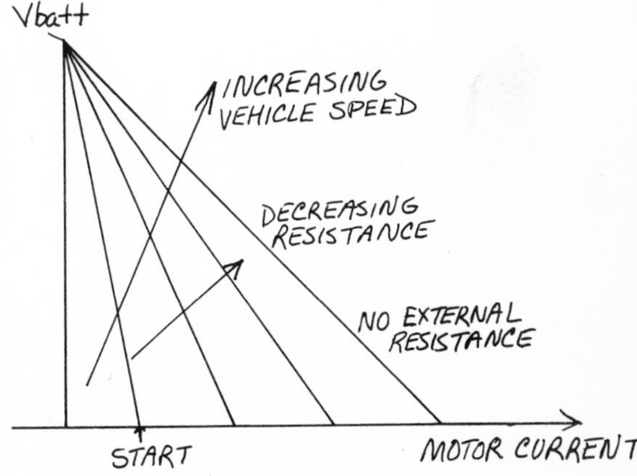

Fig. 5–2. Battery voltage divided by a varying total-circuit resistance results in a varying current.

Battery Switching Control

One might suggest, use battery switching; i.e., start out with the battery voltage at a low setting and then progressively increase it. See figure 5–3. This control method works, but before long one would notice that the batteries in this arrangement discharge unevenly. For instance, if the lower voltage were used extensively, they would discharge faster than the less frequently used batteries in the higher-voltage condition. Therefore, if after a while, the higher voltages are used (at higher speed), the lower-voltage batteries would be discharged sooner, with the result that the lower-voltage batteries would be charged in reverse by the other batteries with a simultaneous drop in motor voltage (and speed). This reverse charge causes excessive gassing and heating and eventually leads to overheating and battery failure. Even if the discharge were to be terminated before this occurs, there remains the problem of properly charging the batteries. Each battery in a series battery pack would essentially require its own charger. At least one system was proposed whereby a small computer would sense each battery condition and switch around the battery units to try to discharge them evenly over a period of cycles. However, this concept sounds too complex to be practical.

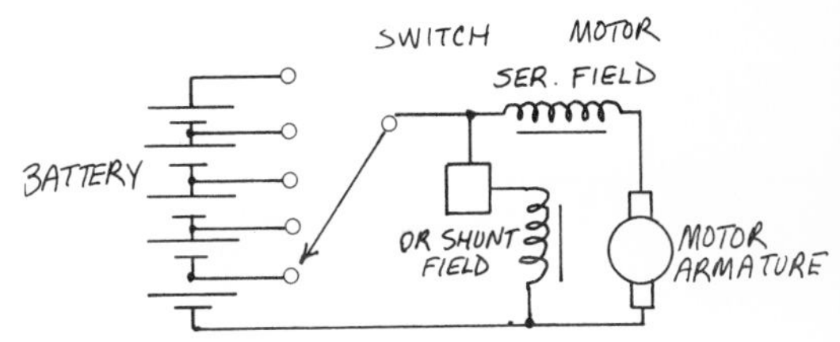

Fig. 5–3. Battery switching to vary current input to motor

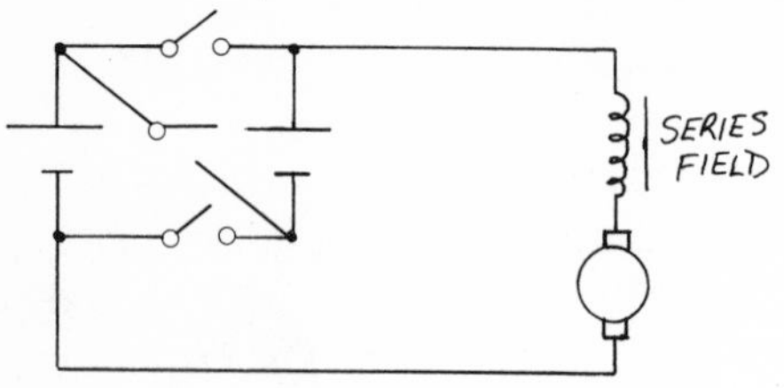

Fig. 5–4. Two-step series-parallel control

SERIES-PARALLEL CONTROL

Another battery switching method, which has been used quite effectively, is the use of series-parallel switching of the battery units. See figure 5–4.

CAUTION: Be sure there is some way the electric current can be interrupted should a relay (contactor) get stuck. The minimum requirement is a fuse rated for the continuous maximum current expected. This fuse should be as close to the battery source as possible so that it can interrupt the current flow should any short circuit develop further down the circuit.

In the case of separate battery packs (i.e., one in front of the car and one in the rear), or in series-parallel controls, there should be a fuse for each battery pack used. A better method, especially recommended if the motor is directly coupled to the differential or wheels (i.e., no neutral or clutch disconnect) is to use a circuit breaker, an extra safety switch or a panic switch in addition to the fuse to interrupt the power circuit.

Before working on or doing anything to an electric vehicle, the transmission should be put in neutral or the drive wheels raised from the ground to prevent sudden accidental runaway. In mechanical systems, a good solid connection has to occur for appreciable power to be transferred. In electrical circuits, a small short might cause enough current to flow to weld wires together or to weld tools to metal surfaces which have power across them. Enough power could be developed to cause the electric motor in series to run away.

In the case of accidental short circuits, sudden very high temperatures and airborne glowing metal particles may be encountered which might affect the most sensitive part of your body—your eyes. **WEAR SAFETY GLASSES!**

Parallel-series battery control is a method to compel the batteries to discharge evenly so that full power, under high efficiency, will be realized under all driving conditions. In a contactor-type series-parallel controller, the power lost in the coils might be about 2% to 5%.

This control technique is also easy to understand by almost anybody with only a minimum knowledge of electricity.

As shown previously, to keep starting current low, we have to reduce the voltage across the motor. One approach is to use large switches or relays to connect the batteries; i.e., 12V, 24V, 48V. See figure 5–5.

Advantages are high efficiency, excellent regeneration, and fairly low cost.

Disadvantages are maintenance of many relay or switch contacts, complexity of wiring, and jerky performance. Operation is jerky because of the relatively large steps of voltage. Each time you go from 24V

Fig. 5–5. Three-step series-parallel control system for DC motor

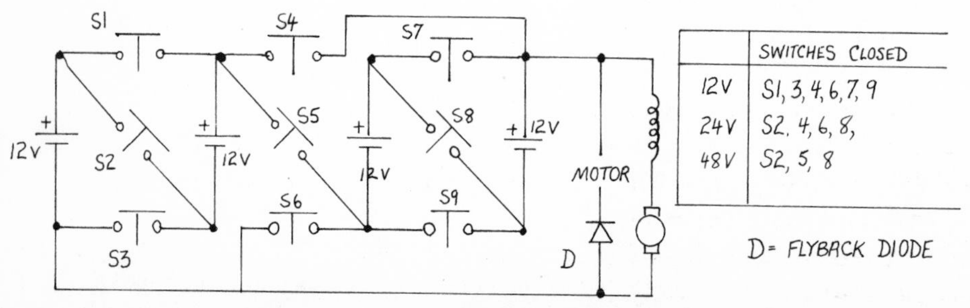

to 48V, for instance, there is a sudden surge of power applied to your electric motor and a resultant "jerk" forward.

THREE-STEP PARALLEL-SERIES CONTROLLER

The practical upper limit is a three-step parallel-series type controller. With one more step, a total of 21 relays would be required! A three-step controller would allow a 4:1 power-level control, which was found to be adequate. But even a three-step controller requires nine relays, as

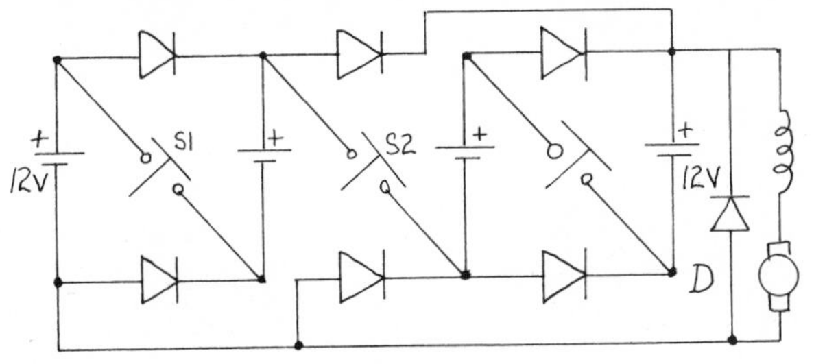

	SWITCHES CLOSED
12V	NONE
24V	S1, S3
48V	S1, S2, S3

Fig. 5–6. **This variation of the series-parallel method is the rectactor, a combination of rectifiers and contactors, therefore the name rectactor.**

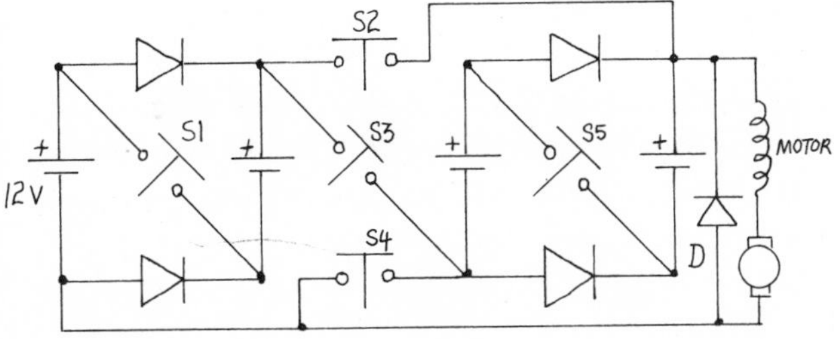

	SWITCHES CLOSED
12V	S2, S4
24V	S1, S2, S4, S5
48V	S1, S3, S5

Fig. 5–7. **Variation: combination relay-series-parallel, and rectactor-series-parallel**

shown in figure 5–5. These relays have to be interlocked to prevent short circuits if the relays were accidentally operated out of sequence. Also, maintenance of many contacts might prove to be a problem.

A variation of this series-parallel circuit has been developed using solid-state diodes to minimize some of these difficulties. Called a "rectactor," a word coined from the words rectifier (diode) and contactor (relay), this circuit appears schematically in figure 5–6.

Only three relays are required; efficiency is fairly high (it is reduced by the voltage drops across the diodes; 75% at 12V, 90% at 24V, and essentially 100% at 48V); cost and maintenance are fairly low; and there is no gear backlash kick. The efficiency would be higher with higher voltage systems.

However, there is no regeneration at lower voltages, and the system is less efficient than an all-relay system.

A variation would be to combine relay-series-parallel, and rectactor-series-parallel circuits. This variation appears in figure 5–7.

The principal advantage is that effective regeneration at 24V is retained while only five relays are used.

RECTACTOR CONTROL

The rectactor parallel-series control circuit has considerably reduced maintenance since many fewer relays are used. For instance, a three-step all-relay controller uses nine relays, while a three-step rectactor unit uses only three. The diodes (rectifiers) have theoretically no maintenance requirement if properly sized. The relays in an all-relay control should be electrically, or preferably mechanically, mutually exclusively interlocked to prevent short circuits. Rectactor controls have no such requirement. Rectactor controls also overcome a dead band in switching from parallel to series, which otherwise causes high shock loads on the gears used in the transmission or differential because of the play in the gears. The rectactor switches instantly from lower to higher voltage.

The main disadvantage of the rectactor control is the loss of regeneration in half or one-quarter voltages. One other minor disadvantage is the voltage drop (approximately one volt) in the diodes in the lower voltages. As an example consider a 3-step series-parallel control for 12, 24, and 48V. In the first step (12V) 1V out of 12V would be lost, which would give an efficiency of approximately 90%. In the second step (24V), the loss would be 1V out of 24V so the efficiency rises to approximately 95%. All the diodes are out of the circuit in the third step (48V), (reverse biased by their respective batteries), and the only loss is in the coils, which might be 1% at the most.

SUMMATION OF PARALLEL-SERIES CONTROLLERS

Series-parallel controllers for electric cars are practical and efficient, allow quite effective regeneration if the proper motor (generator) is used, and are reasonably inexpensive. They can also be built and maintained by anybody with a minimum of electrical knowledge. Drawbacks are maintenance requirements of the contacts, a complexity of wire interconnections to the batteries, and a rather discontinuous (jerky) performance.

Electronic Chopper

All methods previously described have some undesirable features. In search for a better approach to control DC motors supplied from DC sources (batteries), a concept using an inductor was proposed. An inductor is a coil made of insulated copper or aluminum wire. To keep size to a practical level, an iron core is normally inserted into the coil, so that for a given performance, size is reduced by approximately a thousand times. When DC voltage is impressed across an inductor, a magnetic field is generated around it. While increasing from zero to some value, the field is also cutting the coil and inducing a voltage in it. This voltage has the same polarity and opposes the applied DC voltage. It can be shown that this slows down the growing magnetic field as well as the current through the coil.

If the applied voltage is suddenly removed, the magnetic field collapses very rapidly. Since there is nothing to oppose it, a very large voltage, possibly hundreds of times that initially applied, is generated across the coil terminals. To protect other components in the circuit, means must be taken to prevent this high-voltage spike. The extreme measure would be to short out the coil, which would allow the energy in the magnetic field to dissipate in the form of a large current at low voltage.

The amount of energy that can be stored in the motor inductance is limited, and so is the power delivered to the motor in the off time. Thus, the off time must be short. A switching rate of 100 to 300 times per second is required with a typical motor, which rules out a mechanical switch. Practical solutions are to use solid-state devices for fast, reliable, efficient switching.

The most sophisticated solution to the problem (using a very basic principle) is a solid-state speed control or chopper. In this method, a variable width and frequency pulse train of full battery voltage is applied to the motor. A diode connected in parallel with the inductive motor path provides a circuit path for the inductive motor current when the switch is opened. A diode is used, since it provides high current capability without dissipating too much energy. This path prevents abrupt current changes and resultant harmful high voltage across the switching device. The current decreases only in response to motor and diode losses, as shown in figure 5–8.

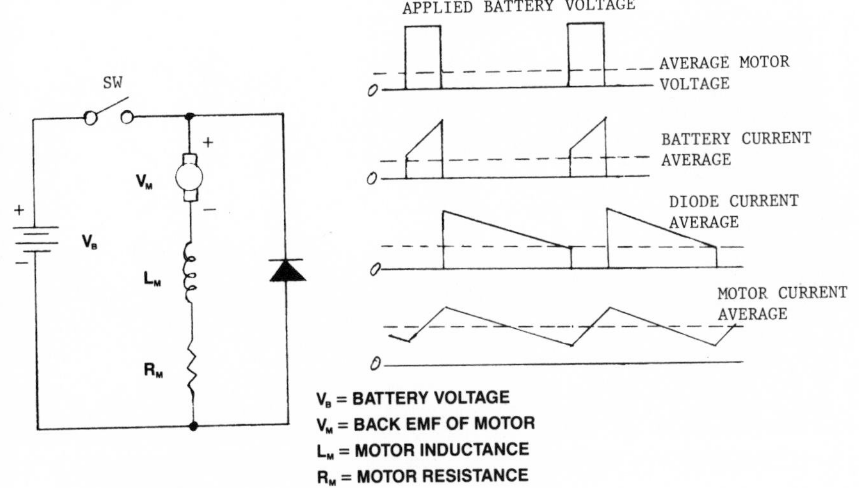

Fig. 5–8. Basic chopper circuit operation

The shunt diode will allow a higher average-level current to flow through the motor than is taken from the battery. However, the power taken from the battery is approximately equal to the power delivered to the motor, indicating that the energy stored in the coil at battery voltage is delivered to the motor at a high current level, but at a much lower voltage.

Effectively, the system is a DC transformer converting high voltage at low average current to low voltage at high average current. If the chopper operates at a high enough frequency, the motor inductance (series field) is strong enough to provide this current multiplication effect.

Commercial Sources of Control Systems for EV's

The Sevcon Mark 7 control system is supplied by SEVCON Division of Tech/Ops, Inc., 40 South Avenue, Burlington, MA 08103, phone (617) 272-2000. This control system is also available through affiliated companies in Great Britain, France, and West Germany.

A simplified schematic of the Sevcon Mark 7 system is shown in figure 5–9. The logic unit shown in this diagram contains all the circuits which control the chopper function and monitor its operation. Sevcon supplies ten different logic units to match various motor and vehicle

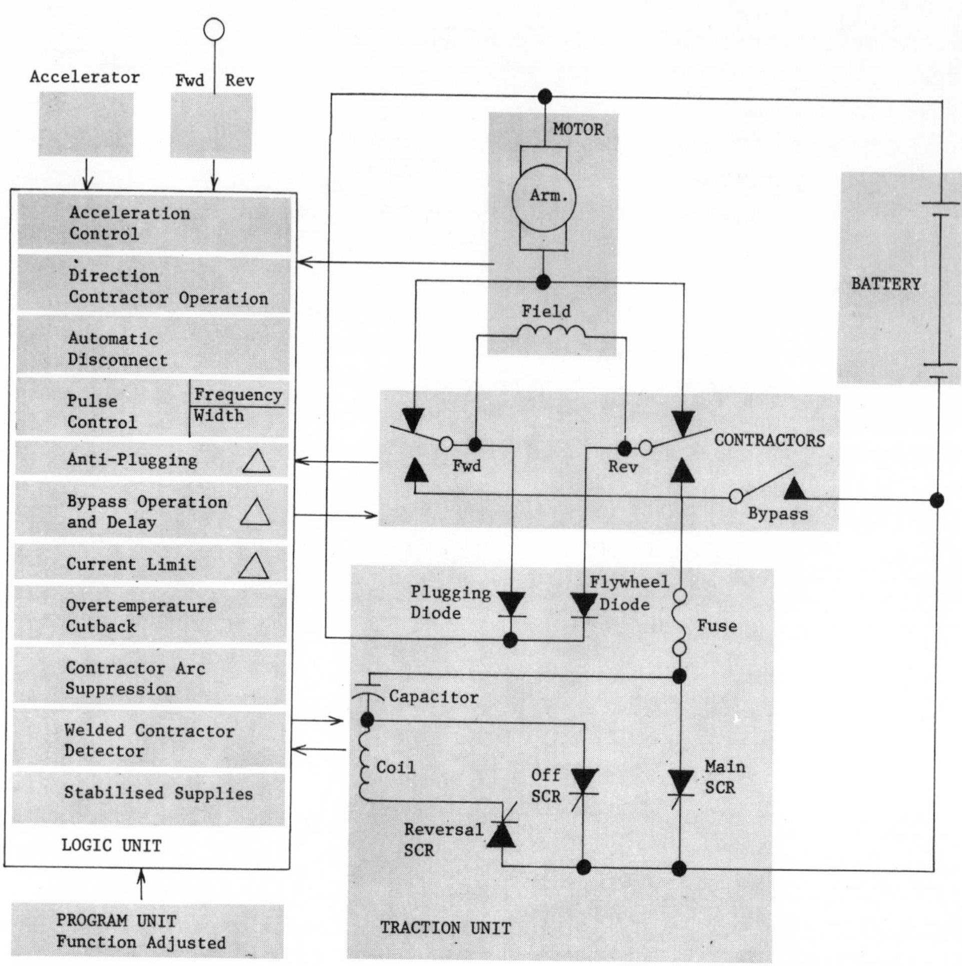

Fig. 5–9. Sevcon Mark 7 control system for DC traction motors

characteristics. The variations available in logic units include control of: pulse width, pulse frequency, bypass inhibit level, plugging, and reversing.

In many applications, especially at low voltage, a fixed pulse width is satisfactory and gives the simplest system at lowest cost. In applications where a bypass contactor is not used, or at higher voltages when cooling is a problem, a variable pulse width is advantageous.

The Sevcon Mark 7 system includes a variable-frequency chopper, the maximum frequency being a function of the pulse width. At maximum frequency with fixed pulse width, the motor voltage is approximately 85% of battery voltage. With variable pulse width, the motor voltage is 93% of battery voltage at maximum frequency.

This system includes in its logic a bypass delay, which is the minimum time delay before bypass closure occurs after start-up. Also, the bypass is prevented from closing if the pulsing level is below a preset minimum. At 30% pulsing level, the bypass is prevented from closing if the chopper system is not operating. The SCR commutating circuit drives the bypass connector arc current through zero instantly following the contact opening, so that bypass contactor-tip arc erosion is virtually eliminated, according to the manufacturer. The pulsing circuit senses the direction of contactor coil voltage and anticipates the contact opening. This prevents the pulsing system from passing current at the instant the contact tips separate.

The logic circuit has an automatic emergency disconnect. If the control system fails, full power would be applied to the motor, but power to the main direction contactors would be interrupted within milliseconds. This assures clearing of a dangerous fault before the driver even becomes aware that a fault might exist. Another feature of this design is that the rate of increase of voltage to the motor is controlled. The period of time over which the motor voltage is gradually applied can be adjusted over a wide range.

For safety, the circuit shuts down and immobilizes the vehicle until the fault is removed if a bypass or direction contactor should weld closed. Also, overheating of the control semiconductors is prevented by a thermal trip that reduces the current limit when the temperature becomes critical. This feature, in conjunction with the standard bypass inhibit, can be arranged to prevent bypass operation when the control system is cut back because of high temperature.

Current limiting is also an important characteristic of this control circuit. The maximum current in the motor is limited by a circuit that senses the armature current and prevents the chopper frequency from increasing when the motor current reaches the desired limit.

By limiting the motor current rather than the battery current, the supplier of the Sevcontrol Mark 7 claims that it provides a constant torque characteristic. By permitting you to apply maximum voltage to the motor even at high speed, this is a definite improvement over control circuits which limit the battery current and reduce the applied voltage to the motor when higher than normal running currents are required. The difference between the two types of control circuits is indicated in figure 5–10.

This kind of circuit also permits an operation called "plugging." Plugging is braking the car by using the energy produced by the motor, now become a generator, as a partial brake. (See the section on Regenerative Braking at the end of this chapter.)

When you want to reverse the direction of travel while the vehicle is in motion, with the Sevcontrol Mark 7, the motor generates a braking torque to slow down the vehicle. That is, you slow down the vehicle with this control before reversing. Two methods of plug-braking are available:

1. Constant current plugging may be used as a means of braking the vehicle electronically because it maintains a controlled braking torque until a complete stop is reached.

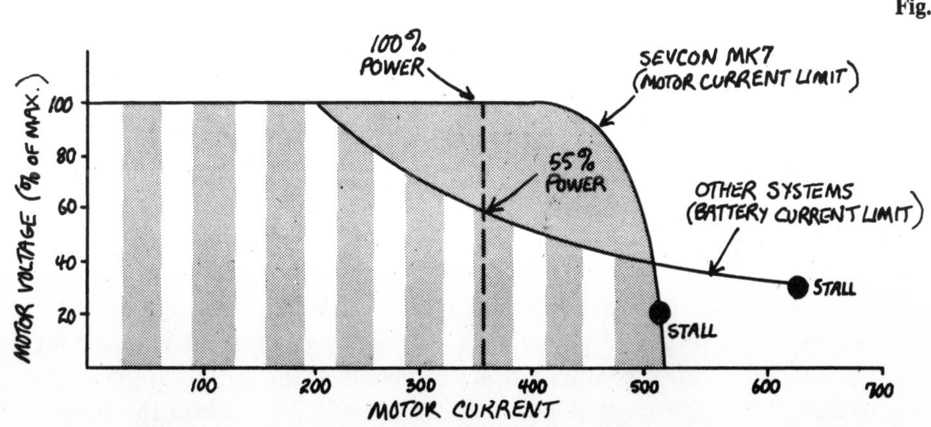

Fig. 5–10. Typical motor current/voltage curves showing how Sevcon's motor-current limit gives more high-speed power for better grade-climbing performance

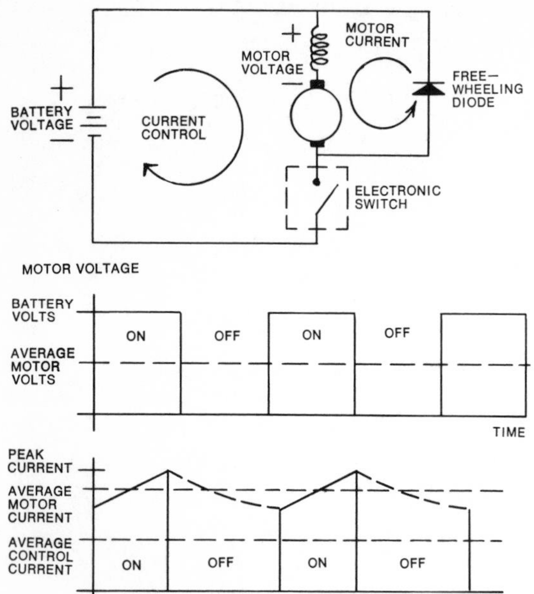

Fig. 5–11. Actronic control system developed by Allis-Chalmers

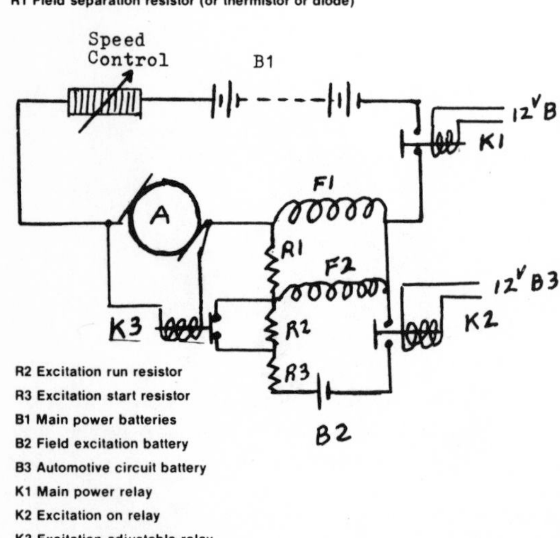

Fig. 5–12. Zubris control system

2. Pulse narrowing is a modification of the constant-current system used on motors with unstable characteristics in the plugging mode.

Reversing the vehicle with this control is possible with three different kinds of connections:

1. Normal reversing is accomplished with a connection that, as you change the direction switch, will allow your EV to freewheel. To apply plug-braking, you must release the accelerator completely to recycle in the opposite direction.
2. Automatic reversing. Even with the accelerator fully depressed, the direction switch can be reversed and the vehicle will be plug-braked to a standstill and reaccelerated in the new direction, that is, in reverse.
3. Semiautomatic reversing. This is a combination of the two previously described systems. The reversing is automatic at low speeds, but after the bypass connector contactor is closed, the accelerator must be released to recycle the controller in the opposite direction.

The Actronic control system has been developed by Allis-Chalmers, Material Handling, 21800 S. Cicero Avenue, Matteson, IL 60443. This system is a silicon transistor integrated-circuit-controlled, pulse-width modulated traction control system. It is composed of a control module, two or three regulator modules, and two or three power modules. A block diagram of the system is shown in figure 5–11.

A series of electronic control systems called the EV-1 SCR controls is available from General Electric Company, Industrial Control Department. GE also supplies directional switches for forward and reverse, accelerator switches, and low-voltage battery indicators, among other components supplied by this department to help you create an electric vehicle.

A small company that specializes in SCR control systems for EV's is Flight Systems, Inc., P.O. Box 25, Mechanicsburg, PA 17055, phone (717) 697–0333. Flight Systems is offering used and carefully rebuilt 36-volt solid-state controllers made by General Electric, International Rectifier, Allis-Chalmers, and Sevcon at an economical price.

If you are going to use a higher battery supply voltage and decide not to build your own control system, you might consult this company about availability of a used and rebuilt system for higher voltages.

Another control system has been developed by Joseph R. Zubris, of Zubris Electrical Company, 1320 Dorchester Avenue, Boston, MA 02122, phone (617) 282-1545. Zubris designed the circuit shown in figure 5–12, which is a simplified version of one used in electric cars made by Zubris and his son Joseph Jr. The Zubrises have converted a Mercury Comet and a Renault.

Relays K1 and K2 are worked through micro-switches. K3, normally closed, is set to activate at about 60% of the maximum counter-EMF voltage. This is a point where acceleration from standstill is leveling off and the current is reduced. When K3 is opened, the excitation of the field coils is weakened and the vehicle is able to achieve a higher speed.

The excitation battery B2 may be two to six volts or higher, depending upon the amount of current that you want to pass through the field. The B1 battery and circuitry are patented by Zubris. R3 is a resistor set for about 250% of the nameplate current of the motor. A check on starting surge currents during adjustment will best reveal the proper setting for the motor. R2 is an optional resistor. F1 is a shunt coil in the circuit so that a failure of the parallel shunt coil F2 would not prevent the vehicle from functioning. F1 can be switched out and replaced by a resistor or a jumper and the motor will run as a shunt motor. Zubris considers, however, that if you try this, the need to protect the armature circuit becomes greater. Licensing is available for his design; some 60 licenses have been issued to date.

As is the case with most devices developed by individual inventors, and covered by patents or patent applications, the Zubris control system is available for use by do-it-yourselfers if you pay a modest license fee. However, not all designers require a license—for example other circuits described in this chapter and not identified by company name. Some of the control circuits previously described were developed and tested by Fred Riess for use in small electric cars. When in doubt, write to the inventor or designer and ask permission to use his design. It may be freely given or you may be asked to pay a license or royalty fee.

Other sources of control systems for EV's include:

Eltra Corporation, 511 Hamilton Street, Toledo, OH 43694. Phone (419) 244-2811.

Mercury Electric Limited, P.O. Box 135, Goodwood 7460, Textile Road, Parow Industrial, England.

Power Functions Engineering, P.O. Box 2312, Garland, TX 75041. Phone (214) 278-0996.

Regenerative Braking

Potentially, effective regenerative braking is also realized with a shunt, permanent-magnet, or compound motor. Regenerative braking is a term used to describe how a moving vehicle (electric) is slowed down by returning the kinetic energy to the batteries (after converting it back to electric energy).

By applying current to the shunt field, or automatically in a PM field, while also reducing the battery voltage, the motor may be run as a generator. The voltage difference thus created between the generator and the batteries causes current to flow to the batteries. As the vehicle speed drops, the generated output voltage also decreases until it is below the battery voltage and the current drops to zero. Four ways of maintaining this regenerative current during deceleration to lower speeds are:

1. Further decrease the battery voltage.
2. Increase the generator output voltage by increasing its magnetic field.
3. Mechanically increase the rotational speed of the generator.
4. Use a fly-back converter to step up the generator voltage. This consists essentially of a switch and an inductor, as shown in figure 5–13.

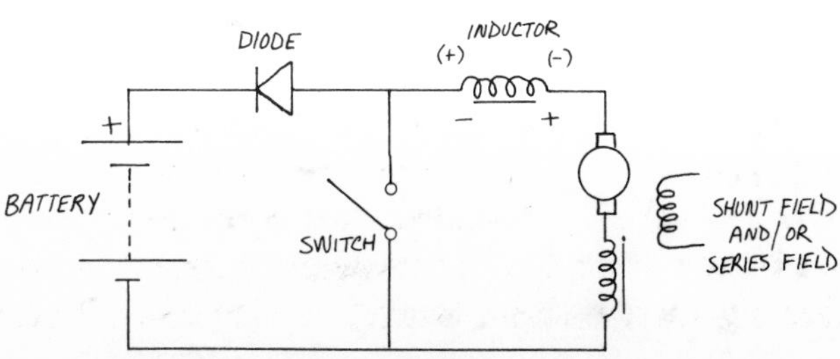

Fig. 5–13. Circuit for stepping up generator voltage with a flyback inductor to cause regeneration

OPERATION

The switch is closed momentarily to allow current from the generator to build up in the inductor in the polarity shown. The diode is reverse-biased and prevents current from flowing from the battery. When the switch is opened, the collapsing magnetic field produces a high reverse-polarity voltage, which is in series with the generator and forward-biases the diode, thereby causing current to flow into the battery from the generator. If the switch (SCR or transistor) is operated properly, regenerative braking can be achieved at a controlled rate down to very low speeds without doing variations 1, 2, or 3. This has actually been demonstrated. Figure 5–14 shows test results.

Since the kinetic energy in moving vehicles is proportional to the square of the speed, little is gained in using regenerative braking to a speed below one-half the initial value since most (about 75%) of the kinetic energy would have been recovered at that point. The main advantage in regenerating to lower than one-half speed would be in the braking effect (feel) of the car and in reduction of brake wear (slight gain).

A two- or three-step series-parallel speed control, used with a PM, shunt, compound or brushless motor, would therefore be quite effective in the regenerative mode. This would apply to an all-relay (contactor) type only, as shown previously in figures 5–4 and 5–5.

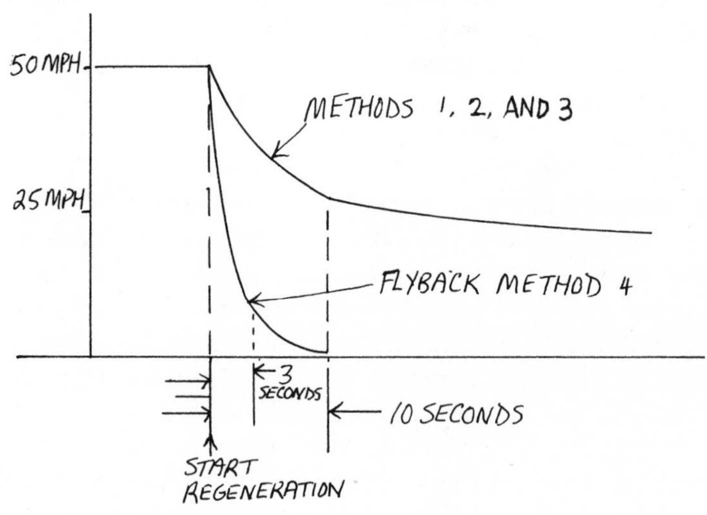

Fig. 5–14. Flyback regeneration (4) vs. series parallel regeneration (1, 2, and 3)

6 Batteries for Electric Vehicles

Although many different kinds of batteries appear to be promising for use in electric cars, at present, most authorities agree with our experience that lead-acid batteries are the most economical choice you can make. For this reason, an extensive research program is being financed by the Department of Energy through the Argonne National Laboratory, with the objective of improving lead-acid batteries. The key contractors in this federal program to develop advanced lead-acid batteries are:

ESB, Inc., Yardley, PA
C&D Batteries Division of Eltra Corporation, Plymouth Meeting, PA
Gould, Inc., Rolling Meadows, IL
Globe-Union, Inc., Milwaukee, WI

Also, in Japan and other countries a considerable amount of work is being done to improve lead-acid batteries. A new design by Shin-Kobe Electric Machinery Company is reported to have a capacity in excess of 50 watt-hours per kilogram (20 watt-hours/pound). Also, the Japanese company claims that this new battery can be recharged as many as 700 times. An active program is under way to reduce its cost and make it competitive. In a road test an electric pick-up truck made by Toyo Kogyo, the maker of Mazda vehicles, used this new battery and achieved a range of 127 miles at a steady speed of 25 mph.

Basics of a Lead-Acid Battery

As shown in figure 6–1, a cell of a lead-acid battery is composed of two electrodes that are placed in a liquid solution called an electrolyte. Both electrodes or plates are lead sulfate in a conventional lead-acid battery. The electrolyte consists of a strong solution of sulfuric acid (H_2SO_4) and water. In the charging process, the positive plate changes from lead sulfate into lead peroxide due to electrochemical action. Meanwhile, the lead sulfate of the negative plate changes into spongy lead. Also during this charging process, the sulfuric acid solution in the electrolyte becomes stronger.

During discharge, the reverse of the electrochemical process occurs. That is, the negative plate changes from spongy lead into lead sulfate, and oxygen is formed at this negative terminal. Meanwhile, the positive plate is transformed from lead peroxide into lead sulfate, along with evolution of hydrogen. The hydrogen from this plate and the oxygen from the negative plate combine to form water that dilutes the sulfuric acid electrolyte.

The voltage you can expect from the electrochemical action within a fully charged lead-acid cell is about 2 volts. When you apply a DC charging voltage that is somewhat greater than 2 volts across the electrodes, usually from 2.1 to 2.5 volts, the lead-acid cell accepts energy and becomes charged.

With the battery cell fully charged and a small current drain, you can expect discharge voltage to be slightly in excess of 2 volts.

If large amounts of current are withdrawn from a lead-acid cell or the cell is nearly discharged, the cell voltage drops below 2 volts. It is generally considered that a level of 1.7 volts per cell of the standard

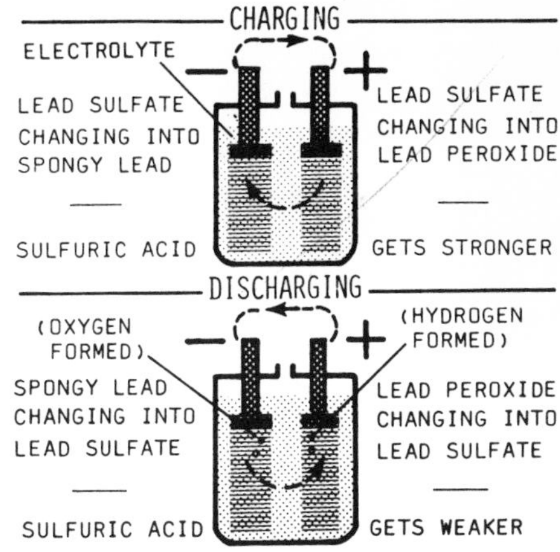

Fig. 6–1. A lead-acid storage battery

lead-acid type is the lower useful limit. When a cell of your lead-acid battery reaches this lower limit, you can consider it to be discharged.

Capacity Rating

The capacity rating of a battery obtained from the manufacturer is expressed in ampere-hours. Abbreviated as AH, this tells you that the battery has a minimum capacity in terms of the amount of current it will deliver for a number of hours.

In general, for electric vehicle use, you will want to get batteries with the highest AH rating; greater than 220 AH is desirable. You should also make sure that the battery has a discharge rate capability of 6 to 8 hours.

Suppose, for example, that you have a battery with a rating of 240 AH, available at a discharge rate of 8 hours. Divide 240 by 8 and you find that you can get 30 amperes per hour for 8 hours from that battery. The battery will actually deliver more current than that for a brief period, but at this higher rate, the time during which it will deliver power will decrease.

All suitable batteries for EV use have thick plates and are classed as deep-cycle types. That means that the battery can withstand a discharge to a very low value, as low as 15% of its capacity, on repeated occasions without major damage or destruction. If you go through many deep discharge cycles with a conventional automobile battery, it will soon fail. However, good deep-cycle batteries will handle as many as 800 cycles of charging and discharging without destruction.

Voltage of Batteries

Most EV batteries supplied at present operate at 6 volts. This means that the battery has three cells, each with an approximate output of 2.2 volts when fully charged. It is most desirable to use batteries of the deep-cycle type. A 6V battery, with an ampere-hour rating of 220 AH, weighs about 75 pounds, while a 12V type weighs about 50 pounds and has a 90 AH capacity. While there are some 12-volt deep-cycle batteries available for EV use, the 6-volt variety is generally more readily available. Six-volt batteries were originally developed for low-voltage electric golf cart use.

Connecting Batteries in Series and in Parallel

Figures 6–2, 6–3, and 6–4 show how you can connect batteries in series, parallel, and in a series-parallel combination. In figure 6–2, where eight 6-volt batteries are connected in series, the total voltage is 48 volts. In figure 6–3, the same light 6-volt batteries are connected in parallel, but the output is only 6 volts. However, if each of the batteries has an ampere-hour rating of 250 AH, the eight batteries have a combined storage capacity of 2,000 AH. While this would generally be an impractical way of operating, the series-parallel combination shown in figure 6–4 may have some advantages. Some of these are:

1. As pointed out before, the price for a lower AH battery is less than for one with a very high ampere-hour rating.

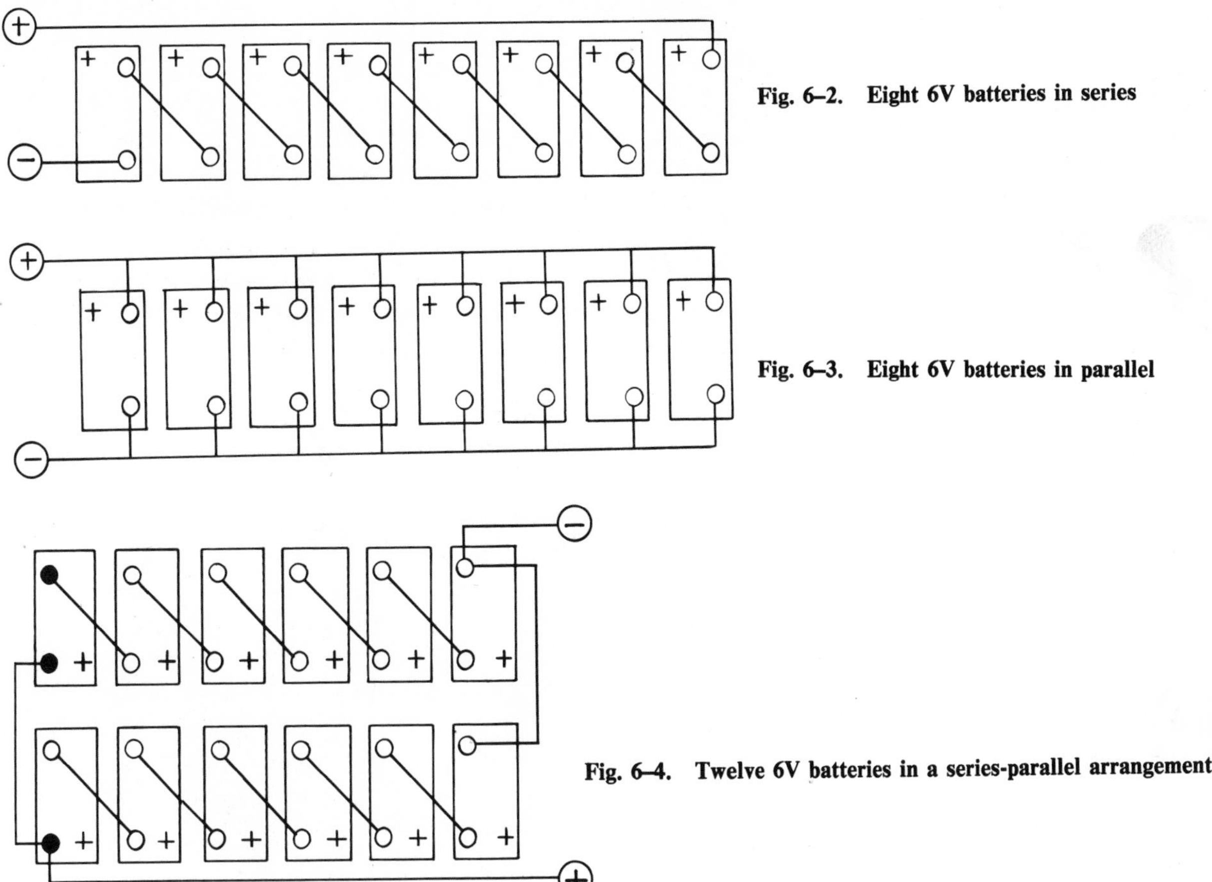

Fig. 6–2. Eight 6V batteries in series

Fig. 6–3. Eight 6V batteries in parallel

Fig. 6–4. Twelve 6V batteries in a series-parallel arrangement

2. The battery with the lower AH rating is smaller and weighs less. This means that you will have less trouble placing your battery in your vehicle.
3. Because the line losses in the cables carrying current in your electric car are directly proportional to the resistance of the cables and the current squared (I^2R), less current will be lost with more batteries having lower AH capacities.

That is, with this series-parallel arrangement you may use EV batteries that are light, but have low ampere-hour capacity, and still save money. (Be careful not to go below about 220 AH in rating, however, if you want your electric-car batteries to have long life and serve you for a large number of charge-discharge cycles.)

Effects of Aging on a Battery

When your lead-acid EV battery is new, its capacity is actually well below its nominal rating. This may seem surprising, but it is a fact that the battery will not deliver as much output as when it has been half "used up." This is shown in figure 6–5.

Therefore, it is good practice to operate your batteries in such a way that you do not fully top off each time you charge your batteries after driving your electric car. Also, you should minimize discharging your batteries beyond, perhaps, 25% of full charge. For example, as shown in figure 6–5, if your batteries are only discharged to 70% on a regular basis, the life of your batteries may be increased by as much as 20%.

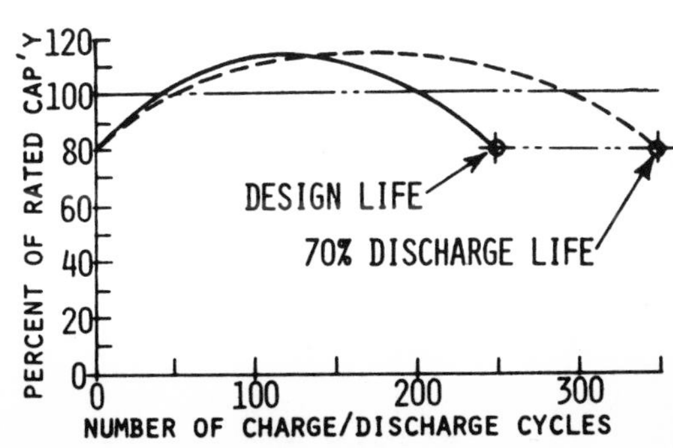

Fig. 6–5. An example of battery-cycle life

Fig. 6–6. Ideal battery arrangement in longitudinal tunnel

Mounting the Batteries in Your Car

Several important factors must be considered in mounting the batteries in your electric car. One of the most important to evaluate is what will happen in case of a crash. You will usually find it desirable to locate your batteries in the trunk or in the normal engine space mounted in a very sturdy frame. Then, in case of a relatively minor road accident, your vehicle will be intact and your batteries will be preserved with minor damage.

You should place your batteries so that you will have easy access for checking electrolyte level and also for removal of the batteries when maintenance or replacement is required. If you are completely redesigning your vehicle, one good way to mount your batteries is in a rack which can be removed by means of a tray on wheels that pulls out of the chassis of your car. One way this may be done is with an opening in the side of the car. Most designers have found it desirable to place the battery pack in a longitudinal tube in the center of the car, as shown in figure 6–6. This arrangement gives enough room in a compact car for 12 or more deep-cycle 6-volt batteries. Located on a wheeled rack, they can be removed very easily for filling with electrolyte water or for replacement. Alternative battery positions are shown in figures 6–7 and 6–8.

Since your batteries will account for a considerable percentage of your car's total curb weight, their distribution is an important additional consideration. If you place too much of your battery weight in the rear of your vehicle, response to controls may be slow. Driving will be difficult and the car will possibly be unstable at high speeds. On the other hand, placing more batteries in the front of the car seems to be a stabilizing factor, according to expert designers of EV's, if the car has a rear-wheel drive and your electric motor is in the rear, replacing the engine.

One important factor in selecting the vehicle area or areas where you mount your batteries is to keep vehicle weight balanced. Also, mount batteries as close to the center of gravity of your car as possible. Otherwise, because batteries are heavy, if you mount them outboard, the centrifugal effect can make your car try to spin, particularly going around sharp curves or corners at high speed.

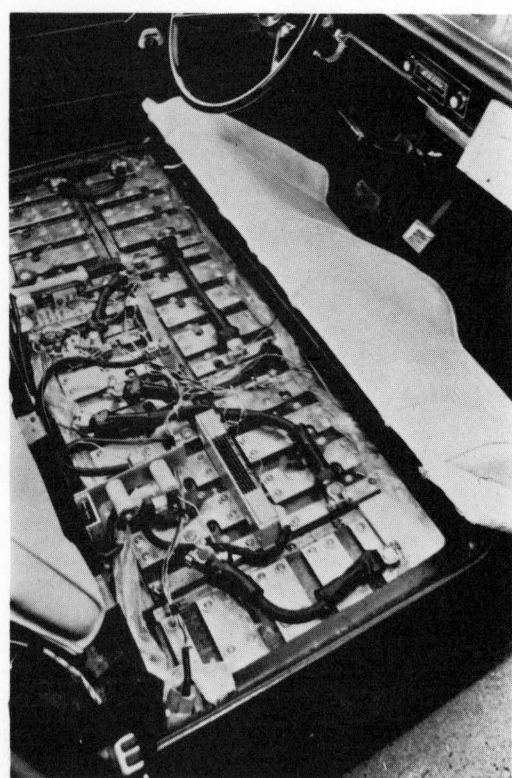

Fig. 6–7. Experimental Yardney nickel-zinc batteries installed under CitiCar seat

Care of Your Car's Lead-Acid Batteries

One of the most important things to know about your lead-acid battery is the specific gravity (SG) of the electrolyte, the mixture of sulfuric acid and water. You should have a good-quality hydrometer for determining the SG of each battery. When your battery has an SG of 1.260, it means that the electrolyte solution is 1.26 times as heavy as pure water and that the battery is fully charged.

In a discharged battery, some of the acid has been exhausted and additional water has been created. At this point, the SG may be as low as 1.160. If any of the batteries in your EV show an SG as low as 1.160, you should immediately charge them.

In practice, it is desirable not to charge your batteries to the maximum, because they will last longer, but at the expense of shorter range. In general, it is desirable to charge your batteries to the point where the SG is about 1.250. If you have an automatic battery charger in your

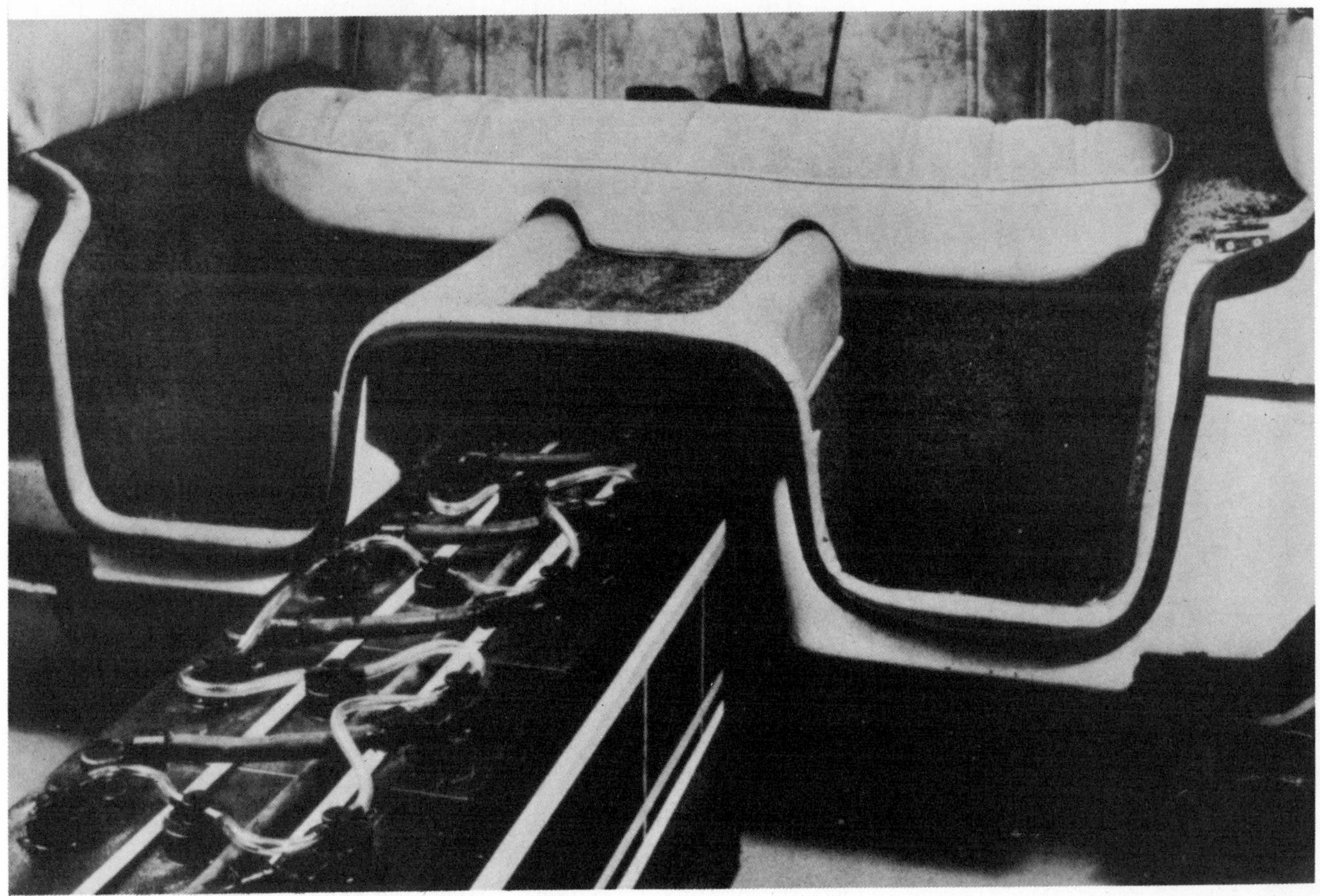

Fig. 6–8. How batteries are mounted in the Copper Electric Runabout, designed by the Copper Development Association, Inc.

car, it will usually shut off at a point just below full charge. An occasional full-value "equalizing" charge, which you can give your batteries at night when you know you are going to drive your car a considerable distance the following day, will not harm your battery. This equalizing charge is usually of short duration, to top off an existing charge.

SAFETY PRECAUTIONS

Because both oxygen and hydrogen gases are common by-products when batteries are charged and discharged, you must make sure that there is adequate ventilation for your batteries. Don't work on your batteries or change connections when the charger is connected and operating because you may generate a spark that could cause an explosion. An open flame or a cigarette in the neighborhood of a battery is also dangerous.

Because the electrolyte is a sulfuric acid solution, it must be considered a dangerous liquid. If you should spill or spatter electrolyte, dilute it immediately with cold water.

Keep your batteries clean and dry. Remove dust and dirt accumulations from the tops of your batteries and from the terminals. If the electrolyte should overflow from the battery or spill, wash the area with a saturated solution of baking soda and water, but be sure none gets into batteries. You can use a ratio of one pound of soda per gallon of water.

As a general maintenance procedure, it is a good idea to apply such a neutralizing solution of soda and water with a clean paint brush to your battery terminals about once a week. Dry these battery terminals and the top of the battery after you've cleaned them.

When adding water to your battery, be sure to use distilled or purified water. You'll find that new batteries require very little water to be added. Old batteries require more frequent checking and will need addition of water far more often. How often you check battery water in old batteries will depend on how far you are driving your electric car each day, and hence how often you are charging the batteries. In very hot, dry weather, you must add water frequently, probably two or three times a week, depending again on your driving needs. If electrolyte level is very low, add a small amount of water just before you start charging your batteries. Do not top off after the batteries are discharged because the electrolyte level in your batteries rises during the charge, and could overflow if you have filled a discharged battery.

TEMPERATURE CORRECTIONS FOR SPECIFIC GRAVITY READINGS

When your battery temperature is higher than 80°F, you should add 0.004 to the SG reading for each 10°F rise in temperature. For example, if your battery hydrometer reads 1.220, and the battery temperature is 90°F, the corrected hydrometer reading should be 1.224.

When the battery is colder than 80°F, you should subtract 0.004 for each 10°F below this temperature.

If the SG readings of all the cells of your batteries are relatively uniform and the voltages of the batteries are approximately equal, your batteries are in good operating condition. Should you find a difference of 0.025 to 0.040 in SG readings for the cells of any one battery, you will almost certainly have a weak cell. That is, if two of the cells in your three-cell, 6-volt battery have an SG greater than 1.220 and the third cell is reading 1.190, you have to be suspicious of the cell with the low SG.

CHARGING A BATTERY

A lead-acid battery is relatively easy to charge. The most important concerns are to avoid excessive battery temperature and battery gassing, yet to obtain a full battery charge.

The ability of a lead-acid battery to accept a given charging rate is approximately proportional to the state of discharge of the battery. It is also dependent on some other factors such as battery temperature, battery type, and gassing rate. Thus, under a given set of conditions, a battery with 100 AH to be replaced might be able to accept a charge current of 200 amperes. When this battery reaches a charged state in which only 10 AH remain to be replaced, the battery more likely will be able to accept a charge current of only 20 amperes. Therefore, most chargers are designed to deliver a tapering charge current to the battery. That is, the charge current is reduced proportionately to the amount of ampere-hours remaining to be delivered to the battery for a "full charge."

Specifically, the 8-hour battery charger usually used with an electric car will start charging at a rate of 20 to 25 amperes per 100 ampere-hours of rated battery capacity. This will taper to a finish current of about 5 amperes per 100 ampere-hours of rated capacity.

Two major factors should be considered when selecting the kind of battery charger you want to use. One is the battery duty cycle. Your primary concern should be to avoid excessive battery temperature due to high charge rates coupled with rapid battery cycling. Leading manufacturers recommend that the battery electrolyte temperature should not exceed 120°F. Rapid charging can increase the internal heating of the battery and could, if done improperly, create excessive gassing of the battery. This can shorten battery life and increase the amount of electrolyte maintenance required.

The second major factor in selecting your battery charger is cost. The more rapid the charging requirement, the larger the charger must be to supply power to your batteries. As charger cost is proportional to the required power output, charger costs will increase with decreased battery charge time. Another factor affecting cost is the electrical service installation required. This cost also increases as the charger's size increases. The cost of electric power that you buy is another consideration.

Following are some recommendations from a leading manufacturer of batteries, ESB, Inc., P.O. Box 6949, Cleveland, OH 44101.

Catch-up Charge. Where an electric car is used hard, it may be necessary at times to employ a catch-up charge. That is, on a rainy day or off day, when you're not going out in your EV, you should check your batteries for charge level. Any batteries that are not in a good state of charge should be recharged.

Amount of Charge. To avoid getting batteries into a condition of low charge, a car should be put on charge early enough in the evening to allow for the full-time schedule of the charger. On the other hand, it may not be necessary to charge batteries every day the car is not used. If you do, you may overcharge them and shorten their life. Overcharging batteries corrodes the positive grids, resulting in the disintegration of the positive grid structure.

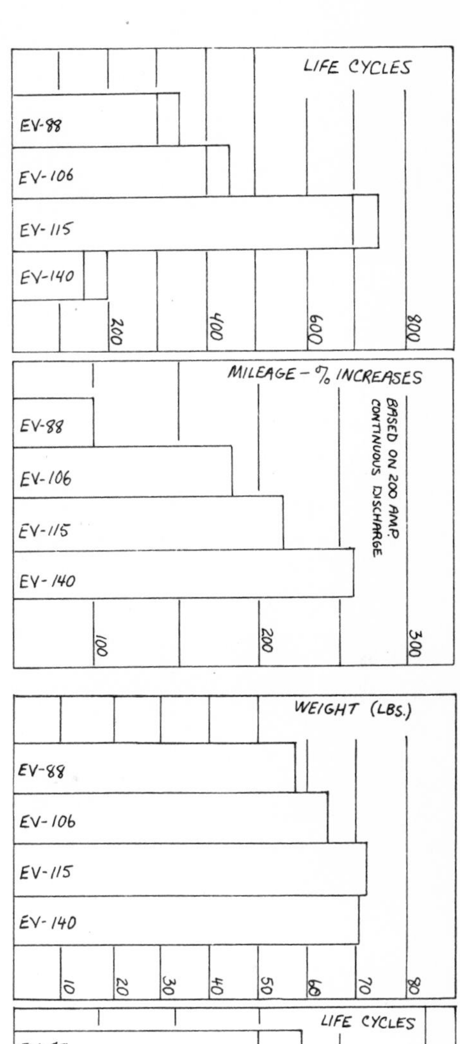

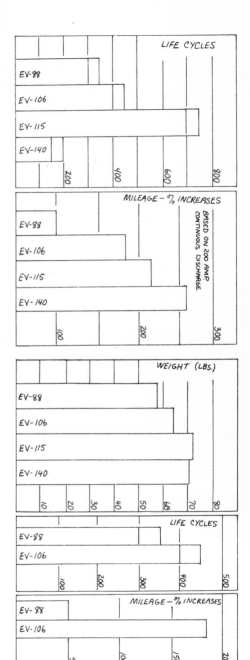

Fig. 6-9. Comparison of four different ESB lead-acid batteries for electric cars, comparing them in terms of weight, life cycles, and mileage

Variations in Types of Batteries

In the four bar charts of figure 6-9 are typical comparisons between weight, life cycles, and mileage obtained with electric cars for four different types of lead-acid batteries made by ESB.

LOWEST-WEIGHT BATTERY

Of the four Exide (ESB) electric vehicle batteries, the EV-88 has the lowest weight—about 17% lighter than the heaviest of the four. Yet the battery has an energy density that gives it a power capacity roughly 17% higher than the industry standard for electric vehicles. This battery may be your best choice for use in certain small vehicles where the load requirement is limited and the desired range per cycle is modest.

HIGHER-CAPACITY PRODUCTION BATTERY

For many moderate-range vehicle applications, the EV-106 may be your best all-round performance battery. It offers a power capacity roughly 41% higher than the industry standard, yet its weight is only 8% greater than that of the EV-88. At the same time, this battery offers substantially greater life potential—400–450 cycles compared with 300–350 for the EV-88.

LONGEST-LIFE BATTERY

In laboratory tests, the EV-115 has shown a life capability of 700–750 cycles—better than twice that of the EV-88. Also, it has a power capacity roughly 118% higher in typical electric vehicle service (200 amperes discharge). The EV-115 features a new-design positive plate that more effectively retains its power-producing materials. This battery is ideal for most heavy-duty applications where long battery life is desired and the user prefers to keep replacements to a minimum.

GREATEST-MILEAGE BATTERY

The EV-140 is said to be the most advanced electric vehicle lead-acid battery yet developed for energy density. It enables an electric vehicle to be driven further, or at higher speeds for a longer distance, than any of the other batteries. The specific range capability of any electric vehicle battery depends also, of course, on the vehicle's speed, the hardness of the tires, the type of terrain, and certain other considerations. It should also be noted that the EV-140 has the lowest predicted life of any of the batteries. The designer must decide, therefore, which battery performance characteristics he wants most.

Performance of an Experimental Electric Car Powered with Lead-Acid Batteries

The Sundancer is a high-performance electric car powered by production lead-acid batteries of the Model EV-106 type. The top speed of the Sundancer is between 60 and 65 mph.

The distance traveled by the Sundancer electric car varies with velocity. The range, when driven at a constant speed, is shown in the following table.

Range at Constant Speeds

Sundancer's Speed	*Sundancer's Range*
30 mph	**95–100 miles**
40 mph	**75–80 miles**
50 mph	**60–65 miles**
60 mph	**50–55 miles**

"Fuel" economy of this electric car is indicated in the subsequent table.

Fuel Economy

Driving Mode	*Miles/kWh*
Constant speed—30 mph	**5.4**
Constant speed—60 mph	**3.6**
Residential area cycle	**4.3**
Metropolitan area cycle	**3.2**

Another investigation with this electric car, powered with production lead-acid batteries, followed a proposed urban-driving cycle test, designed for electric cars by the Society of Automotive Engineers (SAE). This test combines periods of rest, acceleration, constant speed movement, and deceleration to simulate the kind of driving you would do in a city. Driving around the neighborhood where you live, if you are in the suburbs, is imitated by the "residential area" driving cycle. Going to and from work, or shopping, is simulated by the "metropolitan area" driving cycle. During the residential-area period, the normal acceleration is from 0 to 30 mph in 14 seconds, reaching a top speed of 30 mph. In the metropolitan-area portion, the acceleration is the same but the top speed is 45 mph. Both cycles last for 2½ minutes, during which the car travels approximately one mile. Sundancer's performance: the distance traveled, and the total elapsed time are shown as follows:

Sundancer's	*City Driving Cycle*	
Performance	*Residential Area*	*Metropolitan Area*
Driving Range	**70–75 miles**	**50–55 miles**
Total Continuous Driving Time	**2 hrs. 53 min.– 3 hrs. 7 min.**	**2 hrs. 5 min.– 2 hrs. 17 min.**

Advanced Lead-Acid Batteries

Considerable work is being done by various manufacturers to improve the quality of lead-acid batteries for use in electric cars. ESB, for example, has a contract with the Department of Energy, which is being monitored by the Argonne National Laboratory, Chicago. The objective is to design better lead-acid batteries for use in EV's. The first phase of this contract calls for developing improved state of the art (ISOA) batteries. In the second phase, which will extend for three years, the objective will be to develop advanced batteries.

During the ISOA phase of this program, two approaches are being examined. One utilizes a flat-pasted plate-type lead-acid battery, and the second is designed around a tubular positive-plate type. At present, according to ESB, the flat-pasted plate battery shows the lowest cost and highest specific energy (Wh/kg), while the tubular battery has the longest life.

Effort is also being applied to a bipolar or pile-type battery. The major goal in this research is development of a suitable partition. It seems likely that the advanced tubular concept will be the most successful.

Another aim in this research effort is evaluation of certain single-point watering systems for lead-acid batteries. Such systems are important in the convenience of operating an electric car with numerous lead-acid batteries because adding water is a considerable chore. This will continue to be true until deep-cycle, maintenance-free batteries are available. Without a single-point watering system, the driver of an electric car must be prepared to check and refill about 60 individual cells with water as a routine maintenance procedure.

The following table shows the estimated performance characteristics of ISOA and advanced lead-acid batteries.

Performance Characteristics of ISOA and Advanced Lead-Acid Batteries

	ISOA	*Advanced Lead-Acid*
Duty cycle	2–4 hr discharge 4–8 hr charge	2–4 hr discharge 4–8 hr charge
Energy efficiency (turn-around)	<60%	<60%
Cycle life	800 cycles	1,000 cycles
Installed cost (1976 dollars)	$50/kWh	$40/kWh
Specific energy	40Wh/Kg (18Wh/lb) @C/3 rate	60Wh/Kg (27Wh/lb) @C/3 rate
Specific power	20W/Kg sustaining (9 W/lb) 99 W/Kg peak (45 W/lb)	30 W/Kg sustaining (13.6 W/lb) 150 W/Kg peak (68 W/lb)
Typical installation size	30–30 kWh	20–30 kWh
Environmental impact	Minimal	Minimal

Nickel-Zinc, the Most Promising New Battery for EV's

It is generally agreed among those with considerable experience in the use of storage batteries for electric vehicles that nickel-zinc batteries are the most promising replacement for lead-acid batteries. The electrochemical reactions for this kind of system are illustrated in figure 6–10. These cells are assembled in a discharged state with potassium hydroxide in solution as an electrolyte. The cell must be charged before it is put into service.

According to Otto von Krusenstierna and Mats Reger of AGA-Tudor, the performance of a 350-AH nickel-zinc "Vibrocel" has been very good. The cell is vibrated during charging. This vibration prevents zinc dendrites from forming. Thus, there is no penetration of the separator nor shorting of the cell, characteristics which have limited the

Fig. 6–10. Charging of nickel-zinc batteries without and with vibration (AGA—Tudor, Sweden)

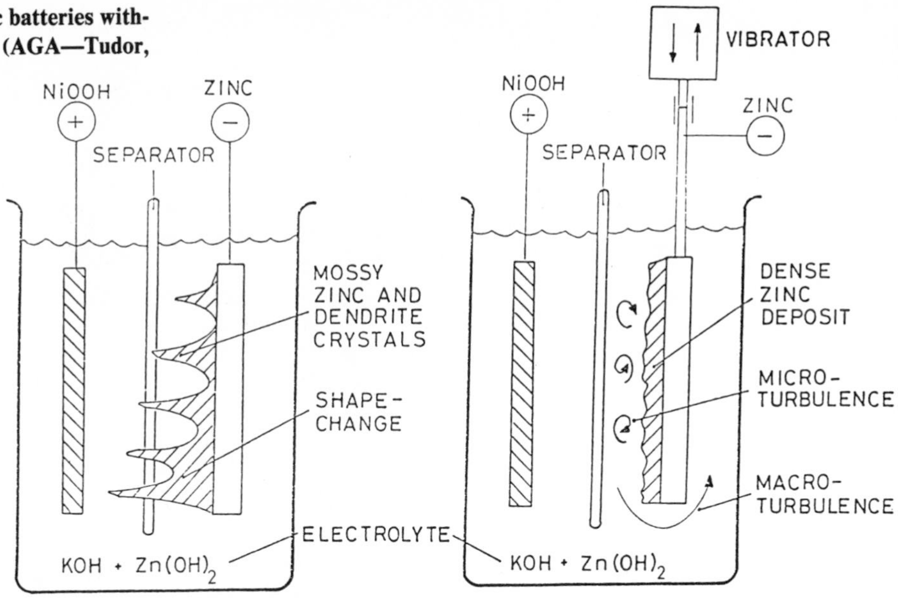

performance of nickel-zinc batteries in the past. The specific energy of these cells has reached a level of 18 Wh/lb at a two-hour rate. The construction of a practical nickel-zinc cell with vibrating electrodes is very simple. The cell, enclosed in a nickel-plated steel can or a plastic container, is assembled from thin perforated steel anodes, separators of open plastic-net type, and nickel cathodes with parts. After a thick, white potassium hydroxide-zinc oxide suspension is poured in, the cell is ready for charging. The vibration is usually performed with a mechanical arrangement having a rotating axle. According to AGA-Tudor, the weight of the vibrating parts can be made less than 5% of the total battery weight. (AGA-Tudor is a Swedish subsidiary of ESB, one of the world's largest manufacturers of storage batteries for automobiles.)

When put into production, these nickel-zinc batteries are estimated to cost $100 per kilowatt-hour with practically no separator cost; about 40% is due to the nickel plates. However, the possible lifetime of these batteries is estimated to be 2,000 cycles. Therefore, the low lifetime cost of $100 per 2,000 cycles amounts to only 5¢ per cycle. This is very competitive with existing deep-cycle lead-acid batteries.

Quoting from a recent paper by Krusenstierna and Reger:

> In a nickel-zinc battery using vibrating zinc anodes during charging, the problems of zinc dendrite formation and shape change are eliminated to such an extent that the nickel cathodes become the life-determining part of the battery. Practical tests with deep-cycling during four years of a 2 kW Ni-Zn battery have confirmed these results.
>
> With this type of nickel-zinc battery with vibrating electrodes, energy densities from 60 Wh/kg up to 90 Wh/kg seem possible if high-capacity, long-life nickel cathodes can be developed. Equivalent driving ranges in urban traffic are 150–250 km (90 to 155 miles).
>
> These batteries using soluble zinc anodes and simple plastic nets as separators can to a large extent be produced by mechanical industry.
>
> The lifetime/kWh cost of these batteries can be low due to possible lifetimes of 2,000 cycles or more.

Another leader in nickel-zinc battery development, the Yardney Electric Corporation, 82 Mechanic Street, Pawcatuck, CT 02891, makes the following comments about nickel-zinc batteries. (Yardney has been a pioneer in the development of many kinds of high-quality batteries, including the silver-zinc batteries used for many aerospace applications as well as in the "Eagle," which still holds the land speed record for electric cars.)

> Yardney Electric Corporation has been applying high-energy battery technology to electric vehicle propulsion for many years.
>
> We are presently in the development stage for nickel-zinc batteries for electric vehicle propulsion. These have been widely acknowledged as the leading "intermediate-term" candidate for EV propulsion and our work has been partially funded by DOE (Argonne National Labs) to further develop these batteries. As is shown in the table from a paper presented by Dr. Albert Landgrebe of DOE last year, nickel-zinc has the highest overall "figure of merit" ratings, from an economic and technical standpoint, of any near or intermediate-term battery system.
>
> We are still approximately 1–2 years away from the manufacture of commercial traction batteries; however, we are now considering a program to manufacture a number of experimental state-of-the-art 300AH, 6.4-volt nickel-zinc battery modules and make them available for test in selected electric vehicles.

Yardney has also supplied information about a small 6-volt battery consisting of four series-connected 300-AH cells, which actually will supply 6.4 volts. Yardney suggests that a typical 15-cell arrangement, connected in series, would yield a battery with a total energy content of 28.8 kWh at a nominal 96 volts. This kind of a battery pack would give your electric compact car a top speed of 60 mph or greater as well as a range of more than 60 miles. Figure 6–11 shows the projected performance at various discharge rates of 300-AH nickel-zinc cells designed by Yardney.

A most interesting comparison is contained in figure 6–12, which was prepared by Dr. Albert R. Landgrebe, Division of Conservation Research & Technology, Department of Energy. Note that the nickel-zinc batteries shown in the center of this table have a higher figure of merit than the other so-called intermediate-term batteries for electric vehicles.

A BATTERY CHARGER FOR NICKEL-ZINC BATTERIES

Yardney has developed a nickel-zinc battery charger which is basically a voltage-controlled current source with preregulation to minimize internal power dissipation and maximize efficiency. During the initial and final charge-rate steps, this unit serves as a constant-current charger.

Initially, the nickel-zinc batteries are charged at a high rate of about 60 amperes until the gas flow from a single pilot cell reaches a specific level. At this point, the charger automatically switches over to a lower final charging rate, about 20 amperes, which is continued until gas evolution reaches a second specific level. At this point the charge is automatically terminated. An SCR (thyristor) located at the output of the battery charger prevents reverse charging from the battery and thus prevents destruction of active semiconductors in the charger due to improper connection to the battery. This charger also includes overvoltage protection for the battery pack.

If you should decide to obtain some of the 300-AH, 6.4-volt nickel-zinc battery modules from Yardney for tests in your electric car, and

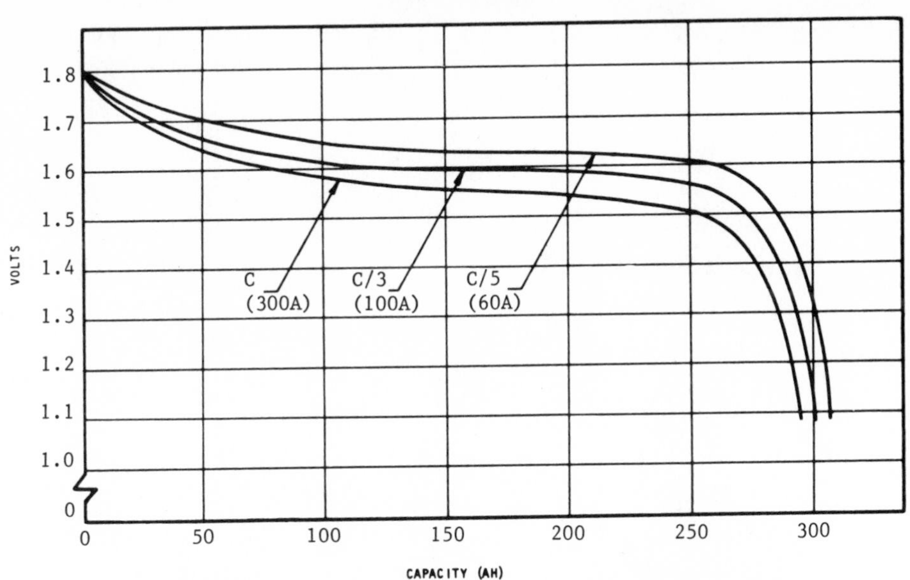

Fig. 6–11. Projected performance at various discharge rates; 300 ampere-hour nickel-zinc cells

BATTERIES			CURRENT (January 1976)				PROJECTED				
SYSTEMS	ELECTROLYTES	TEMP. °C	W-hr/kg	W/kg (PEAK)	CYCLE LIFE	COST. $ /KWH	W-hr/kg	W/kg (PEAK)	CYCLE LIFE	COST. $ /KWH	RELATIVE FIGURE OF MERIT*
Near Term (1–2 yr)											
Lead/Acid (SOA)	Aq. H_2SO_4	Rm.Amb.	30	50	700	100	50	150	>1000	60	1.0
Ni/Fe	Aq. KOH	Rm.Amb.	44	110	>800	1800	60	150	>1000	120	2.2
Intermediate Term (3–5 yr)											
Lead/Acid (Advanced)	Aq. H_2SO_4	Rm.Amb.	--	--		--	50	150	>1000	60	2.9
Ni/Zn	Aq. KOH	Rm.Amb.	77	110	200	800	110	150	>1000	50	4.6
Long Term (5 yr)											
(Zn,Fe)/Air	Aq. KOH	Rm.Amb.	80–120	40	<150	2000	90	80	>1000	60	2.5
Zn/Cl_2	Aq. $ZnCl_2$	Rm.Amb.	<66	<60	<100	>2000	130	150	>1000	50	4.5
Li/MS	LiCl-KCl eutectic	400–450	100	120	<250	>2000	150	300	>1000	40	7.2
Na/S	α-alumina	300–350	90	100	<200	>2000	170	200	>1000	40	6.3

***"Relative Figure of Merit" is a function of driving range capability, power capability, battery and cycle life costs, and the number of years to commercial deployment, based on the projected performance of the battery systems. The higher the figure, the better the system is.**

SOURCE: "Secondary Batteries for Electric Vehicles," Dr. Albert R. Landgrebe, Div. of Conservation Research & Technology, ERDA, April 1976.

Fig. 6–12. Potential electric vehicle batteries

want to obtain a battery charger from Yardney, the following information would also be helpful. Charger dimensions for a 96-volt battery charger are about 20" (508 mm) deep x 19" (483 mm) wide x 28" (711 mm) high. Weight is about 140 pounds (63.5 kg) so the unit may be mounted in the car.

Figure 6–13 shows the improved performance you can get with nickel-zinc batteries for a typical small van and a four-passenger compact electric car.

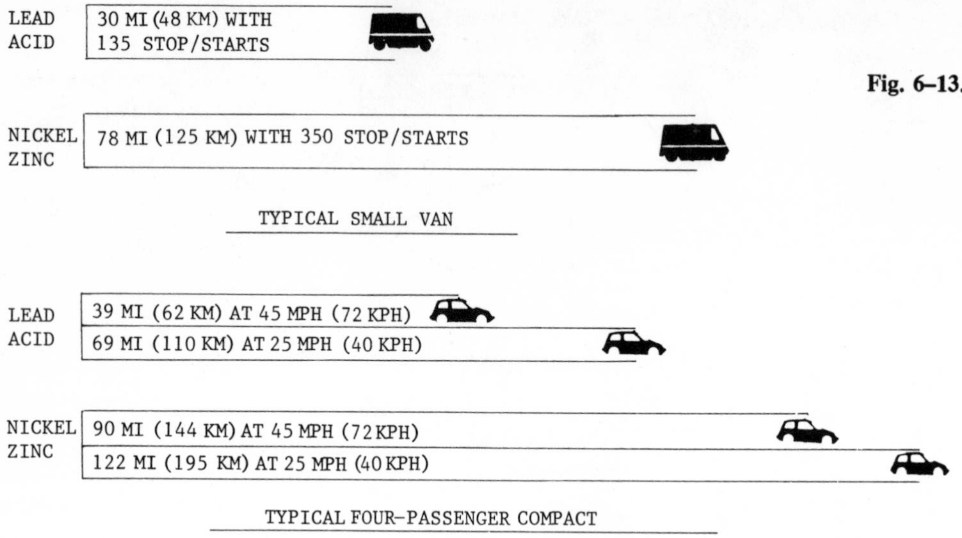

LEAD ACID — 30 MI (48 KM) WITH 135 STOP/STARTS

NICKEL ZINC — 78 MI (125 KM) WITH 350 STOP/STARTS

TYPICAL SMALL VAN

LEAD ACID — 39 MI (62 KM) AT 45 MPH (72 KPH)
69 MI (110 KM) AT 25 MPH (40 KPH)

NICKEL ZINC — 90 MI (144 KM) AT 45 MPH (72 KPH)
122 MI (195 KM) AT 25 MPH (40 KPH)

TYPICAL FOUR-PASSENGER COMPACT

Fig. 6–13. Improved performance with nickel-zinc batteries

Figure 6–14 shows comparative CitiCar (a commercial electric car) performance with lead-zinc and nickel-zinc batteries.

The superiority of nickel-zinc over lead-acid, more energy and power per pound as well as smaller volume per watt-hour, is shown in figure 6–15.

Among leading companies now manufacturing lead-acid batteries, but doing considerable work on nickel-zinc batteries for electric vehicles, is Gould, Inc., Vehicle Power System Department, 30 Gould Center, Rolling Meadows, IL 60008. This manufacturer estimates that the advanced lead-acid, as well as nickel-zinc, batteries for electric vehicles will be available in production quantities in 1981.

An interesting point relative to the nickel-zinc batteries being developed by Gould is that their research engineers estimate 300 cycles of charge and discharge in 1979 and at least 1,000 by 1981. These might be conservative figures in view of the fact that with the vibrating tech-

Fig. 6–14. Comparative CitiCar performance with lead-acid and nickel-zinc batteries

	Pb-Ac Stock Test	NiZn Proto Test	NiZn Production Design
Type	8 EV Traction	28 EV1X Cells	8 EV 4-Cell Traction
Gross Vehicle Weight	1826 lb (828 kg)	1550 lb (704 kg)	1728 lb (785 kg)
Battery Weight	556 lb (252 kg)	280 lb (127 kg)	458 lb (208 kg)
Stored Energy	5875 Wh	7475 Wh	13728 Wh
Energy Density	10.6 Wh/lb (23.3 Wh/kg)	26.4 Wh/lb (58.8 Wh/kg)	30 Wh/lb (66 Wh/kg)
Range @ Speed	32mi @ 35mph (51km @ 56kph)	41mi @ 39mph (66kkm @ 63kph)	70mi @ 45mph (113km @ 72kph)
Acceleration	18sec to 30mph (48kph)	13sec to 30mph (48kph)	15sec to 30mph (48kph)

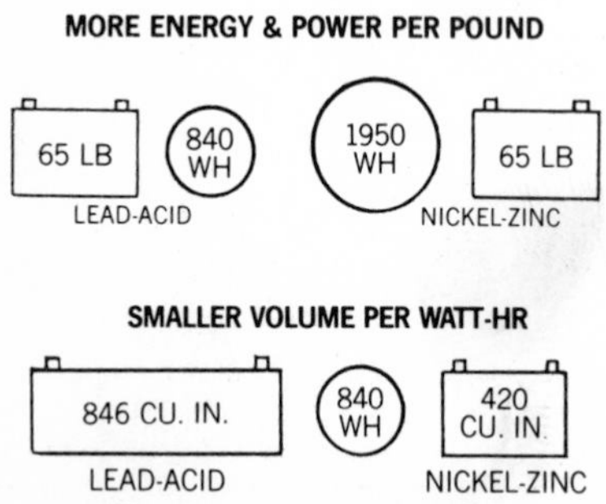

MORE ENERGY & POWER PER POUND

65 LB — 840 WH — LEAD-ACID

1950 WH — 65 LB — NICKEL-ZINC

SMALLER VOLUME PER WATT-HR

846 CU. IN. — LEAD-ACID

840 WH

420 CU. IN. — NICKEL-ZINC

Fig. 6–15. Graphic comparisons between lead-acid and nickel-zinc batteries for electric cars

nique Vibrocel, developed by AGA-Tudor, as many as 2,000 cycles have been achieved.

A recent table prepared by Harvey J. Schwartz, Manager, NASA Electric & Hybrid Vehicle Project Office, Lewis Research Center, Cleveland, Ohio, indicates the improved performance which can be gained from nickel-zinc batteries and also shows other potential types of advanced batteries. The comparison is shown in figure 6–16.

A TECHNIQUE FOR USING TWO DIFFERENT BATTERIES

A system designed by Fred Riess that can be used to improve the performance of the batteries in your electric car at relatively low cost is shown in figure 6–17. This is a technique in which the principal source, which will normally provide most of the energy through the diode, as shown, to the controller and electric motor, consists of conventional lead-acid batteries. However, when more power is needed to produce a greater amount of energy to the electric motor, the nickel-cadmium (NiCad) batteries are cut in through a diode to the controller. Normally, when you are cruising, you would be using only the lead-acid batteries. The NiCad batteries, which are much smaller but considerably more expensive, will cut in only when you need surges of power for high speed, acceleration, or climbing a hill.

A similar design, shown in figure 6–18, was used by the research engineers of Gulton Industries for powering an AMC electric car. The lithium-nickel fluoride battery provides energy for cruising and recharging the bipolar battery, while a bipolar nickel-cadmium booster battery provides the high-peak power necessary for acceleration. Cruising at about 35 mph, the motor and other electrical systems in this car draw about 50 amperes from the lithium battery. At this point, the battery's terminal voltage is 100 volts and the 69-cell (1.45V per cell) nickel-cadmium booster is on trickle charge. When the car accelerates, up to 450 amperes may be required. During acceleration, the lithium battery's potential drops, the discharge control senses the increasing

Battery	Vehicle	Range/Speed (km)/(km/h)	Range Relative to Lead-Acid
Nickel-zinc	Otis P-500 (NASA)	54.7/40.2	1.97
		43.4/J227-B	2.05
	Otis P-500 (USPS)	54.7/48.3	1.59
		17.7/postal cycle	1.75
	CDA Town Car	235/64.4	1.83
Nickel-iron	Daihatsu	259/40.2	1.48
	Fiat 128	96.5/45.1	1.50
	0.25-tonne van	114/48.3	1.51
Zinc-air/lead-acid	Toyota	455/40.2	2.53
	Nissan	496/40.2	2.25
Iron-air/lead-acid	Daihatsu	261/40.2	1.48
Zinc-chlorine hydrate	Vega	243/80.4	----
Sodium-sulfur	Bedford	161/--	----

Fig. 6–16. Performance of vehicles with experimental batteries

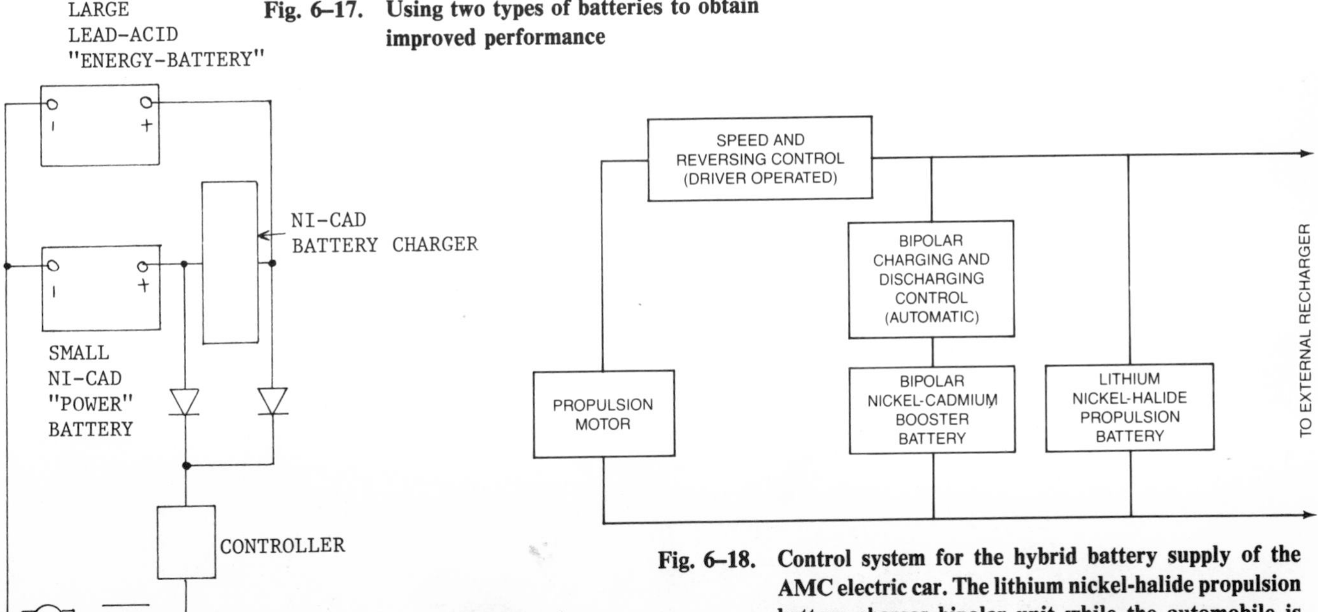

Fig. 6–17. Using two types of batteries to obtain improved performance

Fig. 6–18. Control system for the hybrid battery supply of the AMC electric car. The lithium nickel-halide propulsion battery charges bipolar unit while the automobile is cruising.

load and connects the nickel-cadmium battery in parallel with the lithium unit. After acceleration, the charge control disconnects the NiCad battery from its on-line position and reconnects it for charging by the lithium unit.

Promising New Battery

A promising *new* battery design is the lithium-titanium disulfide battery, which will operate at ambient temperatures, and is being developed by the Advanced Battery Project of Exxon Enterprises, Inc. in Bound Brook, NJ. This group is working with a battery using a negative electrode made of lithium and a positive electrode of titanium disulfide (TiS_2). The advantages of this system, according to the research team, which includes Lewis H. Gaines, Senior Application Engineer, are:

1. Excellent room temperature rate capability and a high theoretical energy density of 215 Wh/lb when coupled with a lithium negative.
2. Substantial insolubility in organic electrolytes.
3. High electrical conductivity.
4. A charge-discharge mechanism involving only the intercalation (insertion) of lithium ions between the TiS_2 layers. This mechanism contributes to long battery life by minimizing the physical changes that occur during battery use.
5. An attractive cost level.

Exxon Enterprises, Inc. (EEI) is testing an operating engineering prototype illustrating some of the performance capabilities of the lithium-titanium disulfide battery. Figure 6–19 compares the Exxon Enterprises electric vehicle design demonstration using a lithium-titanium disulfide battery and an AC control and propulsion system, with an existing EV powered by a lead-acid battery and DC propulsion system. Because the battery operates at ambient temperatures, relatively inexpensive construction techniques and materials can be used. EEI projects that, when applied in a vehicle with a range of 100 miles, a lithium-titanium disulfide battery system would deliver 60 Wh/lb at a manufacturing cost of approximately $35/kWh in large-volume production. These values compare favorably with current extended-cycle-life lead-acid battery technology, which provides an energy density of approximately 10 Wh/lb at a comparable energy cost.

For a 2,000-pound compact car, $LiTiS_2$ batteries would occupy about 3.02 cubic feet of space and weigh 350 pounds. EEI modeling studies made in 1978 showed that electric vehicles with a range of 100 miles, costing about $5,000, could be constructed with either a moderately expensive high-energy system, that is, $62/kWh at 60Wh/lb or slightly less expensive, lower-energy system consisting of batteries at $48/kWh at 31 Wh/lb. It appears that, from the economics of electric cars and batteries, electric cars will not be competitive in price if the cost of batteries is greater than $70/kWh. However, although the price of an electric car must be greater than this 1978 estimate now because of inflation, the price of gasoline has increased far more drastically. It's becoming increasingly more attractive in dollar savings to own an electric car.

ADVANCED EV'S (Li/TiS_2 TECHNOLOGY and AC CONTROL and PROPULSION SYSTEM)

RANGE	100. M LA CYCLE	MOTOR WEIGHT	5.6 LB/KW
BATTERY COST	50. $ /KWHR	CONTROLLER EFFICIENCY	72.0 PCT
BATTERY ENERGY DENSITY	60. WHRS/LB	BATTERY LIFE	500.0 CYCLES

PURCHASE PRICE	4556.
OPERATING COST	6.9 CENTS/MILE
VEHICLE TEST WEIGHT	2411.0 POUNDS
ENERGY CONSUMPTION	358.8 WHR/MILE

	WEIGHT DISTRIBUTION		*COST DISTRIBUTION*	
	PCT.	POUNDS	PCT.	DOLLARS
BATTERY	19.	470.	40.	1816.
CHASSIS	60.	1440.	48.	2195.
MOTOR/CONTROLLER	6.	151.	12.	546.
TEST LOAD	15.	350.		
	100.	2411.	100.	4556.

PRESENT EV'S (Pb/ACID TECHNOLOGY and DC PROPULSION SYSTEM)

RANGE	25. M SAE METRO	MOTOR WEIGHT	7.0 LB/KW
BATTERY COST	40. $ /KWHR	CONTROLLER EFFICIENCY	40.0 PCT.
BATTERY ENERGY DENSITY	10. WHRS/LB	BATTERY LIFE	250.0 CYCLES

PURCHASE PRICE	3204.
OPERATING COST	15.7 CENTS/MILE
VEHICLE TEST WEIGHT	3000.2 POUNDS
ENERGY CONSUMPTION	803.6 WHR/MILE

	WEIGHT DISTRIBUTION		*COST DISTRIBUTION*	
	PCT.	POUNDS	PCT.	DOLLARS
BATTERY	30.	900.	14.	464.
CHASSIS	53.	1593.	71.	2264.
MOTOR/CONTROLLER	5.	158.	15.	477.
TEST LOAD	12.	350.		
	100.	3000.	100.	3204.

Fig. 6–19. Exxon Enterprises electric-vehicle design demonstration

Other Batteries of the Future

Ford of England built a small car to test a sodium-sulfur battery several years ago. At present, an English battery company with a U.S. branch called Chloride, 3001 Fairfax Traffic Way, Kansas City, KS 66115, has been doing a considerable amount of work with sodium-sulfur batteries. These are being tested in Britain in city buses, delivery trucks (including milk trucks), and vans. The sodium-sulfur battery has an advantage over lead-acid in power storage by a factor of 6.3:1. This means that every pound of sodium-sulfur battery provides 6.3 times as much power as a pound of lead-acid battery.

The biggest problem with sodium-sulfur batteries has been design of a suitable separator for the two materials. The present configuration consists of a cell that is in the form of a large tube with a white cylinder made of an exotic ceramic material called Beta alumina in the center. The sodium is placed inside the white tube and the sulfur outside. Another problem with the sodium-sulfur battery is that it needs a temperature of around 600°F in order to operate. Self-contained heating elements can keep it warm while generating power to operate an electric car, but it eventually needs additional heating from the outside to keep going.

There are also lithium-metal sulfides different from the Exxon type. In particular, a lithium-iron sulfide unit being tested by General Motors looks quite promising.

Zinc-chlorine energy storage systems are being developed by such companies as Energy Development Associates, 1100 W. Whitcomb Avenue, Madison Heights, MI 48071, phone (313) 583–9434. This battery requires a pump and chiller and is therefore a very complicated assembly to create. It is also fairly expensive. It would appear at present that batteries of this kind will prove to be useful as supplementary storage of electrical energy for utility companies, but it will be several years before this type of battery can be considered for electric vehicle use.

Another type of battery that is under development is a lithium-copper sulfide battery. Such units, as well as lithium-copper sulfide designs, are being tested in a research program by the Atomics International Division of Rockwell International Corporation, Canoga Park, CA. This concept appears to have a potential of as much as 81 watt-hours per pound.

Still another approach is a lithium-water-air battery, which is being studied by a research team at Lockheed Missiles & Space Company, Palo Alto, CA, under a contract with DOE.

A basic research program on the characteristics of various kinds of batteries containing lithium is being conducted at the Lawrence Livermore Laboratories of the University of California. This study includes an examination of techniques for producing and recycling lithium so as to make batteries containing lithium more economical.

Iron Redox Battery

Important news has come to the author from Peter H. Rubie, president of Electric Passenger Cars, Inc., 7954 Convoy Court, San Diego, who said that, in his opinion, the most useful battery for EV's will soon be the iron redox battery, developed by GEL, Inc. for manufacture by New Resources Group, both North Carolina companies. Rubie's opinion has real merit because he has been designing and building electric cars for many years. The following is a summary taken from a brief article on iron redox batteries prepared by GEL and New Resources Group.

The iron redox battery has been under development since 1971 by GEL, Inc., Durham, NC. Its basic components are plastic and carbon, and the system utilizes electrodeposited iron as a fuel and an aqueous solution of ferric chloride as an oxidant. All the elements of the storage system are plentiful and are harmless to man and his environment, according to New Resources Group, Sanford, NC, now developing a manufacturing process for this battery patented by GEL. The president of GEL is Ralph Zito, Jr., a research physicist largely responsible for this new battery.

Other important features include:

1. Unlimited charge-retention time and storage life.
2. Unlimited charge/recharge cycle capability (including discharge to zero with no adverse effects).
3. Long system life.
4. Reversible electrochemical reaction in which no material elements are consumed or dissipated.
5. Component materials are inexpensive and readily available.

Performance data from the evaluation of laboratory systems developed for the U.S. Army and EPRI (Electric Power Research Institute, Menlo Park, CA) indicate that the iron redox battery is a viable energy storage system. The United States Department of Energy, Division of Solar Technology, has provided financial assistance to support the research and development of the iron redox battery. This was through a pilot program to solar-power a new campus for the Mississippi Community College in Blytheville, Arkansas. Also, a development program is currently under way through DOE Contract Em–78–C–05–6050.

In September 1977, GEL embarked on the Mississippi County Community College project. This effort was to adopt the iron redox system to the 250-kW photovoltaic-powered campus. During a 10-month program, much valuable data was gathered and several laboratory-constructed modules were built and tested. The last, a 4-kW unit, consisted of eight 41-cell arrays. This unit achieved 50% total energy efficiency during 6- and 10-hour charge/discharge cycles. Single cells were performing at 55–65% efficiency at the end of the program. Since September 1978, GEL has continued to explore and optimize the iron redox system under a Department of Energy research contract. This research has yielded much important information on polarization, membrane behavior, diffusion losses, and electrolyte control. Efficiencies of 60–65% have been achieved with multiple cell arrays and computations with independent parameter data indicate 70% total energy efficiency is possible with presently available technology.

Most of the recent improvement in performance is due to an increased understanding of membrane properties. Detailed information on the recent development of iron redox is documented in the reports from GEL under the present DOE contract. According to GEL, there are many areas of research that could improve the performance even further.

The next step, according to James C. Pate, P.E., president of New Resources Group, will be to enter into manufacturing these promising batteries for large-scale use in EV's and for utility standby service.

DETAILS OF IRON-REDOX BATTERY

The iron redox battery system consists of an electrochemical cell (shown in figure 6–20) or energy converter, an anolyte flow circuit and a catholyte flow circuit. Electrodeposited iron serves as the fuel and a ferric salt serves as the oxidizing agent. On discharge a ferrous salt is formed by the reaction.

Each cell of the battery is made from five physical elements, which are: (1) a conducting carbon electrode, anode, upon which iron is electrodeposited during charge and dissolved during discharge; (2) a circulating anolyte containing only the ferrous salt of iron; (3) a microporous barrier that passes electrons freely while strongly impeding the cross-flow of anolyte on one side and catholyte on the other; (4) a circulating catholyte, which consists of ferrous and ferric salts of iron with greater ferric proportions at higher electrical charge; and (5) the cathode, which is a conducting carbon electrode. When the battery is discharging, metallic iron is dissolved from the anode surface. Each molecule of iron becomes a positively charged bivalent ion and, in so doing, releases two electrons. At the same time, ionized ferric salt in the catholyte is reduced to ferrous salt. The iron ion in this reaction is

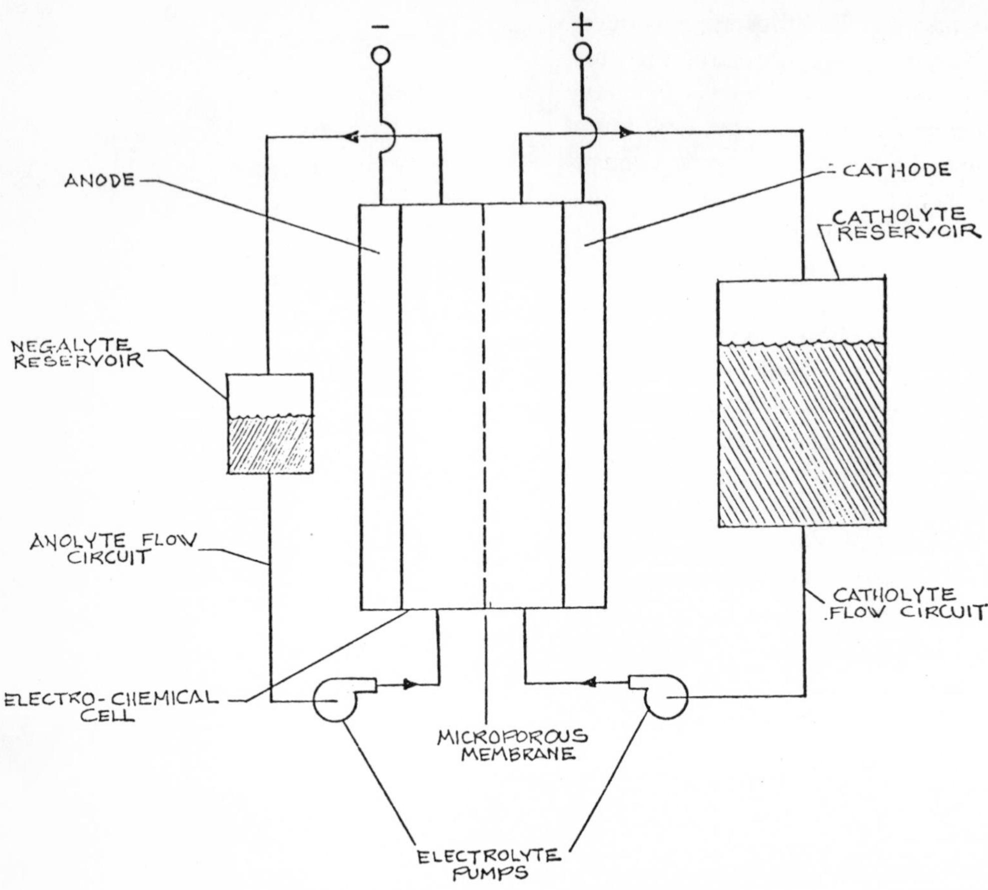

Fig. 6–20. Iron redox battery system, single cell, from New Resources Group

reduced from a trivalent state to a bivalent state and, in so doing, absorbs an electron. These electrons are obtained from the cathode plate and, in completing the internal circuit, are conducted through the catholyte, microporous barrier, and anolyte to the positively charged anode surface. The iron redox chemical reactions follow.

$$\mathbf{Fe + 2FeCl_3 \underset{charge}{\overset{discharge}{\rightleftharpoons}} 3FeCl_2}$$

During the charging mode

$$\mathbf{Fe^{+2} + 2e^- \longrightarrow Fe^o \text{ at anode.}}$$
$$\mathbf{Fe^{+2} \longrightarrow Fe^{+3} + e^- \text{ at cathode.}}$$

During the discharging mode

$$\mathbf{Fe^o \longrightarrow Fe^{+2} + 2e^- \text{ at anode.}}$$
$$\mathbf{Fe^{+3} + e^- \longrightarrow Fe^{+2} \text{ at cathode.}}$$

The iron redox battery is fully charged when the available plating volume in the negative compartment of the cell is filled with iron and is fully discharged when all the iron has been plated off the electrode. A complete discharge does no harm to the recharging capability of the battery and no inherent cycle life exists. The catholyte is pumped out of the cells and into external storage tanks when the battery is not in use. No reaction can occur in this inoperative mode, so the charge can be stored indefinitely without degradation.

The iron redox battery has low internal resistance and can therefore operate at high current density. The amount of energy storage per cell can be varied because of the external storage of catholyte.

Advantages claimed for the iron redox battery include:

1. Higher energy density than lead-acid over the entire range of design configurations on a Wh/lb or weight basis (about the same on a volume basis).
2. Lowest-cost secondary energy storage device to produce.
3. Cannot be damaged by discharge to zero.
4. Efficiencies on the order of 70%, which can probably be increased slightly with further product development.
5. Unlimited charge-retention time.
6. Power density in terms of watts per pound or watts per cubic foot generally higher than lead-acid systems.
7. Cannot be damaged by reverse-charge potentials.
8. No degradation evidenced after hundreds of charge/discharge cycles (200 cycles represent 80,000 miles of propulsion for an electrical vehicle at 400 miles per charge).
9. Uses no internal metal except current-carrying conductors.
10. Unlimited storage life (charged, discharged, or dry).
11. Terminal potential zero when switched off and thus no residual voltage hazard.
12. Direct metering of residual (or expended) energy.
13. Electrolyte volume may be increased to enhance capacity without increasing converter volume, through a range of 18:1 from 0.3 cu ft to 6 cu ft per cu ft of converter.
14. The electrolyte has several advantages. It is (a) water-based, (b) completely stable, (c) nonvolatile, (d) hazard-free, (e) odorless and, (f) degradable in nature; it has a (g) wide range of operating temperatures and, (h) unlimited storage life and charge retention; it is (i) inexpensive (cheap enough to be considered expendable), and (j) reusable indefinitely, without handling constraints.

Fuel Cell Battery for EV's

In the August 10, 1979, issue of the *New York Times,* an article by Malcolm W. Browne described some new developments applicable to future EV's. One significant new battery is a fuel cell designed by Dr. J. Byron McCormick and his associates at the Los Alamos Scientific Laboratory of the University of California, Los Alamos, NM. This fuel cell combines oxygen and hydrogen, with methyl alcohol as a "starter." The alcohol is broken down by a catalyst to provide hydrogen (H_2).

A flow of H_2 is used as one battery electrode, while a continuous flow of air—which contains about 20% by volume of oxygen (O_2)—is the other electrode. Separating the two gases is a porous carbon barrier in which tiny particles of platinum act as a catalyst to force the H_2 and O_2 to combine. In this reaction, electrons from the H_2 are separated and flow to the O_2 in the air. This creates a flow of electricity (which of course is an electron flow) through the carbon/platinum barrier impregnated with phosphoric acid as an electrolyte.

According to Browne:

> Dr. McCormick said his group had made calculations from their experiments [using these fuel-cell batteries in a golf cart] showing that a small car could be built right now using fuel cells that would not entail any major new technology.
>
> An electric car the size of a VW Rabbit drawing its power from fuel cells and methyl alcohol could travel about 500 miles at a speed of 55 mph on 13 gallons of methyl alcohol. . . . The car could be built to sell for about $7,500 in 1978 dollars, and the fuel cell system would have a

life expectancy of about 40,000 hours. . . . The power system Dr. McCormick described operates at an efficiency of more than 40% compared to about 16% for the best conventional automobile engines.

This is a particularly encouraging development for two reasons:

1. Because the Los Alamos Scientific Laboratory is entirely financed by federal funds, a license for manufacturing McCormick's fuel-cell battery can be obtained by any reputable U.S. battery manufacturer—or a new entrepreneurial firm—through the Department of Energy. DOE will be glad to get a return on this investment and other inventions developed by federally financed laboratories.
2. There is increasing interest among farmers in the production of methyl alcohol as a fuel, as Dr. Barry Commoner described in his excellent articles in *The New Yorker* in two April 1979 issues. Also, DOE is now looking actively into the various biomass techniques for increasing our nation's homegrown fuel supply.

Thus the golf cart operated by Dr. McCormick and his associated scientists and technicians high in the mountains of northeast New Mexico, where the last thing anyone wants is smog, may be the forerunner of highly efficient future batteries for EV's. Such batteries in mass production can be relatively cheap, and a life expectancy of 40,000 hours sounds excellent to the authors of this book with their experience in EV's constrained by the present lead-acid batteries.

New Design from Old

For several years California Institute of Technology's Jet Propulsion Laboratory (JPL) has been doing work on storage batteries for EV's under the sponsorship of the U.S. Department of Energy. Much of this program has involved evaluation of such new batteries as various nickel-zinc, nickel-iron, and improved lead-acid models developed by American manufacturers, with Jack Roulette as one principal engineer. Another program under experienced EV engineer Howard Vivian involves testing new models of electric cars developed with DOE funds, such as the latest General Electric/Chrysler/Globe-Union EV described in chapter 8 and the Air Research electric van with AC motor and flywheel designed by a team headed by Bob LaFrance, well known in the Electric Vehicle Society of Southern California.

The most promising research activity by JPL scientists applicable to EV's is a new battery design, described by Wally Rippel as "based on a lead-acid battery patent from the nineteenth century." Taking off from an idea almost 100 years old, Rippel, Dean Edwards and a JPL/Caltech team have designed a bipolar lead-acid battery that they say could greatly improve EV performance within the next two years. This design consists of a cell with a negative plate, then a bipolar separator having a positive plate plus a separator element and a negative plate. This 3-element bipolar separator is made with the element separating the positive and negative plates fabricated from a polyethylene/graphite material. The positive and negative plates have a thin Teflon surface coated with lead stripes on the outer surfaces.

"We've used an old idea with modern materials," Rippel says. "We also apply axial pressure, based on a French concept, using clamps to hold the bipolar unit together. Our research results indicate that we may be able to build a lead-acid bipolar battery having an energy density of 23.9 watt-hours per pound vs. the present 13.5 Wh/lb possible with the best present lead-acid EV battery. This 77% improvement means a potential range for a small electric car at 45 mph of 119 miles instead of 71 miles. Power density can be improved still more dramatically, from 40 watts per pound to 150 W/lb. This translates to an ability to accelerate a future subcompact EV from 0 to 60 mph in 8 seconds —comparable to present gasoline-driven cars—as compared with 25 seconds in an electric car with conventional lead-acid batteries."

Rippel is hoping that the bipolar lead-acid battery will permit at least double the present cycle life, lower weight, and significantly lower cost per mile of EV operation. Estimated time before this new battery can go into production is less than two years—perhaps mid-1981. Further details on this battery development may be obtained by serious EV researchers by writing to Wally Rippel, JPL, 4800 Oak Grove Avenue, Pasadena, CA 91103.

List of Electric Vehicle Battery Manufacturers

This list of manufacturers, in the United States, of lead-acid batteries suitable for use in electric cars has largely been taken from a publication of the Lead Industries Association, Inc., 292 Madison Avenue, New York, NY 10017.

Barrett Battery, Inc./Varta Batterie AG
3317 La Grange Street
Toledo, OH 43608
(419) 241–4198

C & D Batteries Division
Eltra Corporation
Walton Road & Township Lane
Plymouth Meeting, PA 19462
(215) 828–9000

Chloride, Inc.
5200 West Kennedy Blvd.
P.O. Box 24598
Tampa, FL 33623
(813) 870–3770

Delco-Remy Division
General Motors Corporation
2401 Columbus Avenue
Anderson, IN 46014
(314) 644–5581

Douglas Battery Manufacturing Co.
500 Battery Drive
Winston-Salem, NC 27107
(919) 788–7561

East Penn Mfg. Co.
Deka Road
Lyon Station, PA 19546
(215) 682–6361

ESB Inc.
5 Penn Center Plaza
Philadelphia, PA 19103
(215) 564–4030

General Battery Corporation
Box 1262
Reading, PA 19603
(215) 929–0771

Globe-Union, Inc.
5757 North Green Bay Avenue
Milwaukee, WI 53201
(414) 228–3155

Gould, Inc.
10 Gould Center
Rolling Meadows, IL 60008
(312) 640–4117

Hester Battery Co.
1300 Martin St.
Nashville, TN 37203
(615) 244–3000

KW Battery Co.
3555 Howard Street
Skokie, IL 60076
(312) OR-3–7710

Mule Battery Co., Inc.
325 Valley St.
Providence, RI 02908
(401) 421–3773

Prestolite Battery Division
511 Hamilton St.
Toledo, OH 43694
(419) 244–2811

Surrette Storage Battery Co., Inc.
Jefferson Ave.
Salem, MA 01970
(617) 745–4444

Trojan Battery Co.
9440 Ann Street
Santa Fe Springs, CA 90670
(213) 945–1471

Yardney Electric Corporation
82 Mechanic Street
Pawcatuck, CT 02891
(203) 599–1100

7 Battery Chargers

In the preceding chapter we discussed many kinds of *traction batteries,* those used to provide electric power for the motor propelling your EV. But there is a second application, usually employing a standard 12-volt automobile battery, to power such accessories as your lights, windshield wiper, horn, radio, and stereo.

Generally, therefore, you need to consider two kinds of battery chargers. First, for the 12-volt accessories battery, many operators of electric cars have found it useful to connect a DC-to-DC converter between their main traction batteries (6 volt) and the relatively small accessories battery. Since it is essential to keep your battery properly charged, such a DC-to-DC converter will automatically take care of this.

Another alternative is to couple a small generator to your traction motor and use its output to charge the 12-volt battery. Or, if your vehicle is designed to provide regenerative braking, some of the electrical energy produced by your traction motor while serving as a generator, as described in chapter 3, can be used to keep your accessories battery fully charged. You may want to consider having both an on-board charger installed in your car and an off-vehicle charger.

If none of these alternatives appeals to you, it is easy to find a standard automotive charger that will keep your 12-volt battery charged. It is not quite so easy to get a suitable battery charger for your 6-volt traction batteries. However, many manufacturers in the United States and abroad make suitable battery chargers for your electric car.

Charger for Traction Batteries

You will want a battery charger that will operate from your normal home electric supply, 115 VAC, 60 cycle, single phase. If you have a 220 VAC, 3-phase supply available—because you have an electric dryer or other appliances in your garage—suitable battery chargers are available for operating from this type of 3-phase power supply.

At the end of this chapter is a list of manufacturers of battery chargers, many of whom you will recognize as leading makers of storage batteries for EV's. This list is obtained from the February 1978 directory issue of *Electric Vehicle News,* P.O. Box 533, Westport, Connecticut 06880. This magazine, published quarterly, contains both technical and business information about EV's that is invaluable to anyone interested in electric cars.

A battery charger for traction batteries usually contains a transformer, a rectifying circuit, and some solid-state control components. Typical efficiency of such a charger will be about 90%. An on-board charger will probably contain an auto-transformer in order to save weight.

At the beginning of the charging cycle, when you first connect the charger to your partially discharged batteries, the efficiency of your charger may be higher than 90%. Then, as the charge progresses, efficiency of the charger decreases. If you don't shut off your charger when your batteries are fully charged, efficiency of your charger goes down still further. However, if you set the timer on your charger correctly, which is easy to do with a little experience, your charger should shut itself off at a suitable time. Also, most chargers are designed to respond to the voltage level of the batteries. As you will recall from the information in chapter 6, you don't want to charge your batteries beyond a certain optimum voltage level. By sensing this level, your charger should shut itself off automatically. This feature of automatic shutoff is highly desirable when you're looking for a battery charger.

If you must get a charger without an automatic timer, you need to estimate the initial state of charge of your batteries and the average charging current in setting a timer correctly. This charging current is determined by the difference between the supply voltage (from the charger output) and the battery voltage divided by the effective circuit impedance (which is largely resistive). Therefore, if you are relying entirely on a timer in your battery charger for correct settings, you must be aware that your timer setting is affected by changes in supply voltage from your charger, changes in battery voltage caused by age, temperature, and other variables that alter battery output.

Similarly, with chargers that sense the rise in battery voltage, performance will vary depending on battery age, temperature, and condition. However, there are some real advantages in an automatic battery charger, since modern designs prevent overcharging and make correct charging easy for the user.

If your propulsion batteries are undercharged, the range of your vehicle will be low. If you overcharge your batteries, you will probably reduce battery life. You'll certainly increase your energy consumption and hence your operating cost per mile.

Expert Information about Battery Charging

The remainder of this chapter contains technical information about battery charging from Gould, Inc. This major manufacturer of storage batteries, battery chargers, control systems, motors, and other components for electric cars offers to supply information on EV batteries from Gould Laboratories, Box 3140, St. Paul, Minnesota 55165.

Note that the accompanying information applies to lead-acid batteries. Information on battery chargers for other types of batteries, including nickel-zinc and nickel-cadmium, may be obtained from manufacturers mentioned in chapter 6 and including Gould, ESB, Yardney, Lucas, and others.

> Charging is always done by the use of direct current, and the voltage of the charger must always be greater than that of the battery. The positive terminal of the charger is connected to the positive terminal of the battery. During charge, the current flows through the battery in the direction opposite of when it is being discharged.
>
> In the discussion below, circuits and calculations are given with reference to the internal resistance of the battery. In most instances, particularly for industrial applications where the battery capacity requirement is large (greater than 10 ampere-hours), the internal resistance is so small that it may be ignored in designing and operating chargers.
>
> A basic charge circuit is illustrated in figure 7–1 where E(I) (source voltage) is a function of the instantaneous current I; $R_i(S)$ (internal resistance) is a function of the state-of-charge; and $E_c(S)$ (counter-electromotive voltage of the battery) is a function of the state-of-charge. Then,

$$E(I) = R_i(S)I + E_c(S) \qquad (1)$$

$$I = \frac{E(I) - E_c(S)}{R_i(S)} \qquad (2)$$

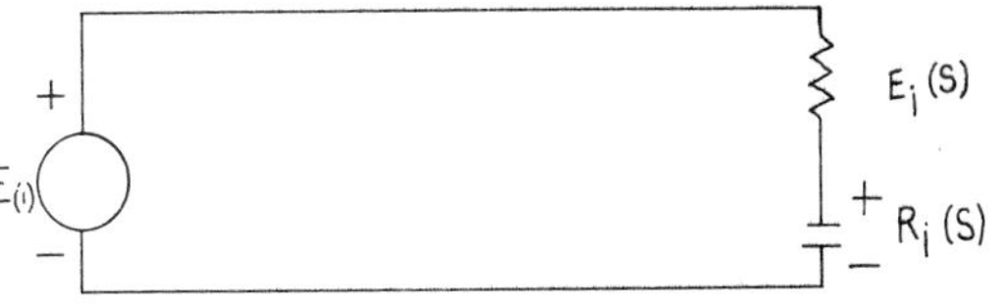

Fig. 7–1. Basic battery charging circuit

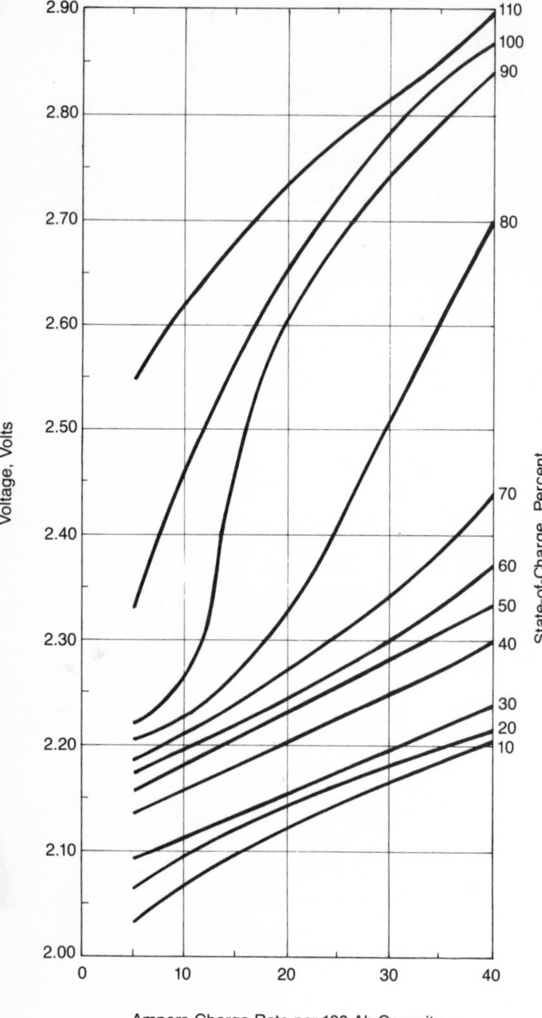

Fig. 7–2. Lead-acid charging voltage per cell vs. charging rate at various states-of-charge

When E(I) = E_c(S), the current will be zero, but when the source voltage is greater than the voltage of the battery, current will flow, its value being inversely proportional to the internal resistance of the battery.

Lead-acid batteries should be charged for a sufficient length of time, and at such a rate as to introduce into the battery the ampere-hours discharged, plus a 5 to 15 percent overcharge. The specific value of overcharge depends almost entirely upon charging temperature, age, and history of the battery. In general, it is more harmful to excessively overcharge at a high rate an older battery, or a battery operating at high temperature, than a freshly manufactured unit, or one being charged at room temperature or lower. Any charge rate is permissible which does not produce excessive gassing or a cell temperature greater than 115°F.

Four methods of charging will be discussed below. These are:

— modified constant-voltage
— taper
— two-rate
— constant-current

The selection of the appropriate method will be governed by considerations such as the type of battery, service conditions, time available for charging, and the number of batteries to be charged at one time. It should be noted that in charging motive power batteries, the end-of-charge rate (finishing rate) is extremely important and should not be exceeded. Normally, batteries can be charged in 8 hours, assuming a normal duty discharge; however, if time permits, a longer period can be used.

VOLTAGE VS CURRENT

Figure 7–2 shows that a discharged battery can absorb high currents at relatively low battery voltages. For example, after the introduction of about 20 percent capacity (20 ampere-hours at 40 amperes), a 100 ampere-hour battery is at a voltage of about 2.22 volts per cell. The curves also show that as the charge progresses at a given rate, the voltage increases; the higher charge rates yielding higher voltages. For example, at 110 percent charge (10 percent overcharge), the voltage at 5 amperes (C/20 rate) is 2.55 volts, and at 20 amperes (C/5 rate), the voltage is 2.74 volts.

The generally used finishing rate for lead-acid batteries is the C/20 rate. With most charging schemes, the normal start-of-charge rate is about the C/5 rate, or 20 amperes per 100 ampere-hours of rated capacity.

MODIFIED CONSTANT-VOLTAGE METHOD

In the modified constant-voltage method, a fixed resistor is in series with the charger and battery. A 2.63 volts-per-cell bus is used for an 8-hour charge. Table 7–1 shows the relationship between volts per cell and time available for charge. In order to use a single fixed resistor, and achieve proper start and finish rate, the voltages indicated in the table are required. For an 8-hour charge, the initial current is 22.5 amperes per 100 ampere-hours, and for a 16-hour charge, 8.5 amperes. It should be noted that the charging resistor should be of sufficient current carrying capacity. The normal "tap" value of the resistor determines the finishing rate. For example, at the 8-hour rate, the "tap" value is 0.022 ohm. This number is calculated as follows: The terminal voltage E_t of the battery at the end of charge, at a finishing rate of 5 amperes, is 2.52 volts (see figure 7–3). Therefore, with a bus voltage E_B = 2.63 volts, the tap resistance must be:

Table 7–1
Modified Constant Voltage
Charging Design Constants

Hours Avail. For Charge	Bus Volts Per Cell	RESIS. VALUES PER CELL: Normal "Tap"	RESIS. VALUES PER CELL: Max. to Provide	RATES (A) PER 100 AH CELL: Start of Chg.	RATES (A) PER 100 AH CELL: Resistor Cap.
7.0	2.60	0.016	0.027	27.5	32.5
7.5	2.61	0.018	0.029	25.5	30.0
8.0	2.63	0.022	0.031	22.5	26.0
8.5	2.65	0.026	0.035	20.0	23.0
9.0	2.67	0.030	0.039	18.5	21.0
9.5	2.69	0.034	0.043	17.0	19.5
10.0	2.72	0.040	0.049	15.5	17.5
12.0	2.84	0.064	0.073	12.0	13.5
14.0	3.00	0.096	0.105	10.0	11.0
16.0	3.27	0.150	0.160	8.5	9.0

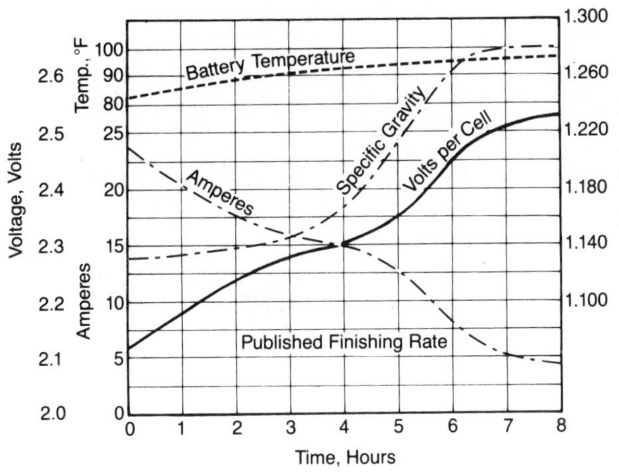

Fig. 7–3. Lead-acid charging typical modified-potential charge profile bus voltage 2.63 volts per cell; 100 AH cell

Design constants based on 100-ampere-hour cell capacity. For cells of other capacity, external resistance per cell will be inversely proportional and ampere values directly proportional to the capacity. Cell resistance values correspond to electrolyte temperature 77°F.

$$R = \frac{E_B - E_t}{I_f} = \frac{2.63 - 2.52}{5} = 0.022 \text{ ohm}$$

When charging several batteries at once, from either a constant-voltage source derived from a motor-generator, or from a rectifier, the modified constant-voltage method of charge is preferred because the current tapers during charge, reducing the possibility of excessive charge currents.

The following formula should be used to calculate the kilowatt requirements when using motor generators to charge several batteries from a fixed voltage bus in 8 hours:

$$kW = \frac{\text{AH} \times 0.225\text{A} \times \text{No. of Cells} \times 2.63\text{V} \times 0.8 \times \text{No. of Circuits}}{1000}$$

Example: Let four banks of 18 series-connected cells be charged in 8 hours, each cell having a capacity of 500 ampere-hours.

$$kW = \frac{500 \times 0.225 \times 18 \times 2.63 \times 0.8 \times 4}{1000} = 17 \text{ kW}$$

The bus voltage would be 18 X 2.63 = 47.3 volts, the initial current 0.225 X 500 = 112.5 amperes, and the total initial current from the generator 4 X 112.5 = 450 amperes.

TAPER METHOD

This method can be used with either a generator or rectifier equipment, and can be considered a variation of the modified constant-voltage charge method. It is employed when only one size of battery is to be charged. Shunt-wound motor-generators, and rectifier chargers can be designed so that their voltage vs current characteristics correspond closely to the modified constant-voltage type charger. No ballast resistor is required. The circuitry of the charger is such that the initial and finish charge rates are matched to the battery. As was previously mentioned, the finish rate is generally C/20, and the initial rate about C/5. Figure 7–4 shows the typical voltage, current, and specific gravity profile of a cell being charged by the taper method. The charge characteristics are nearly the same as those shown in figure 7–3 for the modified constant-voltage method. In order to meet the requirements for charging a single battery from a motor-generator, the following design parameters must be met:

- the nominal voltage of the generator must be 2.25 volts per cell
- the initial load voltage of the generator should be about 2.135 volts per cell
- at the end of charge, the charging current should be 5 amperes per 100 ampere-hours battery capacity, and the corresponding voltage 2.52 volts per cell

To calculate the kilowatt requirements for a single motor-generator set, the following formula should be used:

$$kW = \frac{AH \times 0.225 \times \text{No. of Cells} \times 2.25V \times 0.8}{1000}$$

For example: Let the battery have 12 series-connected cells, each cell with a capacity of 250 ampere-hours.

$$kW = \frac{250 \times 0.225 \times 12 \times 2.25 \times 0.8}{1000} = 1.22 \text{ kW}$$

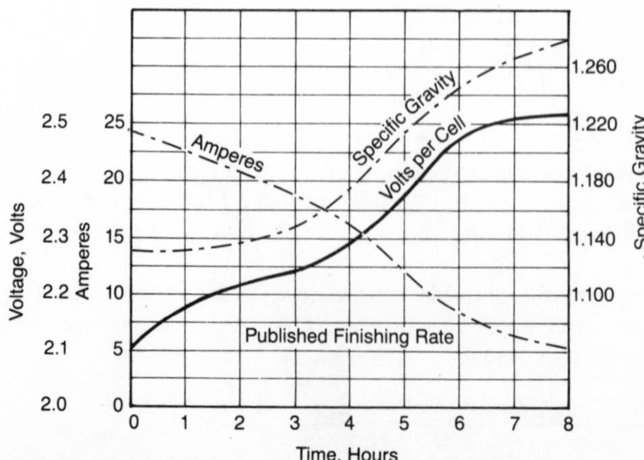

Fig. 7–4. Lead-acid charging typical taper-charge profile for 100 AH cell

TWO-RATE METHOD

The principle of this method is to begin charging at the recommended start-of-charge rate, then switch to a lower rate when gassing occurs (at about 2.37 volts per cell). Two resistors are connected to the source voltage, the first having a value that provides the correct initial current, and the second such that when it is switched into series with the first resistor at the appropriate battery voltage (2.37 volts per cell), the proper finishing rate is produced toward the end of the 8-hour period. Figure 7–5 illustrates the charge curve for the two-rate method. When the second resistor is brought into the circuit, a sharp drop in current occurs.

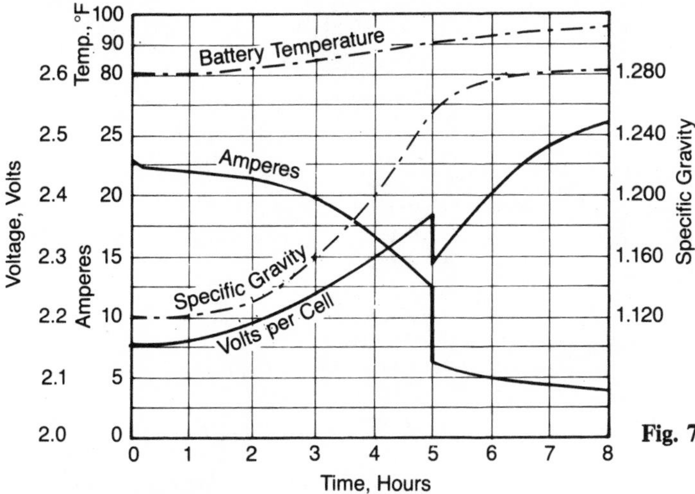

Fig. 7–5. Lead-acid charging charge curves for 2-rate method for 100 AH cell

CONSTANT-CURRENT METHOD

Constant-current charging is seldom used for 8-hour or shift-charging of motive power batteries, because this would require manual control during and at the end of the charge. If, however, the charge time available were about 12 to 16 hours, constant-current charging could be used. Strictly speaking, the charge period is longer, the initial current is lower than for the 8-hour charge rate, and the taper much shallower. As shown in figure 7–6, the initial rate for the 16-hour charge is about 8.5 amperes, and the finish rate 5 amperes, yielding a taper ratio (the ratio of the initial to finish current) of 1.7 to 1, and for the 8-hour charge, the ratio is approximately 4.0 to 1.

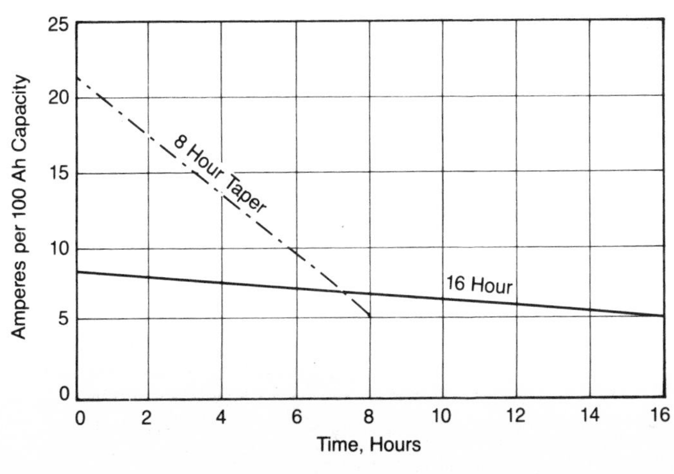

Fig. 7–6. Lead-acid charging constant current at two rates

RECOMMENDED END VOLTAGES FOR VARIOUS BATTERIES

In Table 7–2 you will find suggested end voltages—the voltage levels at which to aim in concluding your charging cycle—for several EV battery types, present and future.

Table 7–2
Recommended End Voltage Per Cell

Type of Battery	Charging or Equalizing	Floating	Pulsing	Discharge
Lead-acid (stationary)	2.33 – 2.37V	2.16 – 2.17V		1.75V
Lead-acid (motive)	2.40 – 2.50V (usually 2.42)	2.16 – 2.17V		1.75V
Calcium lead-acid	2.34V	2.17 – 2.25V		1.75V
Vented nickel-cadmium	1.55V	1.40 – 1.43V	1.55 – 1.65V	1.00V
Sealed nickel-cadmium	1.45 – 1.50V	–		1.00V
Silver-zinc	1.97 – 2.05V	–		
Nickel-iron	1.80V	1.50V		
Silver cadmium (vented)	1.55 – 1.65V	–		
Silver cadmium (sealed)	1.52 – 1.55V	–		

List of Battery Charger Manufacturers

AB Tudor
Accumulatorenfabrik Sonnenschein GmbH
Accumulatorenfabriken Wilhelm Hagen AG
Akkutechnik Ladegerate GmbH & Co.
American Monarch Corp.
Barrett Battery, Inc.
Berix Electric AB
Blake Electronics, Inc.
Brown, Boveri & Cie.
C.D.S. Westinghouse
Camis Electronics, Ltd.
Chloride Industrial Batteries, Ltd.
Christie Electric Corp.
Conde Barao, SARL
ESB, Inc.
EVC, Inc.
East Penn Mfg. Co., Inc.
Electric Auto Corp.
Electric Fuel Propulsion Corp.
Electric Motion Control Corp. Intl.
Electric Vehicle Associates, Inc.
Eltra Corporation
Fox Products, Inc.
Furukawa Battery Co., Ltd.
General Battery Corp.
Gottfried Hagen AG
Gould, Inc.
Hobart Brothers Co.
John R. Hollingsworth Co.
Inducto/Power
Industrial Battery Engineering, Inc.
KW Battery Co.
Kaylor Energy Products
LaMarche Mfg. Co.
Lansing Bagnall (Canada)
Lansing Bagnall, Ltd.
Lawnel Corp.
Lester Electrical of Nebraska
Lester Equipment Mfg. Co., Inc.
Linear Alpha, Inc.
McGraw-Edison Co.
Master Control Systems, Inc.
Morrison Electrical Engineering Ltd.
Motor Appliance Corp.
NDC Netzler & Dahlgren Co., AB
Pluskota Electric Co.
Propel, Inc.
Rectron, Inc.
Ross Engineering Corp.
S.A. Accumulateurs TUDOR
S.A.F.T.
Sigma Electrotenkisk A/S
Sociedad Espanola del Acumulador Tudor
Triple-A Specialty Co.
Unitron Corp.
Watanabe Engineering Corp.
C. H. Waterman Industries
Westinghouse Brake and Signal Co., Ltd.
Wind Kraft A.E.S.C.
Yardney Electric Corporation
Yuasa Battery Co., Ltd.

8 A Wide Variety of Electric Cars

If you don't believe that Americans are experimenting with all kinds of electric cars, just go to a meeting of the Electric Vehicle Society's chapter nearest you. To give you an idea of a small cross-section of this variety, here are some pictures and brief descriptions of electric cars created from clunkers. All these EV's and several others were at a recent meeting of the Southern California chapter of the Electric Vehicle Society in Fontana, about 50 miles east of Los Angeles.

The modified Suzuki pickup shown in figure 8–1 has eight 6-volt batteries to provide power for a compound-wound DC motor mounted under the truck bed. A feature of this conversion is a variable belt drive, providing a theoretically infinitely variable range of drive-train ratios between 1-to-1 to about 6-to-1. The control unit is shown mounted on the left side below the flatbed just to the rear of the driver's door. Just behind the passenger compartment are the on-board battery charger and two of the heavy-duty traction batteries. This handy little truck was converted into an electric vehicle for less than $1,000 in materials. The owner drives it between his home and work every day. It's a highly reliable, economical EV with top speed of about 50 mph. At 45 mph, the range of this electric compact is approximately 45 miles. By adding two more batteries, this range could be extended to at least 60 miles.

Fig. 8–1. Modified Suzuki pick-up makes useful electric commuter car

Mounted in the trunk of the 1969 Simca in figure 8–2 are the control system and two of the eight 6-volt batteries providing power for this neat EV. The other traction batteries are under the hood with the compound-wound DC motor, which is connected to the car's original trans-axle. This converted electric car will do between 45 and 50 mph on a level road, with a range of about 40 miles at this speed. The owner uses it regularly to drive to work, for shopping, and other suburban driving. Cost of operation is less than 2¢ a mile with excellent reliability and practically zero maintenance. (Eventual battery replacement will run the total operating cost up to about 3.5¢ a mile, but then maybe he can use a panel of solar cells to charge his traction batteries and reduce his daily operating costs!)

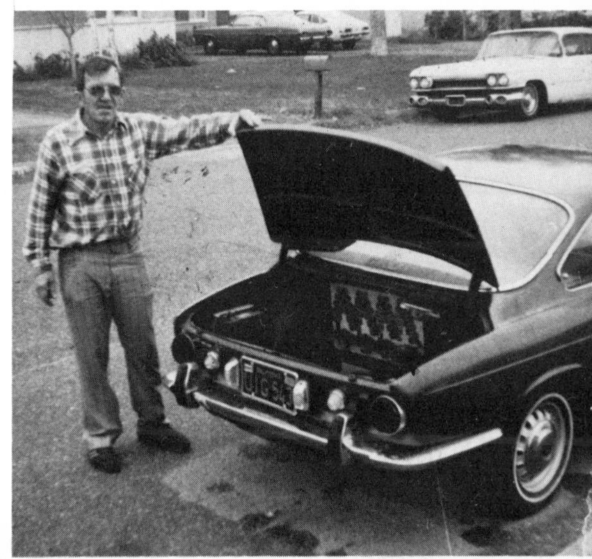

Fig. 8–2. This 1969 Simca is now an electric car with reliable performance

The owner is proud and his daughter looks pleased with the converted Renault Dauphine shown in figure 8–3. The trunk is full of traction batteries, placed over a compound-wound DC motor linked to the trans-axle drive between the rear wheels. The control system and additional batteries are mounted in the former engine compartment, under the hood. This electric car will travel at freeway speed, 55 mph, for about 30 miles. If you reduce its speed to 40 mph, the range is extended to more than 45 miles.

Converting an NSU Prinz into an electric car, the owner used a surplus aircraft starter/generator that serves as either a compound-wound or shunt DC motor. With regenerative braking, this car, shown in figure 8–4, has a range of more than 60 miles in urban driving at 30 mph; or about 35 miles at 45 mph. The electric motor is connected to the standard trans-axle; this drive train and two traction batteries are in the rear, while additional batteries and the control system are under the hood.

Conversion Kits from Several Sources

In previous chapters you've learned one way of converting your clunker into a useful electric car, as well as considerable information about the

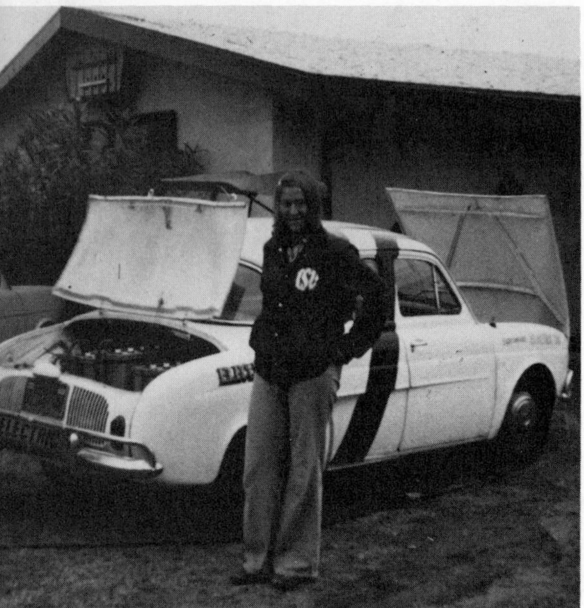

Fig. 8–3. An old Renault becomes a new electric car

components required for such a conversion. Later in this chapter you'll find descriptions of a wide variety of electric cars that may give you some helpful ideas. Meanwhile, here is a list of manufacturers who make EV conversion kits.

Corbin-Gentry, Inc.
40 Maple Street
Sommerville, CT 06072
(203) 749-2238

Electric Engineering
723 Forest Street
East Lansing, MI 48823
(517) 482-9313

Flight Systems, Inc.
P.O. Box 25
Mechanicsburg, PA 17055
(717) 697-0333

Flight Systems, Ltd.
6480 Viscount Road
Malton, Ontario L4V1H3, Canada
(416) 678-9470

Frizzell's Electric Transportation
P.O. Box 59
Maynard, MA 01754
(617) 897-9449

Heald, Inc.
P.O. Box 1148
Benton Harbor, MI 49022
(616) 849-3400

Kaylor Energy Products
1918 Menalto Avenue
Menlo Park, CA 94025
(415) 325-6900

King Engineering
5436 Topsfield Lane
Clay, NY 13041
(315) 699-3534

Pedal Power Division,
General Engines, Inc.
591 Mantua Blvd.
Sewell, NJ 08030
(609) 468-0414

Fig. 8–4. Economical transportation is assumed with this Prinz converted into an EV

Roy Kaylor, who has built several models of a streamlined electric car on a VW chassis, has achieved excellent performance from his Kaylor Kit vehicle. His electric car will travel 50 miles at 50 to 55 mph and has a top speed, for passing, of 70 mph. At 30 to 35 mph, its range is in excess of 120 miles on a level road. In a recent test run, Kaylor drove from Crystal Bay, Nevada, over the 7,200-foot Donner Pass into Auburn, California, a 90-mile trip, including the climb over the pass, on one charge of the batteries in his EV.

Batteries, mounted in the center of the Kaylor vehicle shown in figure 8–5, keep the center of gravity low with the aerodynamically designed body. Based on a VW chassis, the car has 4-wheel independent suspension and weighs only 1,850 pounds. The 30 HP continuous-duty compound-wound DC motor can provide a peak of 100 HP with a 4-speed transmission. Kaylor offers either a controller of the switching regulator type with transistor chopping to regulate armature current, or a mechanical chopper providing both forward and a reverse speed control.

Fig. 8–5. Kaylor electric car

Plans and parts are available from Kaylor Energy Products for converting Volkswagens, including Beetles, Superbeetles, Fastbacks, Squarebacks and buses; Things, Karmann Ghias, Porsches, DKWs; and VW-based vehicles such as dune buggies. Any of these can be converted into an electric car. According to the manufacturer, the simplest conversion involves using the two packages designated as KK-1 and KK-2, with details and prices as of July 1978 on the following list.

As of mid-1979, Kaylor's complete conversion kit for any VW is priced at $1,700.

Kaylor Kits Available

KK-1	Motor with cooling fan, special lightweight flywheel, clutch disc, pressure plate, splined pilot shaft, precision bearings, and machined cast-aluminum adaptor plate to fit VW transmission.	$495
KK-2	Control relays, voltmeter, ampere meter with shunt, heavy-duty charger, battery cables and terminals, control wiring, switches, transistorized field control, headlights, tail-lights, and horn.	$495
KK-3	Fiberglass body with mounting hardwear, seats, windshield, and welded battery racks (will fit any Bug Chassis).	$2495
KK-4	Optional transistorized (switching regulator type) speed controller that regulates armature current.	$595
KK-5	Michelin X radial-ply tires, magnesium wheels, and wheel adaptors.	$495
KK-6	Baja Bug kit which includes 4 lightweight fenders, front end, and rear end.	$145
KK-7	Battery Sets, 6V 220 AH deep-cycle type, shipped dry-charged without acid. (List price $32.00 each.) Batteries weigh 70 pounds each.	6 batteries KK-7A $265 12 batteries KK-7B $495
KK-8	"Starter" VW Conversion kit. This mini kit provides the parts necessary to do a simple conversion of a VW "Bug." You provide your own batteries, flywheel and clutch assembly (standard VW), wire and cable, charger, and battery mounts. Kit includes motor with cooling fan, splined pilot shaft, precision bearings, machined cast aluminum adaptor plate to fit VW transmission, control relay, voltmeter, ampere meter with shunt, and assembly blueprints (can be used with KSR-2 and KR-2).	$495

Kaylor Controllers and Parts

KR-1	SPST 400-amp main safety relay silver contact (18–24 volt coil)	clean $20.00 new $80.00
KR-2	DPDT 200-amp series-parallel relay for controlling battery voltage mechanical interlocked (18–24 volt coil)	clean $100.00 new $238.45
KS-1	SPDT Special toggle switch (end off) to control KR-2 relay	$5.00
KSR-1	200-amp transistorized switching regulator controller. Provides stepless speed control for lighter-weight vehicles. Operates from any voltage up to 72 volts DC and regulates the output voltage from 0 to almost the battery voltage in an efficient switching manner. This will not provide as strong an accelerator as the relay-type control but provides much smoother control than the relay system.	$275.00
KSR-2	20-amp transistorized switching regulator controller for shunt field (for variable speed between relay steps)	$75.00

King Engineering Conversion Kits

As with the Kaylor kits made in California, the King Engineering kits produced in Clay, New York, are designed primarily for standard 4-speed VWs, including bugs, squarebacks, fastbacks and vans. The basic kit shown in figure 8–6 provides all necessary components and hardware, except batteries and battery racks, for converting a VW to an electric car.

The DC motor, mounted directly on the VW trans-axle, is provided with a discrete armature control and continuous field control. Included in the conversion kit are heavy-duty copper cables, a motor cooling fan, and a 40-ampere, 36-volt battery charger for on-board use.

According to Robert D. King, president of King Engineering, safety is improved by internal overload current protection designed into the control system, plus a heavy-duty battery fuse. Electronic control systems are completely assembled, calibrated, and tested prior to shipment. The range of EV's built from King Engineering kits is said to be extended because of controlled acceleration and regenerative braking.

The King Electric GT in figure 8–7 received top honors in the Mt. Washington Alternative Vehicle Regatta in June 1977. With three passengers in this electric car, it successfully climbed this steep mountain, more than 6,000 feet high. Speeds of more than 55 mph, and a range of up to 70 miles, at a constant 40 mph, are achieved with this streamlined electric car.

Fig. 8–6. King Engineering conversion kit

Fig. 8–7. Electric car wins Mt. Washington climb

Electric Vehicles from Mazda

Although a great deal of development work on electric vehicles is taking place in Japan, most manufacturers have been somewhat secretive about their efforts. Therefore we are pleased to be able to provide some data, drawings, and photographs of one EV design developed by Toyo Kogyo Co., Ltd., the maker of Mazda automobiles and Courier and Mazda trucks. This information was provided by Masataka Matsui, Manager of the Automotive Products Planning Division, Toyo Kogyo Co., Ltd., P.O. Box 18, Hiroshima 730–91 Japan (Telephone: 0822-82-1111). See figures 8–8 and 8–9.

Fig. 8–8. Mazda Bongo electric van

Specifications of Mazda Bongo Electric Van

Dimensions	Overall length	3,770 mm
	Overall width	1,500 mm
	Overall height	1,680 mm
	Luggage compartment length	2,000 mm/1,220 mm
	Luggage compartment width	1,300 mm
	Luggage compartment height	960 mm
	Wheelbase	2,000 mm
	Road clearance	170 mm
Weight	Vehicle weight	1,265 kg
	Seating capacity	2 persons/4 persons
	Max. loading capacity	250 kg/100 kg

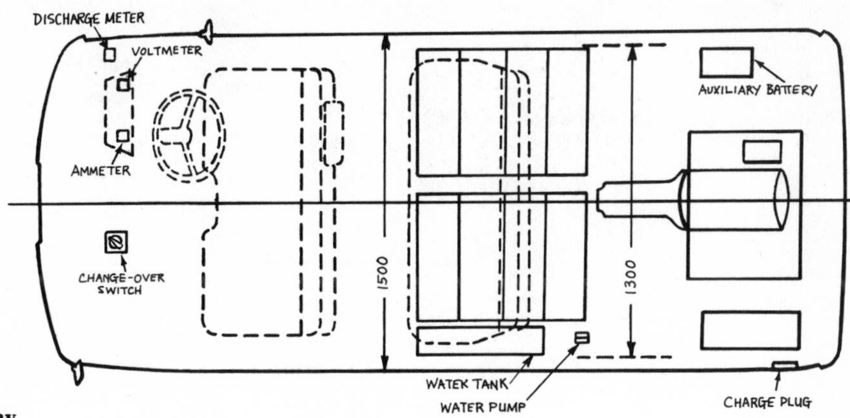

Fig. 8–9. **Mazda Bongo electric van—cutaway drawings showing component placement**

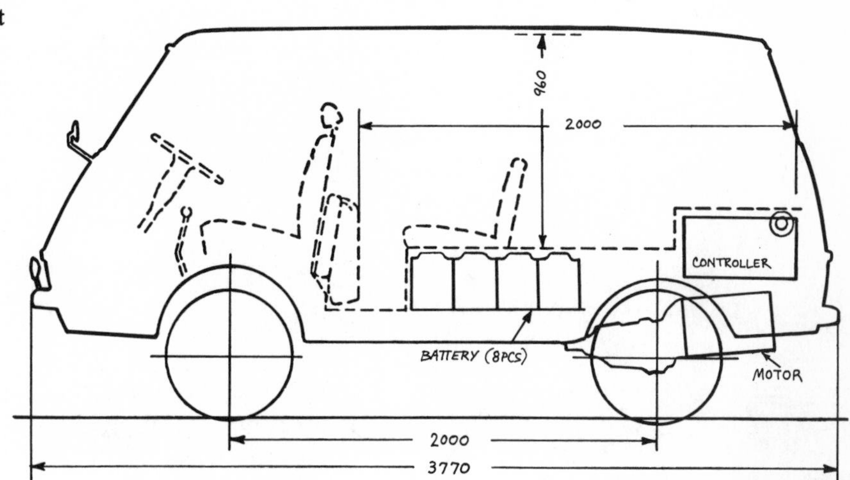

Specifications (cont'd)

Performance	Max. speed Range Acceleration Climbing ability	More than 60 km/h More than 60 km (30 km/h 20 c) Less than 8 sec (0 – 30 km/h) More than 0.25
Electric motor	Type Rated output Rated torque Rated voltage & current	DC motor 8.1/4, 640 kw/rpm 1.7/4, 640 kg-m/rpm 96V, 108A
Control system	Type	Series-parallel switching type or thyristor chopper type
Battery for power	Type Voltage Capacity Number & connecting method	Modified-type lead-acid battery 12V 125 AH (5 hr) 8, series-parallel
Transmission system	Clutch Transmission	Single dry, diaphragm Forward 4 speeds, reverse 1 speed

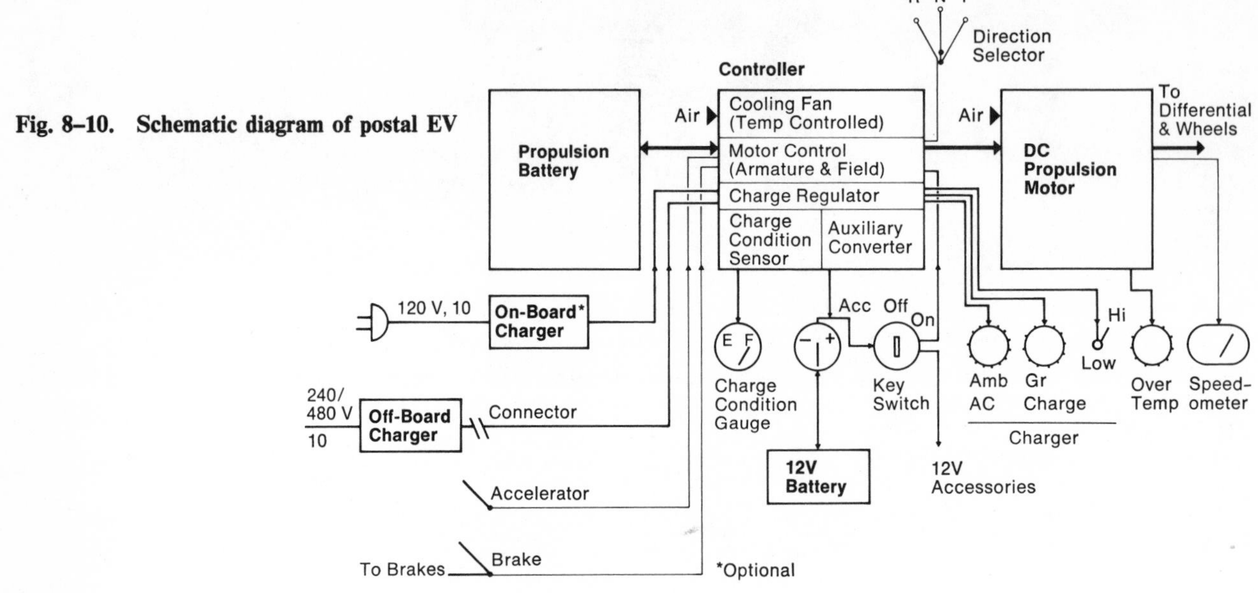

Fig. 8–10. Schematic diagram of postal EV

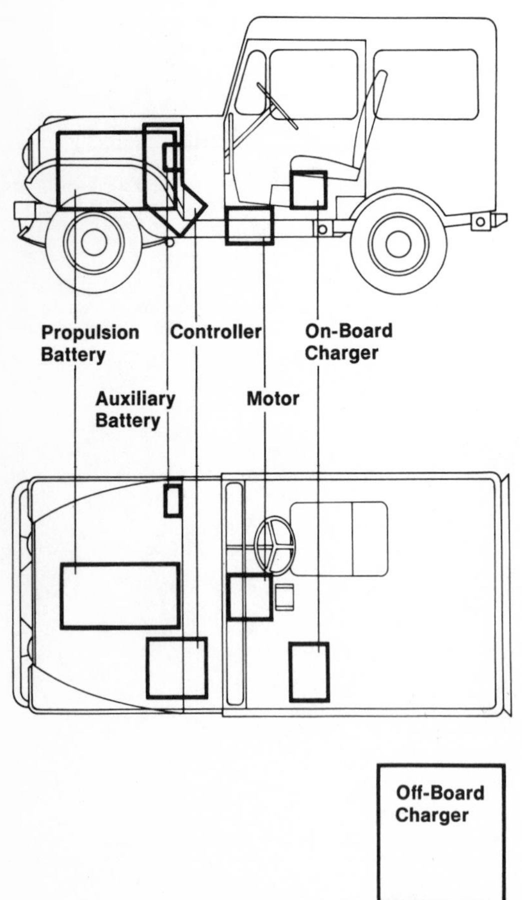

Fig. 8–11. Component positions in postal EV

Electric Vehicles for the U.S. Postal Service

Since December 1975 the U.S. Postal Service has been using a fleet of more than 300 electric vehicles designed with an American Motors chassis and powered by lead-acid traction batteries, a high-torque compound-wound DC motor, and electronic controller made by Gould, Inc. See figures 8–10 and 8–11.

Experience with these EV's has proved them to be extremely efficient and economical. Quoting a recent statement by Gould:

> The fleet of electric vehicles now operating in California (294 of these postal EV's are in the Los Angeles area) has in effect *cut the operating cost* of similar vehicles powered by internal combustion engines *in half.* Down time experienced by the fleet accounted for only 2% of the total operating time.

Postal EV Specifications

Vehicle Performance	
Cruising Speed:	33-40 mph
Acceleration:	0–30 mph/20 sec
Gradeability:	10% grade, 16 mph
Range:	300 stop/starts, 29 miles
Kilowatt Hours per Mile:	.8 to 1.2 kWh
Service Requirements	
Daily Normal charge **Weekly** Clean cell terminals Clean battery terminals Check pilot-cell electrolite level	Check specific gravity on pilot cell after equalize charge Check state of charge gauge reading, after equalize charge Clean controller air intake screen

(if low, check all cells and add water as required)
Equalize charge

Monthly
Check all cells for electrolite level (add water as required)

Semi-Annual
Check motor-brush wear
Check motor electrical connections
Check motor mounts

Components of Postal EV's

Component Descriptions

Propulsion Battery
Type: lead-acid electric vehicle 27–66E–11
No. of cells: 27
Capacity: 330 AH (6-hr rating)
Size: 19 X 32 X 22 in. High
Weight: 1270 lb (including tray)

Propulsion Motor
Type: DC compound, enclosed. Voltage: 54 volts
Insulation: class H
Size: 11.72 in. dia x 16.2 in. long
Weight: 263 lb

Off-Board Charger
Recharge time: 8 hours maximum
Input: 240 or 480 V, 26/13 amp, single phase
Size: 22 X 13 X 24 in.
Weight: 195 lb

On-Board Charger
Recharge time: 10–16 hours
Input: 120 V, 20/15 amp
Single phase
Size: 8 X 10 X 12 in.
Weight: 45 lb

Auxiliary Battery
Type: Gould power breed
Rating: 81 AH (20 hr), 140 min at 25 amps
Size: Group 24–10¼ in. h X 6⅞ in. w X 8¾ in. h
Weight: 45 lb

Controller
Integrated functions:
- Motor speed & directional Control
- Charge regulator
- Auxiliary power converter-regulator
- Battery-charge condition Sensor
- Cooling-ventilating fan

Size: 2.5 Cu Ft
Weight: 100 lb

Controller Operational Characteristics
Speed control
- Time ratio control; Armature voltage control <1400 rpm, ~ 17 mph,
- Field Control > 1400 rpm, ~ 17 mph
- Regenerative braking—above 14 mph
- Current limiting

Charge regulator
- Taper charge
- Temperature compensated
- Overcharge control
- Both off-board & on-board Charge controlled

Auxiliary converter
- Regulated output voltage
- Output current—30 amp max., isolated

Cooling-ventilating fan
- Ventilation during charge
- Controller-motor cooling as needed; temperature controlled

Battery-charge condition Sensor
- Type: voltage sensing
- Current compensated
- Output: meter current

Smaller Manufacturers

Among several smaller manufacturers of electric cars, the most notable in terms of number of cars produced and in service is Sebring-Vanguard, Inc., Sebring Industrial Park, Sebring, Florida 33870, maker of the well-known CitiCar.

Another small two-seater is the Marathon C-300 made by Marathon Electric Car Ltd., 8305 Le Creusot, Ville de St. Leonard, Quebec H1P 2A2 Canada. This car's twelve 6-volt batteries supply power to the 72-volt 8-HP DC motor, and a 12-volt battery is used for accessories. Operating range is 50 miles at a cruising speed of 35 mph, with a payload of 500 pounds. Estimated operating cost is about 3¢ a mile.

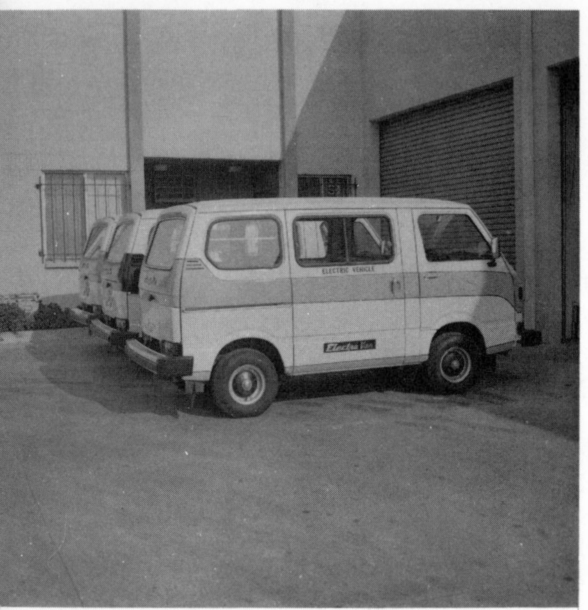

Fig. 8–12. **ElectraVan Model 600**

Fig. 8–13. **ElectraVan Model 1400. This EV carries eight passengers and on one charge will go 60 mph for 30 miles, or 45 mph for 50 miles.**

3E Vehicles, P.O. Box 19409, San Diego, California 92119, provides a two-person streamlined sport commuter and also offers a "Leisure-Town" kit series. These vehicles and others have been designed by Paul Shipps, president of the company and long a designer of EV's. He is also the author of a useful small book, *Electric Mini-Cars for Urban Driving.*

Electric Vehicle Associates, Inc. 9100 Bank Street, Cleveland, Ohio, 44125, has supplied three 4-passenger electric cars for test driving by the U.S. Department of Energy at a price of $9,500 each. These cars have a top speed of about 53 mph, with a range of 28 miles at that speed. At 25 mph, the range is extended to 56 miles.

Electric Auto Corporation, 2237 Elliott Avenue, Troy, Michigan 48084, was formed in 1977 to manufacture and distribute electric passenger cars and battery chargers based on patents developed by Electric Fuel Propulsion (EFP) Corporation (also of Troy, Michigan) since 1966. During the past 12 years, under the guidance of Robert R. Aronson, president, EFP has produced a series of electric cars and delivery vans with good performance. One feature is the use of a tripolar lead-cobalt battery that can be recharged to 80% of capacity in 45 minutes. These batteries are lighter and have more energy density than conventional lead-acid batteries, which require six to eight hours for recharging.

Battronic Truck Corporation, a subsidiary of Boyertown Auto Body Works Incorporated, Boyertown, Pennsylvania 19512, has built a variety of vans and several bus models as pioneer EV's. A current model is called a Minivan and includes an SCR controller made by GE, with 18 heavy-duty 6-volt batteries, made by General Battery Corporation, that supply 112 volts to the compound-wound DC motor. A large hinged door at the rear provides a wide opening for cargo. Batteries can be removed with a fork-lift truck or with a special lift available from the manufacturer.

Some very promising EV's come from Jet Industries, Inc., in Austin, Texas, whose ElectraVans are distributed on the West Coast by Erwin A. Ulbrich, president of Creative Automotive Research. Figure 8–12 shows the ElectraVan Model 600, and a view of the larger Model 1400 appears in figure 8–13. The specifications for the four models available from this small, progressive Texas manufacturer are given in figure 8–14.

The ElectraVan Model 600 utilizes a Suburu van chassis with standard 4-speed forward manual transmission and front-wheel drive, like most modern compact cars made in the United States, Japan, or Europe. Propulsion is by a General Electric 20-HP or Prestolite 22-HP series-wound DC motor, with a GE electronic (SCR-type) controller, and regenerative braking as an option. There is a bench seat for driver and front passenger, a mid-van bench seat for up to three additional adults, and cargo space in the rear. On two test drives in the Whittier area, Ted Lucas found this ElectraVan to be the best commercial EV he has driven. Top speed is 53 mph on level roads, acceleration is adequate for even freeway driving, and this electric car handles extremely well. Its performance is vastly superior to the Elcar—an oversize golf cart—which the author leased from Creative Automotive Research for 30 days in 1977. It is a good product at a fair price, carrying an 18-month warranty on all parts—including the 17 quality lead-acid 6V batteries in the Model 600—that will sell itself, Ulbrich

	600	1000	1400	1000P
Overall Height	64.4"	77.23"	80.8"	67.8"
Overall Length	125.8"	176.0"/1940"	176.0"/194.0"	190.0"/210.24"
Overall Width	54.9"	79.82"	79.5"	79.5"
Wheelbase	71.7"	109.0"/127.0"	109.0"/127.0"	115"/131.0"
Cargo Cu. Ft.	76.56	208.0	8 passenger	n/a
Inside Length				
(motor cover to rear door)	65.4"	117.3"	117.3"	96.0"
Inside Width	48.0"	65.3"	65.3"	70.0"
Inside Height	48.0"	47.18"	53.2"	—
Propulsion Motor				
Type	series	series	series	series
Insulation	H	H	H	H
Size	7"X16"	11"X18¼"	11"X18¼"	11"X18¼"
Weight	105 lbs.	255 lbs.	255 lbs.	255 lbs.
HP Rating	20 at 4900	28 at 3900	28 at 3900	28 at 3900
Propulsion Battery				
Type	lead/acid	lead/acid	lead/acid	lead/acid
Voltage	102	144	144	144
Weight	1190 lbs	1680 lbs.	1680 lbs.	1680 lbs.
Curb Weight	2690 lbs.	4475 lbs.	n/a	n/a
GVW	3340 lbs.	5475 lbs.	n/a	n/a
GAWR (Front)	1410 lbs.	2700 lbs.	n/a	n/a
GAWR (Rear)	1930 lbs.	2700 lbs.	n/a	n/a
Axle Ratio	4.375	3.5	3.55	3.55
Transmission				
First	4.363	2.99	2.99	2.99
Second	2.625	1.75	1.75	1.75
Third	1.809	1.0	1.0	1.0
Fourth	1.107	n/a	n/a	n/a
Reverse	4.272	3.17	3.17	3.17
Steering				
Turn Diameter	25'	36.5'	36.5'	47'
Turning Angle	37°	37°	37°	33°
Wheels & Rims	500X10	15X5.50	15X5.50	15X5.50
Controller	SCR	SCR	SCR	SCR
Charger	On Board	Off Board	Off Board	Off Board
Input Voltage	115/220V	220V	220V	220V
Max Output Amperage	15/30	30	30	30

Fig. 8–14. ElectraVan specifications

says. Average operating cost during this 18-month period is 2¢ per mile, a very attractive figure as gasoline prices continue to climb.

Perhaps the most compact commercial EV is the 3-wheel Free-Way shown in figure 8–15, available from H-M Vehicles, Inc., 9341 Penn Avenue South, Bloomington, Minnesota 55431. This vehicle is 115" long, 53" wide, 51" high, and weighs only 550 pounds without driver or passenger. It is available as an electric car with a top speed of 55 mph, and up to 40 miles per battery charge at 20 mph, according to Vexilar, Inc. The price as of June 1979 is quoted as $2,995. This car is also sold with a gasoline engine and diesel engine. But who wants smelly and costly fossil fuels when electricity is cheaper and more reliable?

Fig. 8–15. The three-wheel "free-way"

Fig. 8–16. Compartment that formerly housed conventional gasoline engine in XDH-1 now holds transverse-mounted rewound aircraft-type starter/generator. Electric motor and five DieHard batteries utilized for power

EV's from Larger Firms

With rapid development of electric cars under way in Great Britain, which has some 45,000 electric vans delivering milk and other products at lower costs than is possible with ICE vehicles, as well as in West Germany, France, and Japan, a bright spot on the American horizon appeared last year with the unveiling of the Sears XDH-1 electric car. This vehicle, developed jointly by Sears and Globe-Union, Inc., maker of DieHard batteries, is shown in figures 8–16 and 8–17.

This electric car was based on a Fiat 128–3P with front-wheel drive. Twenty traction batteries supply power for the 120V compound-wound DC motor, transverse mounted, with solid-state field-weakening controller. The standard 4-speed manual transmission is used, with the electric motor coupled to the original trans-axle. The motor is cooled with a fan supplied by the 12-volt accessory battery.

The Sears XDH-1has exceeded 75 mph and will easily cruise at 55 mph, with reserve power for passing. Its range at a steady speed of 45 mph is more than 90 miles. The car includes a built-in charger, operating from either 115V or 220V supplies. Estimated cost of operation in the Chicago area is stated at from 1 to 1½¢ per mile.

Figure 8–18 shows two views of the 4-passenger ETV–1 or Endura, developed for DOE by the General Electric Research and Development Center, Chrysler Corporation, and Globe-Union. GE provided the propulsion DC motor, controls, and overall management of the program, Chrysler the chassis, and Globe-Union the 18 improved lead-acid batteries and automatic battery charger. Batteries are packaged in a tunnel extending from behind the drive train and front suspension to the rear of the EV. Tunnel width is minimized in the passenger compartment by using a single row of batteries. The body has minimum frontal area for low aerodynamic drag.

Fig. 8–17. Interior of the XDH–1 looks very conventional except for the addition of small center console that houses ammeters, voltmeters, and switch to activate chargers

Fig. 8–18. The GE/Chrysler ETV–1

Technical manager of this program is the Jet Propulsion Laboratory of California Institute of Technology, Pasadena. The Endura uses a similar 20-HP motor supplied by GE for the commercial ElectraVans described earlier in this chapter, and a similar GE control system plus an Intel 8080 microprocessor for propulsion control, sequencing, fuel-gauge computation and display, and programmed battery charging. Actual fabrication of the vehicle, designed by Chrysler, was performed by Modern Engineering Services, Inc.

Total weight of this 3-door passenger car, painted silver, is about 4,000 pounds when carrying four passengers. It has front-wheel drive, a low center of gravity, and with 4 occupants will do 117 miles (187 km) at a constant speed of 35 mph (56 kph). At 45 mph, the range is approximately 100 miles. Endura will accelerate from 0 to 30 mph in about 9 seconds, and from 25 to 55 mph in 17.6 seconds, so you could drive it on freeways, toll roads, thruways, and other high-speed traffic arteries.

Cost of developing this attractive car was considerably more than $1 million in federal funds. The much smaller makers of commercial electric cars like Jet Industries and their ElectraVans, The Electric Auto Corporation, Troy, MI, Electric Passenger Cars, Inc., San Diego (Peter Rubie's Hummingbirds), and others have received little if any federal funding.

Figure 8–19 shows General Motors' Electrovette, which is a Chevette modified to become an EV. GM has also made a commercial van (figs. 8–20 and 8–21). Eliot M. Estes, president of GM, has been widely

Fig. 8–19. The Electrovette from General Motors

GMC BATTERY POWERED COMMERCIAL VAN
GVW.................8100 LBS (3682 KG)
PAYLOAD...............1500 LBS (682 KG)
BATTERY PACK WEIGHT 2500 LBS (1137 KG)
WHEELBASE...............110 IN (279 CM)
OVERALL LENGTH.......178.2 IN (452 CM)
OVERALL WIDTH..........79.5 IN (202 CM)
OVERALL HEIGHT.........81.2 IN (206 CM)
BATTERY TYPE.........LEAD-ACID (DELCO)
BATTERY VOLTAGE...............216 VOLTS
BATTERY MOUNTING........SINGLE PACK: UNDER VEHICLE MOUNTING
DRIVE TRAIN.....DC SERIES MOTOR WITH CHAIN DRIVE GEAR REDUCTION SOLID STATE CONTINUOUS ELECTRONIC SPEED CONTROL
BRAKES......VACUUM ASSIST HYDRAULIC WITH ELECTRICAL REGENERATION
ACCESSORIES
POWER.............DC/DC CONVERTER WITH EMERGENCY ACCESSORY BATTERY
ACCELERATION............0-30 MPH IN 12 SEC (48 KM/HR)
GRADE LIMIT........................20%
RANGE...................40 MILES (64 KM) (SAE SCHEDULE C)
TOP SPEED............50 MPH (80 KM/HR)

Fig. 8–20. GM's commercial van

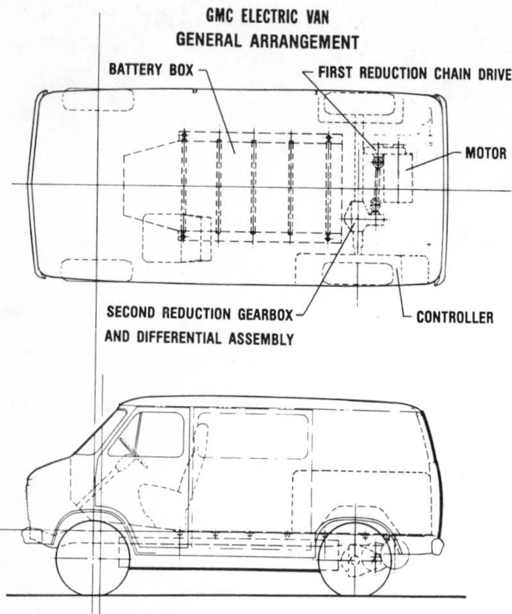

Fig. 8–21. Cutaway views of the GM van

quoted as saying that electric cars will be available by 1985. Ford has modified its Pinto, Maverick, and other compacts, including the Fiesta.

Exxon Industries, active in designing the improved lithium-titanium sulfide battery, has established a separate operation for electric-car research in Somerville NJ. ARCO Solar, moving from its modern solar-cell facility in Chatsworth to a larger plant a few miles west in Camarillo, California, is also developing a battery specifically for electric cars. This is not surprising because Bill Yerkes, vice-president of engineering of this Atlantic Richfield division, not only founded this solar-cell manufacturing business (and sold it to ARCO a few years ago) but also designed and built an electric car for his daughter when she was a senior in high school.

Electric utilities as well as companies in the oil business, electrical equipment, transmission, and battery manufacturers are all becoming increasingly supportive of the EV industry. Ray Kulvicki, a senior engineer at Southern California Edison Company, is one example of a utility engineer who has helped many independent designers of build-your-own electric cars. Through him, this book's authors and many other members of the Electric Vehicle Society of Southern California have received copies of *Electric Vehicle News,* an excellent quarterly publication, and other useful technical data. Creative Automotive Research has been partially financed in development and testing of electric and hybrid cars by Southern California Edison and the Electric Power Research Institute (EPRI), Menlo Park, an organization supported by the privately owned U.S. electric utilities.

To repeat the important statement made in chapter 1 as proof that the United States can gain enormously in the battle against inflation by developing and using electric cars by the millions:

If all the 26 million second and third cars in American garages and driveways were to become electric cars overnight, there would be no additional electric-plant capacity required. This is based on the reasonable assumption that these cars' batteries would be charged between 11 P.M. and 6 A.M., using built-in battery chargers with automatic shutoff. During this period, electric utilities operate at between 45% and 50% of capacity but burn almost as much fuel to keep their turbogenerators going as during peak hours in the daytime. Thus the savings in our national bill for fuel oil would be enormous, as well as the savings in gasoline now consumed largely on short trips by these second and third cars. The total saving could be as much as 15% of our total national oil consumption.

Think what this one advance can do to decrease dependence on foreign oil. If you really care about inflation, write, wire, *and* telephone your congressman and other political friends to help speed usage of electric cars. You'll find benefits in your own pocketbook and could help eliminate waits in long lines at filling stations during another gas crunch.

The general motoring public in the United States—leaving aside the thousands who have built or are building their own electric cars by modifying ICE compacts, as described in chapter 2—*will* respond to EV's. Certainly with gasoline prices on the rise, anyone with a modicum of thrift is going to say: "An electric car will save me enough money in a year or two so that I can't get along without it." Then we'll see some holes in the smog.

9 Motor Vehicle Codes

In most of the 50 states there are no specific laws or regulations applicable to electric cars. Your electric car must meet the standard requirements for all passenger vehicles in terms of brakes (including parking brakes), headlights, taillights and reflectors, windshields and rearview mirrors.

If you are converting a compact car of some recognized make into an electric car, you should have no trouble at all. Like Fred Riess and many other members of the Electric Vehicle Society who have built EV's from selected clunkers, all you need to do is to apply to your state's motor vehicle department. You won't have to worry about meeting low-emission requirements because your electric car doesn't emit pollutants.

You will probably be required to observe special regulations if the top speed of your vehicle is under 40 mph. See the following excerpts from appropriate regulations in the State of New York. Certainly if your electric car won't reach 40 mph, you'll not be permitted on superhighways, freeways or toll roads, where the minimum speed for passenger vehicles exceeds 40 to 45 mph, but you will be able to operate on urban and suburban streets and country roads.

Information from Many States

While writing this book, we asked the appropriate authorities in all 50 states about their motor vehicle codes applicable to electric cars. Following is a summary of the information we can pass along to you. For California, Florida, and New York, we have provided some of the applicable laws. For every state from which we received a reply, we have indicated the address of the relevant department so that you will have a source for further specific local information if you need it.

State of Alabama, Department of Public Safety, Montgomery, Alabama 36130. No specific laws or regulations apply to electric cars. If they are to be used on public highways, they must conform to all rules of the road, licensing laws, and lighting requirements.

State of Alaska, Department of Public Safety, Division of Motor Vehicles, P.O. Box 960, Anchorage, Alaska 99510. No specific regulations for EV's.

Arizona Department of Transportation, Motor Vehicle Division, 1801 West Jefferson Street, Phoenix, Arizona 85007. Electric cars must meet the requirements of a gas- or diesel-powered vehicle—nothing specific for EV's.

Department of Motor Vehicles, P.O. Box 1319, Sacramento, California 95806.

> **4153.** In the event the vehicle to be registered is a specially constructed or reconstructed vehicle, the application shall also state such fact and contain such additional information as may reasonably be required by the department to enable it properly to register the vehicle.
>
> **21654.** (a) Notwithstanding the prima facie speed limits, any vehicle proceeding upon a highway at a speed less than the normal speed of traffic moving in the same direction at such time shall be driven in the right-hand lane for traffic or as close as practicable to the right-hand edge

or curb, except when overtaking and passing another vehicle proceeding in the same direction or when preparing for a left turn at an intersection or into a private road or driveway.

(b) If a vehicle is being driven at a speed less than the normal speed of traffic moving in the same direction at such time, and is not being driven in the right-hand lane for traffic or as close as practicable to the right-hand edge or curb, it shall constitute prima facie evidence that the driver is operating the vehicle in violation of subdivision (a) of this section.

(c) The Department of Transportation, with respect to state highways, and local authorities, with respect to highways under their jurisdiction, may place and maintain upon highways official signs directing slow-moving traffic to use the right-hand traffic lane except when overtaking and passing another vehicle or preparing for a left turn.

21656. On a two-lane highway where passing is unsafe because of traffic in the opposite direction or other conditions, a slow-moving vehicle, including a passenger vehicle, behind which five or more vehicles are formed in line, shall turn off the roadway at the nearest place designated as a turnout by signs erected by the authority having jurisdiction over the highway, or wherever sufficient area for a safe turnout exists, in order to permit the vehicles following it to proceed. As used in this section, a slow-moving vehicle is one which is proceeding at a rate of speed less than the normal flow of traffic at the particular time and place.

22400. (a) No person shall drive upon a highway at such a slow speed as to impede or block the normal and reasonable movement of traffic, except when reduced speed is necessary for safe operation or because on a grade or in compliance with law....

24002. It is unlawful to operate any vehicle or combination of vehicles which is in an unsafe condition, which is not equipped as required by this code, or which is not safely loaded.

24008. It is unlawful to operate any passenger vehicle, or commercial vehicle under 4000 lbs., which has been modified from the original design so that any portion of such vehicle other than the wheels has less clearance from the surface of a level roadway than the clearance between the roadway and the lowermost portion of any rim of any wheel when in contact with such roadway.

24008.5 An "unsafe condition" within the meaning of Section 24002 includes, but is not limited to, the raising of the center of gravity or other modification of a vehicle so as to unsafely affect its operation or stability.

24252. (a) All lighting equipment of a required type installed on a vehicle shall at all times be maintained in good working order. Lamps shall be equipped with bulbs of the correct voltage rating corresponding to the nominal voltage at the lamp socket.

(b) The voltage at any tail, stop, license plate, side marker or clearance lamp socket on a vehicle shall not be less than 85% of the design voltage of the bulb. Voltage tests shall be conducted with the engine operating.

(c) Two or more lamp or reflector functions may be combined, provided each function required to be approved meets the specifications determined and published by the department.

24253. (a) All motor vehicles manufactured and first registered after January 1, 1970, shall be equipped so all taillamps are capable of remaining lighted for a period of at least one-quarter hour with the engine inoperative. This requirement shall be complied with by an energy storing system which is recharged by energy produced by the vehicle.

24400. During darkness, every motor vehicle other than a motorcycle shall be equipped with at least two lighted headlamps, with at least one on each side of the front of the vehicle, and, except as to vehicles registered prior to January 1, 1930, they shall be located directly above or in advance of the front axle of the vehicle. The headlamps and every light source in any headlamp unit shall be located at a height of not more than 54 inches nor less than 24 inches.

24408. (a) Every new motor vehicle registered in this state after January 1, 1940, which has multiple-beam road lighting equipment shall be equipped with a beam indicator, which shall be lighted whenever the uppermost distribution of light from the headlamps is in use, and shall not otherwise be lighted.

(b) The indicator shall be so designed and located that when lighted it will be readily visible without glare to the driver of the vehicle so equipped. Any such lamp on the exterior of the vehicle shall have a light source not exceeding two candlepower, and the light shall not show to the front or sides of the vehicle.

24600. During darkness every motor vehicle which is not in combination with any other vehicle and every vehicle at the end of a combination of vehicles shall be equipped with lighted taillamps mounted on the rear as follows:

(a) Every such vehicle shall be equipped with one or more taillamps.

(b) Every such vehicle, other than motorcycles, manufactured and first registered on or after January 1, 1958, shall be equipped with not less than two taillamps, except that trailers and semitrailers manufactured after July 23, 1973, which are less than 30 inches wide, may be equipped with one taillamp which shall be mounted at or near the vertical centerline of the vehicles. If such a vehicle is equipped with two taillamps, they shall be mounted as specified in subdivision (d).

(c) Every such vehicle or vehicle at the end of a combination of vehicles, subject to subdivision (a) of Section 22406 shall be equipped with not less than two taillights.

(d) When two taillamps are required, at least one shall be mounted at the left and one at the right side respectively at the same level.

(e) Taillamps shall be red in color and shall be plainly visible from all distances within 1000 feet to the rear.

(f) Taillamps on vehicles manufactured on or after January 1, 1969, shall be mounted not lower than 15 inches nor higher than 72 inches.

24601. Either the taillamp or a separate lamp shall be so constructed and placed as to illuminate with a white light the rear license plate during darkness and render it clearly legible from a distance of 50 feet to the rear. When the rear license plate is illuminated by a lamp other than a required taillamp, the two lamps shall be turned on or off only by the same controls switch at all times.

24603. Every motor vehicle which is not in combination with any other vehicle and every vehicle at the end of a combination of vehicles shall at all times be equipped with stoplamps mounted on the rear as follows:

(a) Every such vehicle shall be equipped with one or more stoplamps.

(b) Every such vehicle, other than a motorcycle, manufactured and first registered on or after January 1, 1958, shall be equipped with two stoplamps, except that trailers and semitrailers manufactured after July 23, 1973, which are less than 30 inches wide, may be equipped with one stoplamp which shall be mounted at or near the vertical centerline of the trailer. If such vehicle is equipped with two stoplamps, they shall be mounted as specified in subdivision (d).

(c) Stoplamps on vehicles manufactured on or after January 1, 1969, shall be mounted not lower than 15 inches or higher than 72 inches.

(d) Where two stoplamps are required, at least one shall be mounted at the left and one at the right side, respectively, at the same level.

(e) Stoplamps shall emit a red or amber light and shall be plainly visible and understandable from a distance of 300 feet to the rear both during normal sunlight and at nighttime, except that stoplamps on a vehicle of a size required to be equipped with clearance lamps shall be visible from a distance of 500 feet during such times.

(f) Stoplamps shall be actuated upon the application of the service (foot) brake and the hand control head for air, vacuum, or electric brakes. In addition, all stoplamps may be activated by a mechanical device designed to function only upon sudden release of the accelerator when the vehicle is in motion. Such mechanical device shall be approved by, and comply with specifications and regulations established by, the department.

(g) Any vehicle may be equipped with supplemental stoplamps mounted to the rear of the rearmost portion of the driver's seat in its rearmost position in addition to the lamps required to be mounted on the rear of the vehicle. The supplemental stoplamp on that side of a vehicle toward which a turn will be made may flash as part of the supplemental turn signal lamp.

24606. (a) Every motor vehicle, other than a motorcycle, of a type subject to registration and manufactured on or after January 1, 1969, shall be equipped with one or more backup lamps either separately or in combination with another lamp. Any vehicle may be equipped with backup lamps.

(b) Backup lamps shall be so directed as to project a white light illuminating the highway to the rear of the vehicle for a distance not to exceed 75 feet. A backup lamp may project incidental red, amber, or white light through reflectors or lenses that are adjacent, or close to, or are a part of the lamp assembly.

(c) Backup lamps shall not be lighted except when the vehicle is about to be or is backing or except in conjunction with a lighting system which activates the lights for a temporary period after the ignition system is turned off.

24607. Every vehicle subject to registration under this code shall at all times be equipped with red reflectors mounted on the rear as follows:

(a) Every vehicle shall be equipped with at least one reflector so maintained as to be plainly visible at night from all distances within 350 to 100 feet from the vehicle when directly in front of the lawful upper headlamp beams.

(b) Every vehicle, other than a motorcycle, manufactured and first registered on or after January 1, 1965, shall be equipped with at least two reflectors meeting the visibility requirements of subdivision (a), except that trailers and semitrailers manufactured after July 23, 1973, which are less than thirty inches wide, may be equipped with one reflector which shall be mounted at or near the vertical centerline of the trailer. If such vehicle is equipped with two reflectors, they shall be mounted as specified in subdivision (d).

(c) Every motor truck having an unladen weight of more than 5000 lbs., every trailer coach, every camp trailer, every vehicle or vehicle at the end of a combination of vehicles subject to subdivision (a) of Section 22406, and every vehicle 80 or more inches in width manufactured on or after January 1, 1969, shall be equipped with at least two reflectors maintained so as to be plainly visible at night from all distances between 600 feet to 100 feet from the vehicle when directly in front of lawful upper headlamp beams.

(d) When more than one reflector is required, at least one shall be mounted at the left side, and one at the right side, respectively, at the same level. Required reflectors shall be mounted not lower than 15 inches nor higher than 60 inches. Additional reflectors of a type approved by the department may be mounted at any height....

24609. Any vehicle may be equipped with white or amber reflectors upon the front of the vehicle, but they shall be mounted not lower than 15 inches nor higher than 60 inches.

24800. No vehicle shall be driven at any time with the parking lamps lighted except when the lamps are being used as turn signal lamps or when the headlamps are also lighted.

24951. (a) Any vehicle may be equipped with a lamp-type turn signal system capable of clearly indicating any intention to turn either to the right or to the left.

(b) The following vehicles shall be equipped with a lamp-type turn signal system meeting the requirements of this chapter.

(1) Motor trucks, truck tractors, buses and passenger vehicles, other than motorcycles, manufactured and first registered on or after January 1, 1958.

The requirements of this subdivision shall not apply to special mobile equipment or auxiliary dollies.

(c) Turn signal lamps on vehicles manufactured on or after January 1, 1969, shall be mounted not lower than 15 inches.

24952. A lamp-type turn signal shall be plainly visible and understandable in normal sunlight and at nighttime from a distance of at least 300 feet to the front and rear of the vehicle, except that turn signal lamps on vehicles of a size required to be equipped with clearance lamps shall be visible from a distance of 500 feet during such times.

25500. (a) Area reflectorizing material may be displayed on any vehicle provided: the color red is not displayed on the front; designs do not tend to distort the width or length of the vehicle; and designs do not resemble official traffic control devices, except that alternate striping resembling a barricade pattern may be used.

No vehicle shall be equipped with area reflectorizing material contrary to these provisions.

(b) The provisions of this section shall not apply to license plate stickers or tabs affixed to license plates as authorized by the Department of Motor Vehicles.

26301.5 Every passenger vehicle manufactured and first registered after January 1, 1973, except motorcycles, shall be equipped with an emergency brake system so constructed that rupture or leakage-type failure of any single pressure component of the service brake system, except structural failures of the brake master cylinder body or effectiveness indicator body, shall not result in complete loss of function of the vehicle's brakes when force on the brake pedal is continued.

26311. (a) Every motor vehicle shall be equipped with service brakes on all wheels, except as follows:

(1) Trucks and truck tractors having three or more axles need not have brakes on the front wheels, except when such vehicles are equipped with at least two steerable axles, the wheels of one such axle need not be equipped with brakes.

(2) Any vehicle being towed in a driveway-towaway operation.

(3) Any vehicle manufactured prior to 1930.

(4) Any two-axle truck tractor manufactured prior to 1964.

(5) Any sidecar attached to a motorcycle.

(6) Any motorcycle manufactured prior to 1966. Such motorcycle shall be equipped with brakes on at least one wheel.

(b) Means may be used for reducing the braking effort on the front wheels of any bus, truck, or truck tractor, provided that the means for reducing the braking effort shall be used only when operating under adverse road conditions, such as wet, snowy, or icy roads.

(c) Vehicles and combinations of vehicles exempted in subdivisions (a) and (b) from the requirements of brakes on all wheels shall comply with the stopping distance requirements of Section 26454.

26450. Every motor vehicle shall be equipped with a service brake system and every motor vehicle, other than a motorcycle, shall be equipped with a parking brake system. Both the service brake and parking brake shall be separately applied.

If the two systems are connected in any way, they shall be so constructed that failure of any one part, except failure in the drums, brakeshoes, or other mechanical parts of the wheel brake assemblies, shall not leave the motor vehicle without operative brakes.

26451. The parking brake system of every motor vehicle shall comply with the following requirements:

(a) The parking brake shall be adequate to hold the vehicle or combination of vehicles stationary on any grade on which it is operated under all conditions of loading on a surface free from snow, ice, or loose material. In any event the parking brake shall be capable of locking the braked wheels to the limit of traction.

(b) The parking brake shall be applied either by the driver's muscular efforts, by spring action, or by other energy which is isolated and used exclusively for the operation of the parking brake and emergency stopping system.

(c) The parking brake shall be held in the applied position by mechanical means, spring devices, or captive air pressure in self-contained cells, which self-contained cells do not lose more than five pounds of air pressure during a 30-day period from their standard operating potential as established by the manufacturer. The force to hold the vehicle parked shall be applied through mechanical linkage to the braked wheels when a spring device or captive air pressure in self-contained cells is used.

26453. All motor vehicles shall be so equipped as to permit application of the brakes at least once for the purpose of bringing the vehicle to a stop within the legal stopping distance after the engine has become inoperative.

26454. (a) The service brakes of every motor vehicle or combination of vehicles shall be adequate to control the movement of and to stop and hold such vehicle or combination of vehicles under all conditions of loading on any grade on which it is operated.

(b) Every motor vehicle or combination of vehicles, at any time and under all conditions of loading, shall, upon application of the service brake, be capable of stopping from an initial speed of 20 miles per hour according to the following requirements:

	Maximum stopping distance (feet)
(1) Any passenger vehicle	25
(2) Any single motor vehicle with a manufacturer's gross vehicle weight rating of less than 10,000 lbs. . . .	30
(3) Any combination of vehicles consisting of passenger vehicles or any motor vehicle with a manufacturer's gross vehicle weight rating of less than 10,000 lbs. in combination with any trailer, semitrailer, or trailer coach	40

26700. Every passenger vehicle, other than a motorcycle, and every bus, motortruck or truck tractor, and every firetruck, fire engine or other fire apparatus, whether publicly or privately owned, shall be equipped with an adequate windshield.

26703. (a) No person shall replace any glazing materials used in partitions, doors, or windows in any motor vehicle, or in the outside windows or doors of any camper, with any glazing material other than safety glazing material.

(b) No person shall replace any glazing material used in the windshield, rear window, wind deflectors, or windows to the left and right of the driver with any material other than safety glazing material.

26706. (a) Every motor vehicle, except motorcycles, equipped with a windshield shall also be equipped with a self-operating windshield wiper.

(b) Every new motor vehicle first registered after December 1, 1949, except motorcycles, shall be equipped with two such windshield wipers, one mounted on the right half and one on the left half of the windshield.

(c) This section does not apply to snow removal equipment with adequate manually operated windshield wipers.

26707. Windshield wipers required by this code shall be maintained in good operating condition and shall provide clear vision through the windshield for the driver. Wipers shall be operated under conditions of fog, snow, or rain and shall be capable of effectively clearing the windshield under all ordinary storm or load conditions while the vehicle is in operation.

26709. (a) Every motor vehicle registered in a foreign jurisdiction and every motorcycle subject to registration in this state shall be equipped with a mirror so located as to reflect to the driver a view of the highway for a distance of at least 200 feet to the rear of such vehicle.

Every motor vehicle subject to registration in this state, except motorcycles, shall be equipped with not less than two such mirrors, including one affixed to the left-hand side.

(b) The following described types of motor vehicles, of a type subject to registration, shall be equipped with mirrors on both the left- and right-hand sides of the vehicle so located as to reflect to the driver a view of the highway through each mirror for a distance of at least 200 feet to the rear of such vehicle.

(1) A motor vehicle so constructed or loaded as to obstruct the driver's view to the rear.

(2) A motor vehicle towing a vehicle and the towed vehicle or load thereon obstructs the driver's view to the rear.

(3) A bus or trolley coach.

(c) The provisions of subdivision (b) shall not apply to a passenger vehicle when the load obstructing the driver's view consists of passengers.

27000. Every motor vehicle when operated on a highway shall be equipped with a horn in good working order and capable of emitting sound audible under normal conditions from a distance of not less than 200 feet, but no horn shall emit an unreasonably loud or harsh sound. An authorized emergency vehicle used in responding to fire calls may be equipped with, and use in conjunction with the siren on such vehicle, an air horn which emits sounds which do not comply with the requirements of this section.

28071. Every passenger vehicle registered in this state shall be equipped with a front bumper and with a rear bumper. As used in this section, "bumper" means any device designed and intended by a manufacturer to prevent the front or rear of the body of the vehicle from coming into contact with any other motor vehicle. This section shall not apply to any passenger vehicle that is required to be equipped with an energy absorption system pursuant to either state or federal law, or to any passenger vehicle which was not equipped with a front or rear bumper, or both, at the time that it was first sold and registered under the laws of this or any other state or foreign jurisdiction.

34715. (a) No new passenger vehicle, except a vehicle certified by its manufacturer as having been manufactured prior to January 1, 1973, shall be sold or registered on or after September 1, 1973, unless it has a manufacturer's warranty that it is equipped with an appropriate energy absorption system so that it can be driven directly into a standard Society of Automotive Engineers (SAE J-850) test barrier at a speed of five miles per hour without sustaining any property damage to the front of the vehicle and can be driven at a speed of five miles per hour into such barrier without sustaining any property damage to the rear of such vehicle.

(b) Property damage, within the meaning of this section, shall not include abrasion to surfaces at the point or points of contact of the vehicle with the test barrier when undergoing such testing.

35408. In no event shall a front bumper on a motor vehicle be constructed or installed so as to project more than two feet forward of the foremost part of either the fenders or cab structure or radiator, whichever extends farthest toward the front of such vehicle.

State of Colorado, Department of Revenue, Motor Vehicle Administration, 140 West 6th Avenue, Denver, Colorado 80204. Colorado law is silent on electric cars, but any EV must conform to conventional standards of the state.

State of Connecticut, Department of Motor Vehicles, State Street, Wethersfield, Connecticut 06109. The only exception to standard motor vehicle rules is that the fee for an electric motor vehicle registration is $10 a year—*half* the annual fee for an ICE car.

Government of the District of Columbia, Department of Transportation, Bureau of Motor Vehicle Services, Washington, D.C. 20001. No special rules for EV's, but each electric car must pass inspection.

State of Delaware, Department of Motor Vehicles, Dover, Delaware 19901. Nothing on electric cars.

State of Florida, Department of Highway Safety and Motor Vehicles, Neil Kirkman Building, Tallahassee, Florida 32304. The only special regulations applicable to EV's apply to brakes and windshields. See the following excerpts from the Florida statutes.

Special Florida Statutes

316.267 Brakes on electric-powered vehicles.—When operated on the public streets and roads, every electric-powered vehicle with a rating of 3 to 6 horsepower shall be equipped with hydraulic brakes on the two rear wheels and at all times and under all conditions of loading, upon application of the service brake, shall be capable of:

(1) Developing a braking force that is not less than 43.5 percent of its gross weight.

(2) Decelerating to a stop from not more than 20 miles per hour at not less than 17 feet per second.

(3) Stopping from a speed of 20 miles per hour in not more than 25 feet, such distance to be measured from the point at which movement of the service brake pedal or control begins.

316.295 Windshields required to be unobstructed, fixed upright and equipped with safety glass and wipers.—

(1) Front windshields in a fixed and upright position equipped with safety glass as defined in and required by s.320.062 are required on all motor vehicles which are driven on public highways, roads, or streets except motorcycles and implements of husbandry, and no person shall drive any motor vehicle with any sign or other nontransparent material

upon the front windshield, sidewings, or side or rear windows of such vehicle, other than a certificate or other paper required to be so displayed by law.

(3) The windshield on every motor vehicle shall be equipped with a device for cleaning rain, snow, or other moisture from the windshield, which device shall be so constructed as to be controlled or operated by the driver of the vehicle.

(4) Every windshield wiper upon a motor vehicle shall be maintained in good working order.

(5) Grove equipment, including "goats," "highlift-goats," grove chemical supply tanks, fertilizer distributors, fruit-loading equipment, and electric-powered vehicles regulated under the provisions of s. 316.-267, shall be exempt from the requirements of this section. However, such electric-powered vehicles shall have a windscreen approved by the department sufficient to give protection from wind, rain, or insects, and such windscreen shall be in place whenever the vehicle is operated on the public roads and highways.

State of Georgia, Department of Public Safety, P.O. Box 1456, Atlanta Georgia 30301. EV's must meet the standard requirements for any self-propelled motor vehicle, which include tag, inspection sticker, headlights, left outside mirror, turn signals, taillights, stop lights, and seat belts.

State of Hawaii, Department of Transportation, 869 Punchbowl Street, Honolulu, Hawaii 96813. There "should be no problem with vehicles that meet the requirements of all applicable Federal Motor Vehicle Safety Standards as they will meet all local (Hawaiian) equipment requirements."

State of Idaho, Department of Law Enforcement, P.O. Box 34, Boise, Idaho, 83731. No special rules for electric cars. Fees vary, depending on the age of the vehicle, from $12.60 a year for vehicles over 8 years old to $29.40 for young vehicles, less than 2 years old.

State of Indiana, Bureau of Motor Vehicles, Indianapolis, Indiana 46204. An electric vehicle is titled, plated, and operated in the same manner as a gasoline-powered vehicle.

State of Iowa, Department of Transportation, Motor Vehicle Division, Office of Vehicle Registration, Lucas State Office Building, Des Moines, Iowa 50319. The only motor vehicle law currently applicable to electric vehicles relates to registration fees as follows:

> **321.116** *Electric Automobiles.* For all electric motor vehicles the annual fee shall be $25. When any electric vehicle has been registered five times the annual registration fee shall be $15.

State of Kansas, Department of Revenue, Division of Vehicles, State Office Building, Topeka, Kansas 66626. There are no special rules about EV's except an advantage in registration fees: $6.50 for electric cars, while ICE vehicles are charged higher amounts.

Commonwealth of Kentucky, Department of Transportation, Bureau of Vehicle Regulation, Frankfort, Kentucky 40301. No special laws cover EV's.

State of Maryland, Department of Transportation, Motor Vehicle Administration, 6601 Ritchie Highway, N.E., Glen Burnie, Maryland 21062. An electric car must meet the same Motor Vehicle Safety Standards as a new gasoline-powered vehicle. A passenger vehicle under 3,500 lb is assessed a fee of $20 per year, while the fee is $30 for a vehicle over 3,500 lb. The operator must possess an appropriate Class D license if a resident of the State of Maryland.

State of Michigan, Department of Motor Vehicles, Lansing, Michigan 48918. There are no special requirements for EV's.

State of Minnesota, Department of Motor Vehicles, St. Paul, Minnesota 55155. No special regulations exist that apply to electric cars.

State of Missouri, Department of Revenue, Motor Vehicle Bureau, Jefferson City, Missouri 65101. Section 301.070 states that the horsepower of all motor vehicles, except commercial motor vehicles, propelled by electric power, shall be rated as being between twelve (12) and twenty-four (24) horsepower. The annual fee for this horsepower is $9. (Author's comment: Although most electric cars will not use a motor with more than 24 HP, this Missouri statute may have to be revised in the future.)

State of Montana, Department of Justice, Montana Highway Patrol, 1014 National Avenue, Helena, Montana 59601. There are no special laws for electric cars.

State of Nebraska, Department of Motor Vehicles, Lincoln, Nebraska 68509. The laws pertaining to motor vehicles include electric cars.

State of Nevada, Department of Motor Vehicles, 555 Wright Way, Carson City, Nevada 89711. There is no provision in the Nevada motor vehicle regulations applying specifically to electric cars.

State of New Hampshire, Department of Safety, Concord, New Hampshire 03301. Electric vehicles are taxed and registered in the same manner as any motor vehicle; no special laws nor regulations.

State of New Jersey, Division of Motor Vehicles, 25 South Montgomery Street, Trenton, New Jersey 08666. To be registered in New Jersey an electric car, or any other passenger car, must be capable of a speed of at least 30 miles per hour on a level road. Other requirements match those of ICE cars except that EV's do not have to meet the exhaust emission requirements.

State of New Mexico, Department of Motor Vehicles, Manuel Lujan Sr. Building, Santa Fe, New Mexico 87503. Although no minimum speed is stated, Section 64-18-4 says: "No person shall drive a motor vehicle at such a slow speed as to impede the normal and reasonable movement of traffic except when reduced speed is necessary for safe operation or in compliance with the law." There are no specific laws dealing with EV's.

State of New York, Department of Motor Vehicles, Empire State Plaza, Albany, New York 12228. The following are some relevant excerpts from the Regulations of the Commissioner of Motor Vehicles. In New York electric cars are at present termed "limited use vehicles." Note that if your electric car will travel faster than 40 mph, the subsequent paragraphs will *not* apply.

102.1 Introduction. Article 48-A of the Vehicle and Traffic Law provides for the control and use of motor vehicles which would be subject to registration under subdivision (6) of section 401 or 410 of the Vehicle and Traffic Law (passenger automobile and motorcycles respectively), but which have a maximum speed capability of not more than 40 miles per hour. Article 48-A of the Vehicle and Traffic Law provides that all of the provisions of the Vehicle and Traffic Law apply to such vehicles, which are called limited use vehicles, unless such law or regulations promulgated thereunder provide otherwise. That article and this Part specify those provisions of the Vehicle and Traffic Law which do not apply, or have been altered or modified in their application to limited use vehicles. Any provision of the Vehicle and Traffic Law which is not made inapplicable or is not modified or altered by such article or this Part is applicable to a limited use vehicle as if such limited use vehicle was a passenger automobile or a motorcycle registered pursuant to subdivision (6) of section 401 or section 410 of the Vehicle and Traffic Law respectively.

102.2 Registration and titling. (a) *General.* A limited use automobile is required to be titled in accordance with the provisions of article 46 of the Vehicle and Traffic Law and Part 20 of this Title. A limited use motorcycle is exempt from such titling requirements. In order to be operated on a public highway in this State, a limited use vehicle must be registered with the Department of Motor Vehicles.

(b) *Registration categories.* (1) *Limited use automobile.* A motor vehicle with a maximum performance speed of not more than 40 miles per hour which would be subject to registration pursuant to subdivision (6) of section 401 of the Vehicle and Traffic Law (passenger automobile) must be registered as a limited use automobile in order to be operated on any public highway in this State.

102.3 Inspection and insurance. (a) *Inspection.* The provisions of article 5 of the Vehicle and Traffic Law relating to the periodic inspection of motor vehicles, and regulations promulgated thereunder apply to limited use vehicles except that class B and class C limited use motorcycles are not subject to such provisions of the Vehicle and Traffic Law and regulations promulgated thereunder.

(b) *Insurance.* (1) The provisions of articles 6, 7 and 8 of the Vehicle and Traffic Law relating to insurance shall be applicable to limited use vehicles, except that the provisions of article 6 (the Motor Vehicle Financial Security Act) shall not apply to class C limited use motorcycles.

(2) Any limited use vehicle, including a class C limited use motorcycle, which will be rented to others will be required to submit proof of insurance upon registration and will be required to be continuously insured in accordance with section 370 of the Vehicle and Traffic Law.

102.4 Equipment. (a) *Vehicular equipment.* (1) A limited use automobile is required to be equipped in the same manner as a motor vehicle registered pursuant to subdivision (6) of section 401 of the Vehicle and Traffic Law (passenger automobile).

(b) *Lights-on requirement.* The requirements of subdivision (1) of section 381 of the Vehicle and Traffic Law relating to the display of lighted lamps whenever a motorcycle is operated on the public highways of this State, including daylight hours, applies to the operation of limited use motorcycles.

102.6 Licensing. (a) Section 2266 of the Vehicle and Traffic Law provides for the licensing of operators of limited use vehicles. Parts 1, 3 and 4 of this Title set forth, among other things, the specific requirements and procedures applicable to the operation of limited use vehicles by class 6 and class 8 licensees (Part 1), licensees generally (Part 3) and the holders of learners' permits (Part 4), and those regulations together with the provisions of article 19 and section 2266 of the Vehicle and Traffic Law govern the operation of limited use vehicles with respect to licensing.

(b) The following paragraphs of this subdivision are intended as a summary of the most pertinent provisions of Parts 1, 3 and 4 of this Title as they apply to the operation of limited use vehicles:

(1) A class 6, 5, 4, 3 or 1 license is needed to operate a limited use automobile.

102.7 Restrictions on the use of limited use vehicles. (a) A limited use vehicle may not be operated on any controlled-access highway other than a bridge or tunnel or other portion of such highway on which signs are in place permitting operation.

(b) A limited use vehicle may not be operated on any highway that has been posted to exclude or prohibit such vehicles, or in violation of any prohibition or limitation or use for which appropriate notice has been given.

(c) *Certification.* (1) No limited use vehicle will be registered (or titled, if required) unless a certification of the maximum performance speed of that model (or sub-model, if applicable) limited use vehicle has been filed with the commissioner by the manufacturer and approved by the commissioner. The type of registration issued to a limited use vehicle shall be established by the commissioner based upon a certification submitted and approved for the model (or sub-model, if applicable) limited use vehicle.

(2) A manufacturer's certification may be based upon tests conducted with a production line vehicle either by the manufacturer or an independent testing laboratory. The commissioner may require additional testing by a third party approved by the commissioner in any case in which the manufacturer's certification is based upon tests conducted by the manufacturer, or for the purpose of confirming the validity of a prior certification. All expenses of testing shall be borne by the manufacturer.

(3) Certification submitted by the manufacturer shall contain the following information: name and address of the producer (and manufacturer, if different than the producer); the trade name, model (and sub-model, if applicable), identifying years covered by the certification; the unladen weight of the vehicle, the brake horsepower and displacement of the engine or motor, a description and explanation of the vehicle identification numbers to be assigned by the manufacturer to units of the model (or sub-model, if applicable) tested, including the location of such number on the frame; and a description (name and model number) of all equipment on such vehicle which is required for such vehicle to be in compliance with the requirements of the Vehicle and Traffic Law and this Part. The certification must also contain a statement that the vehicle tested meets all requirements of the Vehicle and Traffic Law and this Part, and with respect to limited use motorcycles, a statement that the seat or saddle for the operator is at least 25 inches above the ground. If the seat or saddle is adjustable, that certification shall apply to the seat or saddle in its lowest position.

(4) The certification shall contain a full description of the test procedures used and shall state the maximum speed attained within one quarter mile from a standing start and the average speed of the vehicle for the next ensuing mile. The certification must contain a statement that the vehicle tested is representative of vehicles of that model (or sub-model, if applicable) as manufactured for sale in this State. In addition, a completed sample of the manufacturer's statement of origin to be used for the model (or sub-model, if applicable), must be submitted for approval with the certification. The certification shall be signed by the person who conducted the test who must vouch for its accuracy.

(5) The certification should be submitted to the Bureau of Technical Assessment, Division of Vehicle Safety, Department of Motor Vehicles, Empire State Plaza, Albany, New York 12228.

(d) *Required testing for certification.* The test required for certification may be performed either by means of a road test or by means of suitable testing equipment which will simulate road test conditions. The following procedures shall be used:

(1) The test shall be conducted on a hard, dry surface having a skid number (hardness) of 50 or less and a zero percent grade with a wind velocity of no more than five miles per hour.

(2) When testing the vehicle it shall be equipped as required for sale in this State, and the head lamps and tail lamps shall be lit throughout the test.

(3) The vehicle shall be tested under a load of 150 pounds, not including equipment, in or on the operator's position, and with the engine operating at maximum output.

(e) *Vehicle identification number.* The vehicle number assigned to a limited use motor vehicle must be unique for each limited use vehicle and must be embossed or engraved upon the frame of each limited use motorcycle and affixed to a limited use automobile in accordance with Federal standards. The vehicle identification number may not consist of more than 13 characters.

(f) *Establishment of maximum performance speed.* If the certification submitted by the manufacturer is acceptable to the commissioner, the maximum performance speed of the model (or sub-model, if applicable) so certified will be based upon the average speed of the model (or sub-model, if applicable) tested for the one mile distance after the one-quarter mile acceleration distance. However, the commissioner reserves the right to determine a different maximum performance speed, if warranted by the test report submitted.

(g) *Alternate certification of certain limited use vehicles.* If an application for registration of a limited use vehicle for which no certification has been approved by the commissioner is made and there is no manufacturer who can provide such certification (examples, manufacturer out of business, homemade vehicle, model no longer manufactured and records not available), the Bureau of Technical Assessment may prescribe and accept alternate methods of approval and certification of maximum performance speed.

(h) Once a certification has been approved, that certification shall apply to all vehicles of the same model (or sub-model, if applicable) manufactured thereafter unless there are changes in the technical specifications or performance standards. Upon any such change, the manufacturer shall submit a new certification. However, the commissioner may, from time to time request a confirmation of the certification for models, (or sub-models, if applicable) manufactured after the identifying years specified in the approved certification. Upon such a request for confirmation, the manufacturer must submit a new certification or confirmation of the continuance of the prior certification.

(i) *Verification of specific vehicles.* A manufacturer must be able to certify to the commissioner or to the owner of a limited use vehicle the maximum performance speed of any limited use vehicle upon submission of the vehicle identification number or other appropriate number. A manufacturer must honor a request for such information promptly upon receipt of such request.

102.9 Vehicles manufactured without a motor to which a motor is later attached. Section 2268 of the Vehicle and Traffic Law, in effect, prohibits the operation on public highways of this State of a vehicle which is primarily designed to be propelled by human power and to which a motor is attached. In accordance with section 2268 of the Vehicle and Traffic Law, the commissioner determines that any vehicle which is manufactured for retail sale without a motor, and to which a motor is attached is a motor-assisted vehicle and may not legally be operated upon the public highways of this State.

State of North Carolina, Division of Motor Vehicles, 1100 New Bern Avenue, Raleigh, North Carolina 27611. All registration requirements such as fees, safety inspection equipment and minimum speed—everything except emission control—are the same for EV's as for ICE cars.

State of North Dakota, Highway Department, 224 Airport Road, Bismarck, North Dakota 58505. No special laws applying to EV's.

State of Oregon, Motor Vehicles Division, Validation Unit, Salem, Oregon 97314. No special requirements are stated for EV's.

Commonwealth of Pennsylvania, Department of Transportation, Bureau of Motor Vehicles, Harrisburg, Pennsylvania 17122. General motor vehicle laws apply to EV's.

State of Oklahoma, Department of Public Safety, Motor Vehicle Inspection Division, 3600 North Eastern, Oklahoma City, Oklahoma 73111. The motor vehicle laws contain no special provisions about electric cars.

State of South Dakota, Department of Public Safety, Division of Motor Vehicles, 118 West Capitol Avenue, Pierre, South Dakota 57501. There are no motor vehicle statutes dealing with electric cars.

State of Texas, Department of Public Safety, Inspection and Planning Division, 5805 N. Lamar Blvd., Austin, Texas 78773. Texas registration laws and other motor vehicle laws do not address electric cars per se. They are treated as other motor vehicles depending on type, e.g. passenger car, motor bus, commercial motor vehicle, etc.

State of Utah, Motor Vehicle Division, State Fairgrounds, 1095 Motor Avenue, Salt Lake City, Utah 84116. Electric cars must be registered and titled like any other passenger vehicle.

State of Vermont, Agency of Transportation, Department of Motor Vehicles, Montpelier, Vermont 05602. There are no special regulations for electric cars.

State of Wisconsin, Department of Transportation, Madison, Wisconsin 53707. No special requirements exist for electric cars.

Summary

We have been able to get information from most of the 50 States. As indicated in the applicable paragraphs from the motor vehicle codes of California, Florida, and New York, cited in this chapter, relatively minor requirements are imposed on some electric cars, particularly those that won't travel over 40 mph.

It appears as though most state officials are trying to help the rapidly rising new industry of electric cars proceed with minimum bureaucratic interference. As sensible Americans, we realize that we must reduce our consumption of fossil fuels; this is a cooperative approach.

A few states are missing from the roster of the preceding pages, because we failed to get a reply from the DMV (or equivalent) personnel in those states. By contrast, the vast majority replied rapidly and courteously to our request for information.

Bibliography

Anderson, E. *Electric Motors.* Indianapolis, IN: Theodore Audel & Co., 1968.

Ayres, Robert U., and Richard P. McKenna. *Alternatives to the Internal Combustion Engine.* Baltimore and London: The Johns Hopkins University Press, 1972.

"A Big Breakthrough in Batteries . . . Almost." *Mechanix Illustrated,* March 1978.

Cost and Design Study to Develop Lead-Acid Batteries for Electric Vehicle Propulsion. Argonne National Laboratory Contract No. 31–109–38–3621, Philadelphia: ESB Incorporated, 1977.

"Directory of the Electric Vehicle Industry." *Electric Vehicle News,* February 1978.

Dvorak, D. Z. *Your Guide to Variable-Speed Mechanical Drives.* West Hartford, CT: Pratt & Whitney Company, 1975.

Esposito, Vincent J. "The U.S. Promotes Electric Vehicles." *IEEE Spectrum,* November 1977.

"EV Controls." *Electric Vehicle News,* August 1973.

"EV Revival." *Machine Design.* Cleveland: Penton Publishing Company, 1974.

Facts About Storage Batteries. Cleveland: ESB Batteries, Inc., 1977.

Gaines, Lewis. "Exxon Enterprises Electric Vehicle Battery Model." Bound Brook, NJ: Exxon Enterprises, Inc., 1977.

Guess, R. H., W. R. Nial, and M. A. Pocobello. "Design of a Current Technology Electric Vehicle." *Electric Vehicle News,* November 1977.

Hackleman, Michael. *Electric Vehicles: Design and Build Your Own.* Culver City, CA: Earthmind/Peace Press, 1977.

Hafer, Paul R., Arthur Dicker, Jr., and Colonel Harry D. Yoder. "The Electric Multistop Fleet Delivery Vehicle—Fact or Fantasy." Warrendale, PA: Society of Automotive Engineers, Inc., 1975.

Harding, G. G. *Design of Electric Commercial Vehicles for Production.* Warrendale, PA: Society of Automotive Engineers, Inc., 1977.

———. *Developing Electric Vehicles.* Birmingham, England: Lucas Industries, 1977.

———. *High Performance Electric Commercial Vehicles for City Use.* Warrendale, PA: Society of Automotive Engineers, Inc., 1976.

———. "A Look at the EV R&D Record of Lucas." *Electric Vehicle News,* February 1978.

Kaylor, Roy. "The Electric Car: A Feasible On-the-Road Proposition." Menlo Park, CA: Kaylor Energy Products, 1978.

Mages, Loren J. *Electric Generating Systems.* Indianapolis, IN: Theodore Audel & Co., 1970.

McClung, John D. "On-Road Type Electric Vehicle Power Systems." Rolling Meadows, IL: Gould, Inc., 1977.

McKee, Robert S., Boris Borisoff, Frank Lawn, and James F. Norberg. *Sundancer: A Test Bed Electric Vehicle.* Warrendale, PA: Society of Automotive Engineers, Inc., 1972.

Naidu, G. M., George Tesar, and G. G. Udell. *The Electric Car—An Alternative to the Internal Combustion Engine.* Acton, MA: Publishing Sciences Group, Inc., 1974.

Petrocelli, A. W., and J. H. Kennedy. *The Nickel-Zinc Battery: A Viable Alternative for Vehicle Powering.* Pawcatuck, CT: Yardney Electric Corporation, 1976.

Port, Frederick J. *Today's Power Source for Tomorrow's Electric Vehicles.* Philadelphia: ESB Inc., 1976.

Power Systems for Electric Vehicles. Public Health Service Publication 999–AP–37, U.S. Department of Health, Education and Welfare, National Center for Air Pollution Control, Cincinnati, OH, 1967.

Santini, John. "The Design and Construction of an Electric Car Using Current Technology." *Electric Vehicle News,* February 1978.

Shipps, Paul R. *Electric Mini-Cars for Urban Driving.* San Diego, CA: 3E Vehicles, 1977.

"Transformer I Electric Car." Troy, MI: Electric Fuel Propulsion Corporation, 1977.

"Variable Belt Transmission Appears First Time in U.S. Car." *Product Engineering,* 1969.

Von Krusenstierna, Otto, and Mats Reger. *A High Energy Nickel-Zinc Battery for Electric Vehicles.* Warrendale, PA: Society of Automotive Engineers, Inc., 1977.

Walker, Peter. "Getting Serious About EV Motors." *Machine Design,* Cleveland: Penton Publishing Company, March 1978.

Wise, Clare E. "Utilities Power New Electric-Car Movement." *Machine Design,* Cleveland: Penton Publishing Company, 1972.

Index

Numbers in italics refer to pages with illustrations